FORGING THE THUNDERBOLT

Other titles in the Stackpole Military History Series

THE AMERICAN CIVIL WAR

Cavalry Raids of the Civil War
Pickett's Charge
Witness to Gettysburg

WORLD WAR II

Armor Battles of the Waffen-SS, 1943–45
Australian Commandos
The B-24 in China
Beyond the Beachhead
The Brandenburger Commandos
Bringing the Thunder
Coast Watching in World War II
Fist from the Sky
Flying American Combat Aircraft of World War II
Germany's Panzer Arm in World War II
Grenadiers
Infantry Aces
Luftwaffe Aces
Messerschmitts over Sicily
Michael Wittmann and the Waffen SS Tiger Commanders
of the Leibstandarte in WWII, Vol. 1
Michael Wittmann and the Waffen SS Tiger Commanders
of the Leibstandarte in WWII, Vol. 2
On the Canal
Packs On!
Panzer Aces
Panzer Aces II
Surviving Bataan and Beyond
The 12th SS, Volume One
The 12th SS, Volume Two
Tigers in the Mud

THE COLD WAR / VIETNAM

Flying American Combat Aircraft: The Cold War
Land with No Sun
Street without Joy

WARS OF THE MIDDLE EAST

Never-Ending Conflict

FORGING THE THUNDERBOLT

History of the U.S. Army's Armored Forces, 1917–45

M. H. Gillie

Foreword by General Jacob L. Devers

STACKPOLE
BOOKS

Published in paperback in 2006 by
STACKPOLE BOOKS
5067 Ritter Road
Mechanicsburg, PA 17055
www.stackpolebooks.com

Cover photo courtesy of the Library of Congress.

Printed in the United States of America

10 9 8 7 6 5 4 3 2 1

FIRST EDITION

Library of Congress Cataloging-in-Publication Data

Gillie, Mildred Hanson.
    Forging the thunderbolt : history of the U.S. Army's Armored Force,
1917–45 / Mildred H. Gillie.
        p. cm. — (Stackpole Military history series)
    Originally published: Harrisburg, Pa. : Military Service Pub., 1947.
    Includes bibliographical references and index.
    ISBN-13: 978-0-8117-3343-4
    ISBN-10: 0-8117-3343-2
    1. United States. Army. Armored Force—History—20th century. 2.
United States. Army—Armored troops—History—20th century. 3. World
War, 1914–1918—Tank warfare. 4. World War, 1939–1945—Tank warfare.
I. Title. II. Series.

    UA30.G5 2006
    358'.18097309041—dc22
                                                    2006004625

Table of Contents

Foreword

During the final months of World War I, tanks created a new combat arm. The combination of field fortifications and rapid firing weapons had stalled the ground troops for four years. The defense had the balance of power when the first combination of gasoline power and armor began to overrun the machine gun nests and help the infantry forward for the decisive attacks.

The lesson is plain to us now, but even after the success of the Allied effort in 1918 there were many wise students of war who overlooked the potentialities as well as the proven capabilities of the clumsy-looking new weapon. They remembered the trenches only. The tendency toward static warfare exemplified in the Maginot Line persisted except in the minds of a few soldiers whose imagination could reach far into the future. These latter realized that in warfare a new offensive was on the way.

Fortunately for the United States we had our share of such prophetic soldiers. Despite peacetime inertia and limited appropriations, they tapped rich wells of American tactical and technological genius and began to make their ideas realities. (Foremost among these men was Lieutenant General Daniel Van Voorhis, the "Grandfather of the American Armored Force," and Major General Adna R. Chaffee, the "Father of the American Armored Force.")

The problem of tank development did not escape the attention of a few patriotic people who spent both their time and money in order to produce better equipment. Outstanding among these men was the forward-looking inventor, Mr. J. Walter Christie, who was responsible for increasing the power and speed of our tanks.

In the final decisive operations of World War II, the Armored Force fulfilled the expectations of those who knew American armor from its infancy. In the rapid advance across France, the thrusts against the Rhine and the race across Germany, armor played a predominant part and established itself without question as a power on the battlefield.

Gen. Jacob L. Devers, USA

Acknowledgments

When Ethel Chaffee and I first discussed the book I proposed to write about the General, she repeatedly said to me that she would prefer that it not be written if it concerned only dry-as-dust facts and figures to the exclusion of a warm personal picture of the man who was her husband. She had in mind a biography that had been written some years before about the General's father, which was a masterly account of the elderly Chaffee's great soldierly exploits, but which practically ignored his non-military personality. All the personal anecdotes and intimate glimpses which this book contains of the man who is known as the "Father of the Armored Force," therefore, came directly from Mrs. Chaffee. Although she is not alive today to see the book in its final form, she read and approved the rough draft of the original biography and consented to its revision as a history of the development of the Armored Force.

My thanks go to Lieutenant General Daniel Van Voorhis, USA (Ret.), to James Wilson Riley, and to Kenneth Hechler, for information which they supplied to me; to Major General C. L. Scott for his comments and criticisms on the galley proofs; Duell, Sloan and Pearce for permission to quote from Robert Ick's *Tanks* and to the various publishers who have allowed me to quote from their books and magazines.

M. H. G.

CHAPTER ONE

Monster of Cambrai

I

When the first British tanks lurched across No Man's Land toward the astonished Germans on that historic day, September 15, 1916, during the Battle of the Somme, they surprised both friend and foe alike. Their appearance was hailed with enthusiasm by the Allied press, and with consternation by the German General Staff. Yet the idea of an armored vehicle in war was far from new. As far back as the twelfth century B.C., a resourceful Chinese Emperor had employed carts armored with leather, and the amazing Leonardo da Vinci, in 1482, had designed and built an armored car which in appearance resembled a Chinese coolie's hat on wheels but for which he outlined tactics "surprisingly modern." Some two centuries later a famous Frenchman was beguiled by the same idea. It was in 1756 that Voltaire presented to the Duc de Richelieu his plan for a horsedrawn, armored wagon to be used to fight the Prussians. In practically every age, someone has suggested an armored vehicle.

To the English Army officer, Colonel, later General, Ernest D. Swinton, however, goes the credit for conceiving the first modern tank. This officer, stationed with British General Headquarters in France, had watched movement go out of war in 1914, when the machine gun had driven soldiers into the trenches and pinned them down. He had also observed the futility of mere artillery attempts to break the stalemate. To him, as to countless other military men, it looked as if the Germans and the Allies might well remain in the trenches until

1

they all had long gray beards, unless——. An idea suddenly came
to him. In his worried peregrinations behind the Allied lines
he had frequently watched with interest the seemingly inde-
structible little American-made Holt caterpillar tractors slosh-
ing powerfully through French mud that was impassable to
ordinary wheeled vehicles. Why couldn't these tractors be
armed and armored, and sent out across No Man's Land to
destroy the guns that had stopped the doughboys?

Granted leave in October, 1914, he scurried home across
the English Channel, to present his plan to a superior officer,
who, in turn, laid the proposal before the Committee of Impe-
rial Defense. Among the members of this committee was Winston Churchill, then First Lord of the Admiralty, who viewed
the new idea with much enthusiasm. He found himself, however, a minority of one in favor of the plan, which was shelved
with cool indifference by the high-ranking brass hats of the
committee. In vain Swinton continued to knock at the doors of
England's leaders with salesmanlike persistence, until his leave
was up and he was forced to return to France. His plan had
been rejected by some of the country's greatest, including
Lord Kitchener, Prime Minister Asquith, Sir Percy Scott, General Scott-Moncrieff, who declared such a vehicle as Swinton
proposed would be wrecked by enemy artillery before it could
be brought into action.

Yet the rude espousals of the colonel proved not to be without good result, for it was only a few months later—February
24, 1915, to be exact—that his idea for a tractored armored
vehicle was adopted, not by the British War office, for whose
benefit he had evolved the plan, but by the British Navy.
Though outvoted by the defense committee, Winston Churchill
had continued to advocate Swinton's proposal by directing persistent notes to all quarters of the government. When the
response proved lukewarm, however, and the War Office, after
feebly experimenting with two Holt tractors, officially abandoned the idea, Churchill took the bit between his teeth and
organized his own committee in the Navy to develop the track-

laying armored vehicle. To silence the criticism of any sticklers who might object that tractors were never meant to sail the seven seas, he dubbed his organization the "Landships Committee" and appointed Tennyson d'Eyncourt, a naval designer, as chairman. It is because of this naval origin that our tankmen of today still refer to the parts of their vehicle in such nautical terms as deck. bow, superstructure, hatch, and hull.

While the War Office was officially unapprised of the unorthodox experiments being conducted by the Navy's indomnitable Lord of the Admiralty, unofficially scores of British Army officers acquired stiff necks from peeping over the fence into the Navy's backyard. After several months of such uncomfortable and highly undignified rubbernecking from the sidelines, the War Office sheepishly invited Colonel Swinton to come back from France to explain his scheme more fully, while they communicated with the Admiralty and suggested that the two join hands in the venture. Both suggestions were accepted with alacrity, though by this time the tank's English godfather had departed the Admiralty because of the failure in the Dardenelles of another of his plans.

For many months of 1915, the common effort produced little but headaches, quarrels, and confusion. Experimental vehicles proved too big, too short, too clumsy, and mechanically deficient. Tracks sagged and came off the rollers. Test after test resulted in failure. Committee members were at odds with each other, while brass hats again began to lose interest. The British Engineer-in-Chief permitted himself to remark: "Before considering the proposal, we should descend from the realm of imagination to solid facts", and Lord Kitchener sneered at what he termed "a pretty, mechanical toy".

It is a singularly heartening fact that the design finally agreed upon was a product not only of combined army and navy efforts, but of international ingenuity as well. Utilizing the gasoline engine invented by the Germans and the caterpillar tractor developed by the United States, to which they added armor and armament, the British War Office and Admiralty produced a weapon which forever altered the course of combat. The tank was finished on January 26, 1916, a little more than a year from the time the idea was first presented by Colonel Swinton. Nine months later it made its debut on the field of battle.

Known variously as the Wilson Machine, Big Willie, Mother, or His Majesty's Land Ship Centipede, the vehicle was produced in two sexes: the female, weighing 30 tons; the male, 31. They were both 32 feet 6 inches long; the male was 11 feet wide, while the female, appropriately enough, was wider in the beam, being three inches broader than her mate. The male tank carried two 6-pounder naval guns and four machine guns, while the female tank, as befitted the weaker sex, was more lightly armed with machine guns only, six in number. The maximum speed was 3.7 miles an hour, and gas tank capacity 53 gallons, sufficient for the vehicle to travel 12 miles; but since the tank was to be fighting with foot infantry, this was considered fast enough and far enough for it to travel.

Following a successful test, a hundred and fifty of the machines were built. These offspring of "Mother" were christened "Mark I's" and began the "Mark" tank series, some 2,700 of which were manufactured by England during the war. In 1917, a light 15-ton tank called the Whippet was developed. Two hundred of these machines, capable of 8.3 miles an hour, were produced.

In a plot that would have done credit to a Hollywood grade B spy thriller, the name of "tank" was acquired for the armored vehicle and the secret of its existence preserved until its appearance at the Somme. In building the experimental model preceding "Mother", shop orders had been divided, the chassis being built in one part of the plant and labeled "Demonstration and Instructional Chassis" for the Royal Marines, the hull being built in another part of the plant and described as a "water carrier for Mesopotamia". Workmen nicknamed it "that tank thing". When the time came to go into production on the first vehicles, the secret became even more precarious and important. One 30-ton monster had been difficult enough to conceal. How could a hundred such elephantine carcasses be hidden from both friendly and enemy prying eyes. Swinton and his colleagues were no prestidigitators; yet they managed the trick very well. It was decided to carry out the idea of the water carrier originally used on the experimental model. Quantities of machinery and war materiel were daily being made and shipped to Russia, and, under the guise of water carriers destined for Russia, the hulking armored vehicles would be built. The word "Tank" was adopted as the official name for the supposed water carriers, and some of the hulls were even labeled in Russian characters "Petrograd with care".[1]

How surprised this little group of British machinators would have been, however, had they been able, in those early months of 1916, to peer through the windows of the workroom of the French company, Schneider et Cie, across the Channel! For there, behind closed shutters, an armored tracklaying vehicle much like their own, though smaller by half, was in the making. Ideas are no respecters of national boundaries or copyrights. They come to every one. In the fall of 1914, the same American Holt caterpillar tractors that had served as the touchstone for Swinton's tank ideas had similarly served the French officer, Colonel (later General) Baptiste Estienne.

Twice the French colonel suggested his ideas to General Headquarters, only to be ignored. A year went by which brought no change in the stalemate on the Western Front. Neither side had moved from the protection of their muddy, bleak trenches. The machine gun still remained king of the battlefield. The colonel decided to try once more, and on December 1, 1915, he addressed a letter to the top man, General Joffre himself. In his communication he described the kind of machine he believed necessary and asked permission to go to Paris to get the work started. The moment proved propitious; the general acquiesced. Twelve days later Colonel Estienne was on his way to interview M. Renault. When this automobile magnate reacted with an undisguised lack of enthusiasm, Estienne at once repaired to the office of M Brillié of the rival automotive firm, Schneider and Company. M. Brillié needed no persuasion; he had long been convinced of the feasibility of such a vehicle. Through the combined efforts of the two men, a week later the project was under way, and in two months production of 400 Schneider tanks began. They weighed 15 tons, went 5 miles an hour, were armed with one short 75mm gun and two machine guns, and were the first French tanks in action.

Simultaneously, production began on the French St. Chamond tank, sponsored by M. Bréton, Undersecretary of State for Inventions, who felt his protégé was far superior to the Schneider. This was a heavier tank, weighing 25 tons and carrying one 75mm gun and four machine guns.

While the British had begun tank development a year sooner than the French, they had squandered many months in red tape and quarrels. Thus it came about that Britain's first tanks were ordered at almost the same time as the French. Such was the secrecy surrounding the work on both sides of the Channel, however, that not until June, 1916, did they discover each other's activities. Estienne immediately hurried to England to view a demonstration of the Mark. The upshot of his visit was a suggestion to both governments that they cooperate in launching a surprise joint offensive with thousands of tanks. This advice was tossed overboard when the British attacked alone at the Somme, with a mere handful of Marks.

Upon his return to Paris, Estienne once again visited M. Renault, and this time succeeded in persuading the auto man to manufacture light tanks. During 1916, 1917, and 1918, five thousand of these tanks, named Renault, were built. They weighed 7.4 tons, could go 6 miles an hour, and carried one 37mm gun or one machine gun and a crew of two.

The United States entered the war the same month the French first used their tanks in action and seven months after the first British tank attack. It would be gratifying to record that soon American tanks were pouring off the assembly lines and being rushed to the Front in thousands. But the plain facts of history are that at the war's end twenty-six American tanks had been built, and none had arrived overseas.

The idea of armoring and arming a tractor was first conceived in this country late in 1915 by Cleve F. Shaffer, a San Franciscan inventor and manufacturer of a small orchard tractor. He offered his plans to the German consul in that city. When this worthy Teuton summarily rejected them on the grounds that his country had no use for such equipment to win the war, he was echoing the official attitude of the entire German General Staff toward tanks. Of the consul's decision Colonel Icks remarks in Tanks, "Its cheapness and the fact that it was already in production would have made it possible to equip the German Army with thousands of these little one-man tanks and easily might have influenced the course of the war.

Though prior to our declaration of war in April, 1917, several experimental models of tanks had been built by American companies, the Army possessed none. The War Department's official attitude was expressed by the American Military Mission in Paris, which, after observing the disappointing performance of tanks through 1916 and the early months of 1917, declared them to be a failure. When General Pershing arrived in France in 1917, he ordered a restudy of tanks, which resulted in a recommendation to organize American tank troops and to equip them with tanks built like the British heavy Marks and the French light Renaults. Though the Allied position was grave and the need for immediate assistance acute, there ensued another shillyshallying delay of six months in adopting the plan. Then, on January 26, 1918, the American Tank Corps suddenly came to life. Plump, marshmallowy Colonel S. D. Rockenbach was appointed the Chief, while Major George S. Patton was chosen to organize and direct the Tank Center at Langres, France. A treaty with England, providing for America to build Mark VIII's, (a miniature of which became the collar emblem of America's tankmen in 1940), and an agreement with France, arranging for the production of modified Renaults in this country, were executed. War plans were out-

lined which called for 23,405 tanks; and an appropriation of
$175,000,000 was approved to pay for them.

The race was on but no course had been set, and the run-
ners scattered in all directions. The A.E.F. had one set of
arrangements; government agencies in the United States, various others. Meanwhile, a dozen private corporations embarked
upon their own tank designs, ignoring the fact that tried and
proven English and French designs were available. Henry Ford
began work on a 2-ton, 3-man, and a 3-man, 7.5-ton tank. Holt
Tractor and General Electric collaborated on a gas-electric
model. Endicott and Johnson, shoe manufacturers, financed a
tank-mounted flame thrower developed by an Army engineer.
The Pioneer Tractor Company of Winona, Minnesota, contrived an ingenious machine out of iron pipe with standard
plumbing connections. It was designated "Skeleton" Tank, and
is very likely still rattling around in the company's closet.

Not until the fall of 1918, on the eve of the war's end, was a
tank coordinator appointed to unsnarl the tangle. But then it
was too late. Millions of dollars and invaluable time had been
squandered, with a mere 26 tanks, none in Europe, to show for
it. When American tankmen rode into battle in machines lent
by the Allies, the pride of "the greatest industrial nation in the
world" was humbled in the dust.

II

"Every tank is to do its damndest." With this simple sentence
a tank commander signaled his only order to his fleet in one
of the most important battles of World War I. Brave words, in
the best military tradition of Wellington and Marlborough,
but scarcely adequate to meet the exigencies of a new mechanized warfare. That the tank survived the mishandling and
mechanical defects of the World War I model is due more to
the farsightedness of a few men than to its performance in
combat.

The battle plan of the Somme, in which tanks were first used, called for them to reach their first objective five minutes ahead of the infantry to demolish the strong points of resistance that lay in their path. Forty-nine tanks only were available for the attack. These were divided into four groups and assigned to different army corps. Ten other tanks, unfit for action because of mechanical troubles, constituted the reserve. Of the forty-nine tanks, seventeen broke down or were stuck before they even reached the line of departure; nine more broke down at the line; another nine were unable to get started in time to leave with the infantry to which they were assigned; and five bogged down during the attack. Nine lonely tanks completed their mission. The only reason the attack was not a complete failure lay in the demoralizing effect the new machine had on the startled German troops.

Though the British and French used tanks in action a dozen times more in the succeeding year, their unimpressive performance led the British War Office to declare officially that tanks were a failure. In the battle of Arras, which was fought on April 9, 1917, the British statement was not disproved. When the required number of tanks for the attack were not found in France, instructional centers were stripped of training vehicles. This improvised fleet was again broken up into small groups and scattered over a long front line area. What tanks did not break down because of inner complaints succumbed to bad weather and boggy ground, and the infantry, trained to work with them, was forced to go forward alone.

Next day at Bullecourt the tanks did nothing to redeem themselves. Assigned to support the Aussies in assaulting Bullecourt, they started out in a blinding snowstorm. By its nature, the tank is a relatively blind animal even in good weather. With their visibility even more limited by the snow, the tanks at Bullecourt were as helpless as eyeless elephants. Their pace was so slow that they failed to reach their positions at the appointed time, and the Aussies had to retreat with heavy casualties. For many months thereafter, the soldiers from Down Under regarded tanks in the same category as Germans.

The Allies, however, were not alone in viewing pessimistically the performance of the new vehicle. Before the Allied venture the German High Command had rejected experimental models of tanks on the grounds of their impracticability, and even after the first British surprise tank attack, though they instituted a study of the possibilities of the new weapon in response to urgent demands from the Chief of the General Staff in the Field, they remained somewhat dubious of its value. Nevertheless, several experimental models of a fairly satisfactory design were developed, and it was decided to proceed with their manufacture in quantity. Labor and material shortages, strikes, and transportation difficulties, as well as the lack of whole-hearted support of the program by the High Command, conspired to delay production, however, and as a result only a handful of German tanks were completed and operating on the front at the war's end. Altogether, the Germans used 45 tanks in action, the majority of which were captured and reconditioned British Mark IV's and Medium A's.

More successful was the enemy in developing antitank measures. It was the practice of the Allies to precede their tank attacks with an artillery bombardment, thereby giving the Germans ample warning of their intentions. When the tanks thereafter appeared before the German lines, they were often met with a hot reception. Most effective antitank weapon was the German artillery, which was thorough and deadly, while the slowness and clumsiness of the tank made it an almost perfect target. The Germans were not long in observing that trenches were a natural tank trap. When they began to dig wider ones, crossing them in a tank became even more difficult and hazardous. French Schneiders and St. Chamonds became the principal victims of this device. With uncanny accuracy, German riflemen soon ferreted out vulnerable chinks in tank armor, and bullet splash, when hot lead entered the vehicle through cracks and openings, blinded and wounded countless hundreds of tankmen. Track exploders and mines were not long in making their appearance, while gas barrages, declared one British officer, had defeated his crew. "When it drifted toward us and began to seep into our bus, we were handicapped and handcuffed. Then I began to vomit, violently, endlessly, and I didn't care a cuss what happened to me."

Life in a tank became not only dangerous but downright suicidal, and it was not long before the tank acquired the unenviable reputation of being a "coffin on wheels". When the Germans discovered the vulnerability of the fuel tank, the tank too often became a "flaming coffin".

Nevertheless, despite the dark fame and gloomy performances attending the wake of the tank, the new vehicle continued to be used, and on November 20, 1917, there occurred a bright day in tank history. It was described thus twelve years later by Adna R. Chaffee, an American tank officer who was trying to persuade the U.S. Army of the importance of an armored force:

"Three hundred and eighty-one tanks were concentrated behind the front of the British Army at Cambrai. At 6:20 o'clock on the morning of the 20th, they jumped off without the preliminary artillery bombardment which had preceded all other tank attacks, and succeeded in surprising the enemy. Their attack went through five miles. However, British GHQ had so little faith in the idea and had lost so many of its men in its offensive campaign in the mud of Ypres that they had no adequate force to take advantage of the penetration. Two cavalry divisions were available to exploit the success, but they were inadequate to the task, for the breach was not wide enough to permit the passage of horsemen through the concentration of fire which fell upon the gap . . . This was the real birth of the tank . . ."

In the battle, conditions favorable to tanks had prevailed. The terrain had been suitable, the weather good, and the enemy surprised. Though seven days later, the British had lost practically all of their gains, tanks emerged from the fight in renewed favor, reviving the drooping spirits of tank proponents and giving pause to doubters. The staid British War Office did a quick about face and began to push the production of tanks instead of discouraging it, while General Pershing delayed no longer but summoned Rockenbach to France to organize the American Tank Corps.

On Germany's "blackest day of the war", August 8th, 1918, the entire British Tank Corps in France—excepting the 1st Brigade—was engaged at the battle of Amiens. In the attack, tanks played a dual role—supporting the infantry by knocking out machine gun nests and assisting the cavalry in exploiting the breakthrough, some tanks being assigned the new job of carrying machine gun crews and their weapons to aid the cavalry in holding objectives until the arrival of infantry. Because the heat and ventilation of the tanks were so bad, however, most of the crews got out and walked to their destination, preferring not to be asphyxiated en route. In accordance with the lesson learned at Cambrai, no artillery bombardment preceded the attack, which went forward seven and a half miles on the first day. But the Tank Corps paid dearly for the success. On that day too tanks were lost to artillery fire, and at the end of four days 70 percent of the tanks were out of action.

Yankee tankers mounted in French machines were baptized by fire in the American show at St. Mihiel on September 12, 1918. Consisting of two battalions, the 344th and 345th, and two groups totaling 24 tanks, the 304th American Tank Brigade, commanded by George Patton, entered the fight in support of the Fourth Corps under General Dickman. Zero hour was set for 5 A.M. A drizzling rain and mist cloaked the movement of the American doughboys as they went over the top. Tanks of the 344th chugged ahead, cutting barbed wire and clearing the path, while tanks of the 345th clanked and wheezed in the rear. Action proceeded according to plan until the first German trench was reached, when large numbers of tanks became stuck. Precious time was lost getting them out, and even more precious gallons of fuel. By three o'clock, the tanks were out of gas, necessitating an unexpected refueling. Total casualties at the end of the day: Of the 174 tanks that started, 23 were ditched, 21 broke down with mechanical troubles, 5 were destroyed by shells and mines. Total bag of prisoners for the tanks—40. Tank history at St. Mihiel shows the brigade stopped in its tracks on succeeding days by mud, lack of fuel, road congestion, and mechanical failures. To the everlasting glory of the American doughboy on foot went the credit for the victory. They bagged 16,000 prisoners and 450 German guns and regained in four days a region held by the enemy for four years.

In the Meuse-Argonne offensive, which began six days later, what remained of the 304th Brigade was assigned to support only a portion of the I Corps line, inasmuch as headquarters deemed much of the proposed battle area too rough and shell torn for tank operations. When intense machine gun resistance was encountered, however, tanks were ordered into action in even the most difficult terrain. The great tragedy lay in the too few tanks available. As the battle progressed, more and more of the tanks were disabled, for which there were no replacements. It was about this time that General Pershing offered "anything in the A.E.F. for 500 additional tanks". When the war ended a month and a half later, every vehicle in the brigade was in the last stages of disintegration, and the personnel riddled with casualties.

By the fall of 1918, the laboratory of war had wrought many changes in Britain's hulking monster of 1916. To neutralize German antitank bullets, tanks wore thicker coats of armor and fire-proof felt packing in their joints to lessen bullet splash. To cross trenches, they carried 1.5-ton portable bridges called fascines. Tracks were wider, and ventilation improved. Cruising radius of the tank was 40 miles instead of 12, and speeds had increased from 3.7 to 6.5 miles an hour.

As to its behavior on the battlefield, a somewhat stuffy code of ethics ruled its conduct. The infantry was the Queen of Battle, and never must the tank forget its subordinate position as handmaiden to the Queen. In combat, it was a ward of the Queen's generals. "An infantry would be dishonored," declared French protocol, "who would subordinate its advance to that of the tanks."[2] Despite such stern pronouncements, however, on May 31, 1918, the elephantine servant of the Queen committed a serious breach of etiquette. In the heat of battle at Ploissy-Chazelle she lost her head and bounded out to the objective far in advance of the infantry. When royal generals were apprised of the treasonous deed, they ordered the tanks back to escort the infantry forward. That such tactics gave aid and comfort to enemy artillery fire and lost impressive gains was of secondary importance to the honor of the Queen.

The seeds of revolution were stirring, however, in the noisy, teeming Central Workshops in France. There, too late to get in World War I, an experimental tank had been built by a young British major that could go thirty miles an hour. Could such a machine ever be tied down to the pace of an ordinary foot soldier?

III

"When war is over, the country at large thinks no more of the means and methods of making war. Its object is to lick its wounds and recover its loss in life and money. The natural tendency is to put aside the weapons with which the last war has been fought as the main supply for the next." Thus wryly observed A.E.F. Colonel Adna Romanza Chaffee who, ten years later, became America's leading exponent of an armored force.

To no other vehicle of war could Chaffee's statement be more truly applied than to tanks, which were strictly a wartime vehicle. Trucks, automobiles, motorcycles, ships and airplanes continued to pour off the assembly lines in large quantities, but not tanks. With the signing of the Armistice, all public interest in armored, tracklaying vehicles ceased. Moreover, military opinion itself was divided on the value of tanks in war. How could one include in cut-and-dried war plans a vehicle that had a tendency to break down when it was most needed and to out-run the infantry when it was in good condition? In view of such undependable conduct, the General Staff was understandably reluctant to include in a threadbare army budget money for a comparatively new and expensive vehicle at a time when the entire army was notoriously underpaid. A report submitted to Congress in 1919 showed that junior officers were receiving $3.00 less per day than stevedores in New York Harbor, while the pay scale of other ranks was correspondingly low. As a result, the regular ranks of the Army were being decimated by an epidemic of resignations of officers who could not support their families on military salaries in the face of spiraling costs of living. "And those who have resigned," sighed General Peyton March, Chief of Staff, "are men of high initiative, force, energy, and self-reliance—military qualities which the Army can ill afford to lose." Thus sorely beset by a variety of vexing problems, the War Department was too occupied to worry about tanks.

For the next year and a half, however, the U.S. Tank Corps under Rockenbach continued feebly to endure. Then, on June 4, 1920, under the provisions of the National Defense Act, which reorganized the entire army, the Tank Corps was abolished, and its equipment and personnel inherited by a somewhat indifferent infantry arm. Its equipment consisted of tanks that had been started during the war but not finished until 1919: 1,000 6-Ton M1917's (American-copied Renaults), which went 5.5 miles an hour maximum and required incessant repairs from the day they left the factory until they were junked; 100 Mark VIII's, modeled after the British Mark series, which went 6.5 miles an hour but were so unreliable that Maj. C. C. Benson, tank equipment expert, said: "Its vibration is so great that engine bolts must be tightened after each three hours of running time"; and 15 Ford baby 3-ton tanks, which could go 8 miles an hour but which were so small inside that even a crew of two was cramped. With the exception of ten experimental models, all unsatisfactory, these were the only tanks possessed by the United States Army until 1930.

The battalions of the Corps were broken up into companies and assigned to infantry divisions; others later formed tank "groups"; and still others became inactive. The tank school was taken over by the Chief of Infantry and located at Fort George G. Meade, Maryland. Here for the next decade, tank doctrine, based on the characteristics of the maladroit Mark and the rheumatoid Renault, taught each successive class of officers and men that the tank was a purely infantry weapon to be used in intimate support of foot infantry battalions in the assault. Except by an embattled few, notably Adna Chaffee, Major Sereno Brett, and Major R. E. Jones of the three iron horsemen, Jones, Rarey and Icks, no independent force of massed tanks, based on a future fast new vehicle, was envisioned.

In England, General J. F. C. Fuller almost singlehandedly rescued the Royal Tank Corps from extinction. The English High Command in 1919, declared this famed English tank expert, did its utmost to abolish the tank altogether, and "undoubtedly would have succeeded but for the strong opposition on the part of myself, supported by a few progressively minded soldiers. After four years of toil, we succeeded in saving three cadre tank battalions out of the thirty-five either in existence or being raised when the war ended. Five years later, that is in 1923, the first new post-war tank—the Vickers Medium—was produced in small numbers (100), to remain for sixteen years the sole medium machine in the British Army."[3]

As in the United States, tank development in the French Army was entrusted to the infantry in the postwar period. Tank tactics were based entirely upon the use of the tank as a close support weapon of the foot soldier. In 1919, General Petain declared in an official bulletin "Infantry will in fifty years time perhaps be carried in tanks", but "for the present the tank is an infantry arm working in the midst of infantry". Light World War Renaults constituted the bulk of French tanks until the late 30's.

The only other tanks produced during that time were some two dozen heavies, ranging in weight from seventy tons to one hundred forty-four tons, and scarcely able to move. These latter tanks were designed, according to another official pronouncement of Petain, to progress "over country which is shell torn or has long been organized for defense in front of infantry, in order to make paths for it and to facilitate the crossing of the light tanks." Thus the top military chief of France visualized the war of the future beginning where World War I ended—in the trenches—and he continued to hold these views when the Germans were knocking at the doors of France with their armored fists twenty years later.

The irony of the defeat of Germany was that her weakness became her strength. By the Treaty of Versailles, Germany was forbidden to manufacture tanks. Thus while the Allies were encumbered throughout the period following the war with thousands of obsolete tanks which a starvation budget did not permit them to junk, the Germans were free to evolve tank tactics to suit their purposes and later to build the tanks to fit them. When Hitler abrogated the peace treaty in 1933 and Germany began to rearm, mass production was immediately begun on a speedy new tank which formed the spearhead of Germany's blitzkrieg plans.

CHAPTER TWO

The Gasoline Brigade

I

Ten years after the appearance of the first Mark tanks at the Somme, the British again made tank history. At the instigation of certain tank-minded officers who foresaw mechanized warfare in the future, an experimental force composed of tanks and armored cars had been organized, and in the summer of 1927 this unique outfit, the only one of its kind in the world, had been assembled at Aldershot, England, to demonstrate what it could do.

Present at one of the maneuvers was the U.S. Secretary of War, Dwight Davis, who was visiting in England. Though the Experimental Mechanized Force was less than one year old and a crude and makeshift affair, nevertheless what Davis saw that day at Aldershot convinced him that the United States needed a similar organization. His orders to the Chief of Staff upon his return to this country, directing that such action be taken, forever altered the development of tanks in America. Proceeding through routine military channels, the Chief of Staff, General Charles P. Summerall, obeyed the instructions of the Secretary by dispatching to G-3 a little pink slip on which was written, "Organize a Mechanized Force. C.P.S."

It is doubtful if any more challenging task has ever been dumped into U.S. military laps during an interlude of peace, and the reaction of the officers of the various arms who constituted G-3 was mixed. Most of them were aware of tanks only as rather smelly, unmilitary monsters belonging to the infantry.

19

Few had ever ridden in one, or desired to do so. And all they
knew about a mechanized force had been gleaned from rather
sparse accounts of the crazy English experiment in the service
journals. Yet if the chief wanted them to pull a mechanized
force out of the hat for him, that they must do. Like good soldiers they set about the task.

Meantime, a soothing announcement was issued,[1] which
assured jittery brass hats of the infantry and cavalry that "motors
and tanks would not displace (them), as the conclusion has
been reached that these branches of the Service must still continue to form the bulk of land forces in time of war . . . The first
step in mechanization . . . will be the development of one completely mechanized unit for experimental purposes, not as a
part of the Infantry or Cavalry, but as a new arm . . ."

The fruition of six months of labor in the War Department
was the assemblage of an Experimental Mechanized Force at
Fort George G. Meade on July 1, 1928. Though the press hailed
the army's newest baby with a frenzy of enthusiasm, there was
nothing to be excited about. What the papers saluted as "the
pride of the Army" with "terrific smashing power" was in reality
a pitifully weak and inadequate conglomeration of old, obsolete equipment.

From Fort Eustis, Virginia, there had come one battalion of
the 34th Infantry, riding in World War Liberty trucks. From
Fort Hoyle had arrived the 2d Battalion, 6th Field Artillery, less
one battery. They were equipped with 75's, and porteed in Liberty trucks also. From other posts in the East there had been
borrowed a company of Engineers, a Signal Company, a Medical Detachment, an Ammunition train, and an Observation
Squadron. Backbone of the force were the 16th Tank Battalion
(light), equipped with Renaults, vintage World War, the 17th
Tank Battalion (Heavy), equipped with Mark VIII's, and the 2d
Platoon, 4th Tank Company, all from Meade and contributed
by the infantry. The cavalry had sent, albeit reluctantly, the one
and only armored car troop in the country from Fort Myer. In
all, there were some 3,000 men included in the original outfit.

The performance of the "Gasoline Brigade", as it was fondly called by newsmen, was no more than could be expected from such an indifferently mechanized organization. The rattletrap trucks and aged tanks made four miles an hour if they were lucky, instead of a scheduled ten. What one writer impressively described as "an ominous rumble" too often was the asthmatic wheeze of a motor in its death agony. To complicate matters, Maryland highway officials put a crimp in maneuver plans by objecting to tanks marching on roads because they might ruin the taxpayers' asphalt. The ambitious objective laid down by the War Department to the commander of the mechanized force stated that he "by practical tests in tactical and strategical employments, will experiment with its organization and equipment with a view to developing correct doctrines with respect to motorization and mechanization of appropriate units of the Army". When, however, the old machines one after another broke down, the ambitious program had to be shelved, and on September 20th, with no money in sight to buy new equipment, "Uncle Sam's Mechanical Army" was hastily disbanded.

To proponents of a mechanized force, the debacle at Meade had not been heartening; yet it could not be considered entirely a failure. It augured well for the future of mechanization that branch jealousies had been submerged in a common effort without the compulsion of war. Moreover, the publicity attendant upon the event had brought the subject of tanks into the spotlight and set the whole army arguing pro and con. "To mechanize or not to mechanize" became the topic of the day. Impassioned brigadiers inveighed against the machine age and voiced their opinion that any continuation of the experiment would be a waste of time. "God invented man's hand and brain," they solemnly declared, "and no machine can ever take their place." More reasonable souls advocated another try, but next time with modern equipment, and found welcome vocal support in the *Washington Post*. "It has been proved", the paper said editorially, "that a motorized force is superior to one that is not. But a force mounted on broken-down equipment cannot prevail against an army mounted in modern, up-to-the-minute machines. It has been demonstrated that the need is imperative for increased appropriations for mechanization. Congress should not refuse any request for such funds."

To all impartial observers, however, it was clear that no tactical doctrines for a mechanized force had emerged from the mock battle of Maryland. "The impossibility of accepting or rejecting any ideas of mechanization based on the [George G. Meade] Force is recognized," stated the *Army-Navy Journal* on July 21, 1928. More study was deemed necessary by the War Department, and once again the matter of mechanization fell into the hands of G-3, where it was assigned to the Training Section.

Thus, to this small group was given the power to set the future course of mechanization in America. Would they agree with the men who had rejected the Meade experiment as folly, or would they blaze the trail for a new kind of army? Now, as never before, mechanization needed a champion.

II

Military history has been made by the right man being at the right place at the right time, George Patton once remarked, and never was this more true than of the Armored Force and of his friend, Adna Romanza Chaffee.

At about the same time that Secretary Davis was watching the tank demonstration in England, this lean, hawk-eyed, high-goal polo-playing cavalry officer reported for duty on the War Department General Staff. There he was assigned to the Training Section of G-3. He was present when General Summerall's pink slip, directing the organization of a mechanized force, arrived, and an interested participant in the lengthy discussions that ensued. Though he had never even ridden in a tank, he found that the more he learned about a mechanized force, the more his enthusiasm grew. He journeyed to Rochester, New

York, to look at a new seven-ton tank, capable of going eighteen miles an hour, that James Cunningham and Sons were building for the Ordnance Department. He witnessed at Meade the demonstration of another new experimental tank built by Walter Christie. This model weighed ten tons and went forty-two and a half miles an hour.

"Should we tie tanks of these characteristics to the immediate front of infantry advancing at two miles per hour? Should they be hemmed in the restricted space between the barrage in front and the infantry in the rear?" he asked himself. To these questions, he believed the answer was "No."

"Can we use this light tank as the backbone itself of a force of given size? Can we view it, rather than the man on foot, as the principal arm in such a force?" He believed the answer to these was "Yes."

When, therefore, a restudy of the whole question of mechanization fell to the Training Section of which he was a member, he was already recognized in the War Department as a strong advocate of a mechanized force. Thirteen years later he wore the title, "Father of the Armored Force."

That Adna Chaffee became the leading exponent of blitzkrieg warfare in America should have occasioned no surprise to those who knew him. No ordinary pace suited him. All his life he did things in a hurry.

On September 23rd, 1884, when he first presented himself to his pretty, golden-haired, young mother at Junction City, Kansas, he did not even wait for his Army father to return from the Indian Wars to attend his birth. The next ten years, which he spent with his mother and sisters chasing the family head from cavalry post to cavalry post on the Southwestern frontier, did nothing to slacken his original tempo. As soon as he could sit on a horse, his father taught him to ride. Thenceforth, young Chaffee went charging over the plains at breakneck speeds, in imitation of his dashing parent. Imprinted forever upon his soul was a love for wild, charging horses and flying hooves on desert sands.

"He rode like an Indian," declared one of his friends.

In 1901, when he was sixteen, his energetic behavior landed him in considerable difficulties with the Japanese health authorities.

His father, the previous year, had gone to China to command the American forces in the Boxer Rebellion. At the close of the war, he was informed by the War Department that his next assignment would be in Manila, where he was to succeed General Arthur MacArthur as Military Governor of the Philippines. Accordingly he had written his family the news and bade them to meet him in Manila in the summer of 1901. Chafing at the long wait of some six months, young Chaffee prevailed upon his parents to allow him to journey off at once to join his father in China instead. All went well on the young man's trip until the boat arrived in Yokohama, where a case of smallpox was discovered aboard. The Japanese health officers immediately placed the vessel under quarantine for two weeks. That night Adna escaped ashore and registered for the night at a Yokohama hotel. There he was discovered sound asleep the next morning by the assiduous health authorities.

"The young gentleman from America will have to take a bath," the Japanese said, smiling toothily, while Adna stared at them in amazement. It was a special kind of a bath, they explained to him, to disinfect his person of smallpox germs.

"And then may I leave for China?" young Chaffee inquired.

"No," replied the Japanese politely. "But we are giving you a big privilege. You may remain quarantined in this room instead of returning to your boat."

Several days later he eluded his Japanese wardens again, and sailed to China on another boat, having learned the efficacy of American dollar diplomacy at an earlier age than most.

At West Point, his dynamic energy found release in fearless and accomplished horsemanship in the riding hall and on the cavalry plain, and "he was considered one of the best riders, if not the best, in the class."[2] It was at the Academy that he learned to play polo, a game which he continued to play for thirty years with considerable zest and distinction. Completely absorbed in such equine activities, however, he was less than impressive in his classroom performances. Among the seventy-eight boys in the graduating class of 1906, Cadet Chaffee ranked number thirty-one.

A fledgling lieutenant in the cavalry, he continued his studies in equitation at the Cavalry School in Fort Riley, Kansas, hard by the scene of his birth. In less than three years, he had acquired the reputation of being the "Army's finest horseman." No horseshow in Madison Square Garden or in Potomac Park was complete without this slim, handsome officer's name on the program; no polo game a success in which he did not star. Recognition of his talents came in 1911, when he was selected, the youngest in years and the lowest in rank of a team of five, to represent the United States in the International Horse Show held in London during the Coronation Week of George V. The following year he attended the French Cavalry School at Saumur, France, reputed to be the best in the world, where he acquired a foreign polish to his horsemanship by learning to jump over fully set dinner tables without so much as overturning a water glass.

Had Chaffee been a man of just average intelligence, he might have been content with such horsy derringdo until he was old enough to retire. As it was, he possessed what magazine-writer Beverly Smith has described as "one of the best brains in the army"—a brain that routine classroom exercises at West Point had not served to kindle. (In the draft of an article which Mr. Smith wrote for the *American Magazine* in 1940, he used this statement. When the copy was submitted to Chaffee for approval before publication, he asked that Mr. Smith omit these words. This Mr. Smith did and substituted instead, "has had many important assignments in the Army.") It was on the eve of our entry into the World War, when Chaffee was a captain and Senior Cavalry Instructor at the Academy, that suddenly he found the glitter of the riding ring and the triumphs of the polo field beginning to pall. He was then 33, married, and the father of one child. For many months, from his rocky, sheltered perch above the Hudson, he had been watching the panorama of world events and, on the map of Europe on the wall of his den, tracing the progress of the war with pins. One night he revealed to his wife the thoughts that filled his mind. "I am through with horseshow riding," he said. "There isn't any future in it. From now on it will be the serious side of the Army for me. I'm going to get on the General Staff."

When the war came, however, he went to Fort Jackson, South Carolina, as a major in the infantry. A few months later came his chance to go to the General Staff College of the A.E.F. at Langres, France. "At the school," reminisced one of his class-mates,[3] "all of us but Chaffee pored over our books all day and half the night. When we saw him finish his work at noon every day and leave, we were sure he would flunk."

Far from failing, Major Chaffee's grades in the course were so high that, much to his disgust, he was retained as an instruc-tor. Thus forced to remain at Langres, he fretted and fumed with impatience, until a few months later he was on his way to Pershing's headquarters, thence to the General Staff at the front. "When I first saw Adna Chaffee," wrote Austen Lake in the Boston *Sunday Advertiser* some years later, "he was a tempo-rary colonel at Chaumont (France), then the general head-quarters of the A.E.F. I used to see Chaffee hustling across the parade grounds where . . . military dudes were wont to stroll between band concerts and guard mount. Chaffee never strolled. Chaffee cantered."

As energetically as he had undertaken equine exploits in his early days, he now pursued his career on the General Staff. For his staff services during the war, he received the Distin-guished Service Medal, which was pinned on his blouse by Per-shing himself in Neuweid, Germany. Upon his return to the United States, he successively taught at the Command and General Staff School at Fort Leavenworth and attended as a student the Army War College in Washington.

His post-graduate education was now complete. He had learned all that the Army had to offer on the art and science of war. At the War College, where each year a select group of hand-picked officers was groomed as potential generals, he had come face to face with the problems incident to high command and to mobilization for war. Here, too, he had probed deeply into the industrial heart of America, from which flowed the tools of war. What use he would make of these valuable lessons was thenceforth more or less up to him. It was at this critical juncture of his career that the Chief of Cavalry, then General Malin Craig, sought to reclaim him for cavalry school service as head of the Horsemanship Department. During the war, cavalry had been eclipsed on the battlefield by the firepower of machine guns, which had proved to be as deadly to horsemen as to rifle-armed infantry. As a result, military horsemanship everywhere had suffered the doldrums. The effect of this war experience still lingered at Fort Riley, and Craig wanted a strong man to restore the school to its former position. He considered Chaffee the ideal man for the job. Despite strong urgings, however, Chaffee declined Craig's offer, demurring that there were younger men than he, and older men who had continued the riding end of cavalry, far better suited for the job.

Craig ceased his blandishments when Chaffee was ordered to duty on the General Staff on July 1st, 1927. Then came Summerall's directive to organize a mechanized force, and Chaffee's course was irrevocably set. The ideas for a future mechanized force, which emerged from the Training Section of G-3 after the Meade maneuvers, were his, and they formed the basis for a written report drawn up by a War Department Mechanization Board of which he was also a member. The last "i" was dotted and the last "t" of this document was crossed on December 5th, 1928, and the same day Chaffee entrained with his wife for Florida to spend a month's leave in the sun. As they sped through the wintry Virginia hills, he said to his wife with a chuckle, "Well, today I turned in a paper at the War Department. When I come back, they'll either meet me with a brass band, or St. Elizabeth's funny wagon."

The paper was noteworthy in that it outlined for the first time for official consideration a definite program leading to the creation of an armored force. Specifically, it proposed a four-year plan to organize as a part of the Regular Army a four-million-dollar, completely mechanized, self-contained, highly mobile regiment—this initial unit to serve as the testing laboratory for similar new fighting outfits which Chaffee predicted would form "a great part of the highly mobile combat troops of the next war." Likewise, it proposed that the new mechanized force be developed as a separate branch of the service, and that a general officer be appointed as its organizer and commander. The time set for the activation of the unit was the fiscal year 1931, beginning July 1st, 1930. 1929 was to be spent testing tank armor and antitank weapons.

Backbone of the force was to be fleets of fast, new tanks. But since tanks were "noisy, blind and their capacity for prolonged defense limited," auxiliary troops, mounted in armored cars, personnel carriers and trucks, would supply their deficiencies. Cannons mounted on tank chassis were proposed for mechanized artillery.

Equipment was to be furnished on the installment plan. Each year for the first three years, the mechanized force would receive one-third of its modern equipment, until by the end of the third year of its existence it would be completely up-to-date—the idea behind this provision being to make the cost of the new organization an easier pill for the War Department budget to swallow.

Like the "Gasoline Brigade" the new force was to be a union of all the arms: cavalry in armored cars for reconnaissance, tanks to strike the enemy, infantry in trucks to hold the ground won by tanks until other infantry could arrive, artillery on tracks to give supporting fire, engineers to build and to clear, chemical warfare to supply fire, smoke and gas, antiaircraft to fight planes, signalmen to transmit orders, supply and repair to keep the vehicles moving—the whole to comprise a unit self-sufficient and self-supporting in combat.

The tactical role of the force would be based on its characteristics of speed, armor, and operating radius. Its missions would include seizure and temporary holding of distant key points, turning and enveloping movements where speed was essential, counterattacks, advance, flank or rear guard actions, and exploitation of a break-through.

"If fast tanks can operate in this manner," declared Chaffee, "we may greatly aid in restoring mobility to warfare, in keeping with the element of operating on the flank and rear and through the gap, in forcing the enemy to make detachments to guard his lines of communications, important bridges, airdromes and bases, and so considerably weaken his main forces in the battle. We may reach quicker decisions in war."

III

Though the Secretary of War approved in principle the proposed program for a mechanized force, no provision was made in the forthcoming budget of the War Department to obtain money for its adoption. A number of reasons conspired to bring this about. Work on the budget which should have included the money had begun even before the maneuvers at Meade in the summer of 1928, and at the time of the completion of the mechanization report, the estimates for the fiscal year, 1930, had already been prepared by the Budget Department and approved by the Secretary of War, and were ready for submission to Congress by the President. To insert an item not included in the estimates required the sponsorship of a member of the Military Subcommittee of the House Appropriations Committee, a procedure which often entailed lively behind-the-scenes manipulation. It was first necessary to reach a congenial Congressional ear and then persuade it of the merits of the project for which the additional money was desired. If the Representative was convinced, then he consented to present the item before the committee members and plead for its adoption. A friend in Congress was quite literally often worth his weight in gold to War Department budgeteers.

To have obtained funds for mechanization in 1929 would have involved such Machiavellian backstage operations. Chaffee had no friends on the Congressional Committee, and no ally appeared to undertake the task.

One is impressed, when reading the service journals of this period, by the number of articles supporting a mechanized force written by lieutenants, captains, and majors. One is even more impressed by the silence of the "big guns." The men who were powerful enough to have come to Chaffee's aid were made conspicuous by their failure to do so. Some were completely disinterested in the experiment, and expressed their attitude in bland indifference. Others jealously regarded the plan as an encroachment upon their domain and openly opposed it. Not a small group opined that the Army could ill afford such an expensive, new gadget as a mechanized force when the ranks of the military were so underpaid.

An undercover dogfight that developed between the infantry and ordnance on the question of tank models injected even more sulphur into the situation. The two tanks involved were the ordnance model, which Chaffee had seen at Rochester, and the Christie model, which had been demonstrated at Meade.

In 1927, the first light tank since World War I had been produced by Cunningham & Sons according to ordnance specifications drawn up at the behest of Chief of Infantry Allen. This tank carried a crew of two, one 37mm gun and one cal. 30 machine gun, and armor 0.25 to 0.375 thick. It weighed 7.5 tons and went 20 miles an hour, and it was called Light Tank, T-1. Though a drastic improvement over World War I U.S. tanks, its performance was still far from satisfactory. A second model light tank, T1-E1 (Type 1—Experimental Model 1), was therefore built and finished in 1928, which proved to be no better—indeed, its speed had been cut down to 18 miles an hour. This was the tank Chaffee had viewed at Rochester.

Meanwhile, another light tank had been presented to the War Department for test by the aging (68), but forward-looking inventor, Mr. J. Walter Christie. In contrast to the 18 miles an hour of the ordnance tank, Mr. Christie's vehicle went 42.5 miles an hour on tracks and 70 miles an hour on its wheels when the tracks were removed. Its armor was a half-inch thick; it weighed 8.6 tons without armament; and its performance across fields and over hills was so spectacular that wherever it was demonstrated, it stole the show from its ordnance competitor. Admirers of the Christie tank called it a "wildcat," while others, notably ordnancemen, claimed it was structurally unsound and only good for "flash demonstrations."

There resulted a sharp division in the official Army family on the question of which of the two tanks should be developed for use by both the infantry and the proposed mechanized force. In the Budget Bill prepared in 1928, and passed by Congress in 1929, $250,000 had been appropriated for the manufacture of six to eight light T1-E2[4] tanks for service test by the infantry. When, however, General Allen left the office of the Chief of Infantry in March, 1929, his successor, General Stephen O. Fuqua, urged a change in the budget provision to permit the purchase of five to six Christie tanks instead. The then Chief of Ordnance, Maj. General C. C. Williams, being agreeable, the matter was taken to the Congressional Committee of Appropriations, which gave its approval of the switch in tanks. Before the Christies could be ordered, however, Maj. General Samuel Hof became the new Chief of Ordnance. General Hof opposed the Christie tank on the ground that it had many engineering and mechanical flaws and, in a special conference with the Chief of Staff, pointed out that it would weigh, when completely equipped, not the 7.5 to 8-ton limit for a U.S. light Army tank, but rather 15 tons. "That," he quoted Summerall as saying, "convinces me. I do not want a medium tank. I want a light tank." Claiming that one, not six, was sufficient to test whether the tank was any good, General Hof thereupon proceeded to spend $62,000 for one Christie tank, and to allow the remainder of the $250,000 to revert to the Treasury unused.

This step by no means quenched the issue; rather, more fuel was added to the fire. The *Chicago Tribune*, upon hearing of the affair, sided with the Christie adherents and spearheaded an attack upon the Ordnance Department with a blazing editorial titled "Another Ordnance Fiasco." The paper took the drastic stand that the Ordnance Department should be abolished and the separate arms be allowed to make their own purchases. More reasonable was the attitude of the *Army-Navy Journal*, which explained the history of the tank problem by giving the views of the successive Chiefs of the Branches. Congressmen inquired, not politely, why only one tank had been purchased when they had specifically authorized more. The upshot of an ensuing Congressional hearing, in which an imposing array of military men testified for and against the Christie tank, was that the $250,000 was made available until June 30, 1932, solely for Christie tanks.

Caught in the maelstrom of such inter-branch bickering, exponents of a mechanized force despaired of its accomplishment. An even greater blow to their hopes was the disbandment of Britain's Experimental Mechanized Force. The reason advanced for the move was that the equipment of the force was desired for experiment by the two older arms [infantry and cavalry], and that there was not equipment or money enough for both. "To discontinue the Armored Force [*sic*] for even one season means the sacrifice of much progress," cried an American devotee of mechanization, who regarded the British action with dismay. If British pioneers were losing ground, what chance had an American force that did not even exist?

Although the War Department had not given him one cent of the four million dollars he had recommended for mechanization, Major Chaffee was far from discouraged. "Despite lost ground due to a setback in the matter of funds at present," he wrote to a friend, "I hope that the War Department will in some way be able to go ahead with the project . . ." And in the year that followed, until October, 1930, this idea was carried along almost solely by the enthusiasm and tireless efforts of this one man. All of his spare time was devoted to its study at home and abroad. His interest in mechanization developments in Britain was intense, and a fellow officer leaving for a post in England has written, "He [Chaffee] loaded me down with a terrible list of things he wanted to know from over there."[5] To another friend, Chaffee wrote, "I have just prepared a memorandum which will result in the War College [planning a mechanized war game] based on the principles that are enunciated in the War Department studies on the subject."

In the budget bill for the fiscal year 1931, the proponents of a mechanized force were more successful. When the bill was signed by the President, it contained $284,999 for mechanization, the money to become available July 1st, 1930. It was but a fraction of the money needed to organize and equip an adequate unit; but Chaffee believed that to wait for more funds would mean to delay so dangerously long that a mechanized force might never be started. The solution lay in "cutting the cloth to suit the money at hand." A feud between two powerful governmental departments and a sympathetic Chief of Staff played into Chaffee's hands. In southeastern Virginia, on the tip of the peninsula between the York and James Rivers near the site of Cornwallis's surrender, was a small army post named Fort Eustis, which, for some time, the Army had considered evacuating and using merely as a place to store guns. When the Justice Department happened to get wind of these plans, they requested that the fort be used as a prison to quarter an overflow of Federal convicts instead. Reluctant to part with the Army post, Summerall settled the matter summarily with one stroke just before he departed the office of Chief of Staff. In October, 1930, he issued his last directive. It read: "Assemble that mechanized force now. Station it at Fort Eustis. Make it permanent, not temporary."

IV

The conglomerate group of men and machines that began to straggle into the Virginia army camp in the fall of 1930 was even less impressive than the original "Gasoline Brigade" that had lived briefly in Maryland two years before. But the new force was the more significant in that, according to the War Department directive, it was to be a permanent army fixture.

There were finally assembled by the middle of November, 19 officers and 519 enlisted men, equipped with 66 trucks, 10 armored cars (one radio equipped), 7 tractors, 22 passenger cars, 15 light tanks (4 T-1s, 6 World War Renaults re-engined with Franklin air cooled engines to give them more speed, and 5 wartime Renaults, unmodernized), and 4 motorcycles. Such was the pitiful handful of vehicles that constituted the "armored might" of the greatest automotive country in the world.

The original outfit included:

TROOP A, 2ND ARMORED CAR SQUADRON. All the armored cars were fairly new, and they had originally been intended for the cavalry. Needless to say, that branch was not happy to lose them.

COMPANY A, 1ST LIGHT TANK REGIMENT. This unit had been transferred from Fort George G. Meade, and was part of the infantry's contribution to the force. "This company," remarked Chaffee, "is furnished, and I may say, burdened with, the best tank carriers that we have." (Tank carriers were tank-transporting trucks. The Christie tank, equipped with a removable track which converted the tank into a wheeled vehicle, was designed to eliminate the necessity for tank carriers.)

BATTERY A, 6TH FIELD ARTILLERY. This group came from Fort Hoyle, Maryland, and was porteed in old wartime Liberty trucks, which could not, "even then, keep their tactical place in the road."

COMPANY H, 34TH INFANTRY. As the home station of the 34th was Fort Eustis, Company H merely transferred its allegiance. This company had been motorized, along with the rest of the 34th, on August 1st, 1929, "the first time in history of our

Army a great unit of infantry moved without the aid of a single horse or mule." It was mounted in 1.5-ton six-wheel trucks and was "a very serviceable organization for the purpose," said Chaffee.

COMPANY C, 13TH ENGINEERS. This was a motorized combat engineer outfit, which came from Fort Humphreys, Virginia.

A detachment of one officer and fifteen men of the 1st Chemical Warfare Service was transferred from Edgewood Arsenal, Maryland. They were the proud possessors of one 4.2 inch chemical mortar on a self-propelled carriage, built in 1928.

A platoon of the 69TH COAST ARTILLERY. Sent from Aberdeen Proving Ground in Maryland, these men were equipped to operate two automobile carriages carrying .50 cal. antiaircraft guns in single mounts and one automobile carriage with guns in double mount.

THE 19TH ORDNANCE COMPANY. This outfit was also from Aberdeen and was mounted in trucks "diverted temporarily for its use."

A Quartermaster mobile repair shop from Holabird, and a headquarters company, including a headquarters platoon, signal platoon, and supply platoon.

The commanding officer of the motley assemblage was an able, aggressive cavalry officer, Colonel Daniel Van Voorhis, who had previously been stationed on the border with the 12th Cavalry Regiment. A general officer had been recommended by the mechanization report for the job, but few generals were interested in risking their careers in the novel undertaking and none could be spared. Van Voorhis had been carefully chosen from a long list of full colonels at a meeting in which the then Lt. Colonel Chaffee had played the deciding role. "Adna knew how important it was to get the right man," recalled Mrs. Chaffee, "and he went over that list again and again, eliminating names until he was sure Van Voorhis was the one." The qualities which led to this choice were Van Voorhis's incomparable organizational and administrative abilities, well known in cav-

alry circles. Mrs. Chaffee also remembered, with a smile, that at
first the colonel was none too pleased with his new assignment.
"You're the one responsible for this, Chaffee," she quoted him
as saying indignantly to her husband, when apprised of his
selection. But before many weeks had passed, Van Voorhis's
enthusiasm for the experiment equaled that of Colonel Chaffee, and time later bestowed upon him the title, "Grandfather
of the Armored Force."

Other names appearing on that list of first officers were:
Major Sereno E. Brett, Executive Officer, former Infantry Tank
School instructor, and for the preceding two years command-
ing officer of the 2d Battalion, 1st Tank Regiment; Major
Robert W. Grow, later the major general who commanded the
6th Armored Division of Patton's Third Army in its dash across
France after the breakthrough at St. Lo in 1944; Captain David
G. Barr and Captain A. R. Wilson, two men whose names
appeared frequently in accounts of the early history of the
force.

Meantime, in a public announcement, the Secretary of
War made clear the purpose in creating the "newest unit of the
Army." "Organized on the theory that modern tanks, on
account of their armament, speed, marching radius and
mechanical reliability are now capable of extended maneuvers
beyond the immediate support of divisional infantry, the proper
role of the Mechanized Force will be those tactical missions
which present an opportunity for those characteristics. In the
conduct of the training of this new Force, its mission will be that
of a tactical laboratory for the determination of the proper tactics which can and must be used in the maneuver of fast tanks
supported by other mechanized and motorized arms. In addition, it will test experimental equipment in the field . . ."

"The employment of this Force," he continued, "will in no
way diminish the role of infantry tanks."

CHAPTER THREE

From Sabers to Monkey Wrenches

I

The activities of the Mechanized Force at Eustis through the winter and spring of 1930-31, in executing the directive of the Secretary of War, were strenuous and engrossing. On January 13th, Van Voorhis and his small armored outfit were arrayed in mock offensive combat against deployed infantry. On January 27th, they marched and bivouacked. On February 3rd, they deployed as an advance guard. A week later, the Force maneuvered on the defensive, the following week as the flank guard of a larger force. In succeeding weeks, there were night marches, raids, and an exploitation of a cavalry breakthrough, while sleepy inhabitants of southeastern Virginia stared in dismay at the new visitors from Mars who rumbled so indefatigably past their doors.

Meantime, in Washington, Colonel Chaffee, with one year left of his four-year term on the General Staff, did not remain quietly on the sidelines. Instead he prepared a lecture on "Mechanization in the Army", which he gave in the ensuing months before the Infantry School, the Cavalry School, the Field Artillery School, the Engineers School, and to the officers of the 1st Division at Fort Hamilton, New York. On October 28, designated by the War Department as "the officer pre-eminently qualified to lecture on the subject of mechanization,"[1] he spoke before six hundred Reserve officers in Chicago. Finally, he pre-

sented his talk before the President and students of the austere
Army War College.

Ignorance regarding the true nature of the Mechanized
Force was one of the bugbears with which Chaffee and its proponents had to contend. This Chaffee sought to dispel when,
in his speech, he described in detail the assemblage at Eustis
and the role of each component.

"The force at present is not properly balanced, however," he
said. "It is apparent now that the tank unit is too small in proportion to the other arms. We shall learn more about organization as we use it more. Its combat equipment of tanks and guns
is far below what is technically possible these days. When we
have sufficient tanks that can get along without tank carriers,
and the day seems not far distant, this should be a very maneuverable force.

"Along these lines," he predicted, "may develop a great part
of the highly mobile combat troops of the next war . . .

"So today we may find two uses for tanks: first, the established usage, to assist the infantry of the combat divisions by
directly preceding them and neutralizing the organized resistance in the main battle . . . and this second possible use in an
armored force." Medium and heavy tanks Chaffee relegated to
the performance of infantry tasks; for the armored force he
claimed the new light fast tanks.

"A completely mechanized fighting unit has distinct limitations as to terrain on which it can be employed and as to the
time and manner of its employment. It is essentially an element
of offense.

"Almost every major offensive operation," he went on
earnestly, "studied in the light of the power of the defense in
modern war, brings out situations which could best be solved
by a self-contained, highly mobile, mechanized unit of considerable striking power and of limited holding power. Equally, it
is shown that on other parts of the front such units would have
no role.

"In carrying out the old principles of economy of force, where we would maneuver and cause movement on one part of a front, we must hold, pin down, and contain the enemy on another. We must recognize that the least stopping means digging in, organizing, and the echelonment of prepared defense. When it is necessary to restore movement again directly through these places instead of turning them, light mobile elements, even armored, will not suffice. The successive neutralization of the heavy bomb, the heavy gun, and tank which is thoroughly protected against all small arms will be required to prepare the way for the infantry, and those infantry will be on foot as before. It must still form the backbone of armies.

"The main point is that we, as soldiers, must recognize the tremendous strides which our automotive industry has made since the last war. If we neglect to study every possible usage of this asset in our next war, we should not only be stupid, we should be incompetent."

As Colonel Chaffee thus concluded his Wellsian picture of wars to come, the silence of his audience was portentous.

"I then had the honor," said Chaffee, "of being told by the President of the War College that my lecture was visionary and crazy."

President of the War College notwithstanding, interest in the mechanized men at Eustis was considerable. Since the post was not far from Washington, brass hats from the War Department were frequent observers of their tortuous gyrations across the sandy Virginia soil. At various times the command was reviewed by such distinguished visitors as General S. D. Embick, General Lesley McNair, and General DeBrees. And on April 27th, there appeared at the fort an impressive group of automotive magnates, among them being Mr. Herrington of Marmon-Herrington, Mr. Holt of the Caterpillar Company, representatives of Cadillac and General Motors, as well as engineers from the S.A.E., to study the Army's brave, new experiment.

Though a Crossley rating might have given the Mechanized Force a fairly high rating for audience interest, behind
the scenes the small force was already fighting for its life.
When, in the fall of 1930, the new Chief of Staff, General Dou-
glas MacArthur, had assumed office, he at once had instituted
a review of War Department policies with a view to moderniz-
ing the entire Army. As a result, mechanization was undergoing an intensive restudy in its relation to all the arms, and how
the experimental band at Eustis would be affected, no one
could then foretell.

Since its inception, there had been an undercover attempt
by the infantry to secure control of the Mechanized Force,
their argument in favor of the move being that under the
Defense Act of 1920 all tank development was in their domain.
And, though the role and mission of the force, as prescribed by
the Secretary of War, were distinctly un-infantryish, the striking
action and quick marches rather more resembling cavalry in
character, yet stout infantry voices were representing to
MacArthur that the force belonged to them. The new, fast T-1
tank had been exclusively developed at the infantry behest,
and they disliked seeing it appropriated by a mechanized
force, or any other arm, at their expense. Moreover, the Mechanized Force contained not only infantry tanks, but motorized
infantry as well. Loyalty to their branch of the service would
not allow them to stand calmly by and watch the infantry be
stripped of any of its troops.

In the restudy of the new Chief of Staff, the Mechanized
Force was not the only military outfit whose life was in jeop-
ardy. A report in the *New York Times* had it that, in a discussion
at the old fishing hole at Rapidan, President Hoover had
ordered a survey by MacArthur to determine whether the cavalry arm was obsolete and ought to be abolished. Squirming
uncomfortably under the coldly inquiring Presidential eye,
horse cavalrymen from Vermont to Texas succumbed to the jit-
ters, and filled their service journal with glowing accounts of
past cavalry exploits intended to prove that the day of the

horse in battle was far from over, in spite of tanks and planes and machine guns.

In Washington, Colonel Chaffee, from his post on the General Staff, surveyed the predicament of both the Mechanized Force and the cavalry branch with anxiety. Unless the cavalry showed more willingness to keep pace with modern warfare, he believed it was doomed. Nor did the future of the Mechanized Force appear to him much brighter. Under the strictures of depression economies in the War Department budget, he foresaw its eventual disbandment through lack of funds, and the return of the tanks to infantry control. After considerable reflection, therefore, he propounded a solution to both problems by recommending that the development of a mechanized force be assigned to the cavalry.

Actually, Chaffee's proposal was not surprising, for many of his utterances regarding the Mechanized Force had borne the stamp of his cavalry training. He often compared the slow, heavier tanks of the infantry to the old heavy cavalry, and the light, fast tanks to the light cavalry.

"Tactical mobility of the highest degree in the past was represented by cavalry," he said in 1930. "There were usually two kinds. The armored cavalry, which gave decisive shock and movement in the main battle, and the light cavalry, which operated on the flanks, on the rear, broke communications, destroyed supplies, which struck at the enemy where he was weak, never where he was strong, and in the end, which stood across his lines of retreat, delaying him, harassing him, and pinning him down till the heavier combat troops again arrived to give the death blow to his armed forces.

"But then, in the years from 1915 to 1917 on the Western Front . . . all element of surprise and mobility was lost, and the ability to strike at vital points and to penetrate quickly in vital directions was gone out of warfare. . . . It is to recover this mobility on and close to the battlefield that we are striving today. Mobility means live men arriving and establishing themselves in possession of the military objectives. To live and to move quickly against the gun requires protection. Armor gives protection. The gasoline engine moves armor. And so we come to mechanization. . . ."

Thus it is apparent that Chaffee saw, in the Mechanized Force, the extension of the powers of cavalry through new and modern methods. Under cavalry control, he believed such a force would be developed along more proper lines than if it should revert to the control of the infantry, and at the same time he saw the new force bringing new life and vigor to the old cavalry arm. Once other cavalrymen understood the nature of the Mechanized Force, he was convinced they would agree with him.

His proposal, however, encountered unexpected resistance from two sources: Van Voorhis, fearing the effect of branch jealousies upon the welfare of the force, declared bluntly that the force should remain outside the control of any one of the existing arms, while certain cavalrymen in high places did not welcome the idea of noisy, smelly tanks in their handsome horse cavalry. Perhaps Colonel Chaffee should have heeded the objections of his colleagues, but instead he overrode Van Voorhis and proceeded to win the support of the Chief of Cavalry, Major General Guy V. Henry, an old friend of his from horse-show days, for his plan. Thereafter, the two worked together to persuade MacArthur to assign the Mechanized Force to the cavalry.

When Van Voorhis learned that his opinion had been disregarded, he immediately penned a strongly worded memorandum to a high ranking member of the General Staff, outlining his objections and urging that the force remain independent of branch control. Time was to prove the validity of his contentions.

II

The official statement of the Chief of Staff announcing the results of the study of War Department policies, which appeared in newspapers throughout the country on May 23rd, 1931, determined the course of mechanization in America for almost the next decade. The force at Eustis was disbanded and remnants assigned to the cavalry for reorganization and development, while all the existing arms and services were directed to carry on the work of mechanization within themselves. "Every part of the Army," said the statement, "will adopt mechanization and motorization as far as practicable and possible." Under this policy, instead of mechanization being centralized in an experimental force, the arms and services went on their independent ways to adapt it to their needs and according to their own ideas. There was to be no over-all coordination of effort.

In assigning the Mechanized Force to the Cavalry, MacArthur declared, "Cavalry acquired its name when soldiers mounted on horses were able to move more rapidly than any other arm. . . . Thus there has grown up a very natural conception that cavalry must include the horse. Modern firearms have eliminated the horse as a weapon, and as a means of transportation he has become, next to the dismounted man, the slowest means of transportation. . . . To enable cavalry to develop its organization and equipment so as to maintain its ability under modern conditions to perform its missions . . . the Mechanized Force will be reorganized as a reinforced cavalry regiment."

Under this plan, the War Department proposed to mechanize one horse cavalry regiment in the fall of 1931, while the tank, armored car, artillery, signal, and maintenance units were salvaged from the original force to serve as the nucleus for the new organization. Thus the important motorized infantry, engineers, and chemical warfare units went back to their parent organizations, leaving the Mechanized Force tactically very much impaired. Ultimately, the artillery succeeded in detaching its two mechanized batteries from the force, thus further weakening it. To permit the assignment of the tanks to the cavalry, an act of Congress would have been required; hence, as a subterfuge to avoid the necessity for such a long, tedious procedure, Colonel Chaffee coined the word "combat car" to apply to all cavalry tanks, as differentiated from those of the infantry, even though they might be the same vehicles.

To the cavalry thus came the greatest challenge of its existence—the opportunity to develop America's blitzkrieg troops.

Newspapers everywhere dramatized MacArthur's announcement of the new mechanized cavalry. "From Sabers to Monkey Wrenches" was the headline of an article in one of the country's leading news magazines. "'Boots and saddles' now means 'crank 'er up'", said the *Louisville Courier Journal*. In a flurry of colorful reporting the *Providence Journal* mourned, "Gone will be the oats and hay. Off with the leather-faced puttees and the spurs. Down with the curry comb and brush to the bottom of Oblivion's well. As for the guidon, proud symbol that fluttered in the van of dust clouds and thundering hooves, the moths may have it even while sabers rust." A popular science journal sturdily declared, "Exit the cavalry, enter the tanks."

Cavalrymen from coast to coast beheld such statements with purpling dewlaps. When the cavalry branch had reluctantly accepted the Mechanized Force, it had been over the objections of those who had predicted its growth at the expense of horse cavalry. Their protestations, however, had been quieted by the assurance that there was no intention of abandoning the horse cavalry in favor of something entirely new and unproven. Now the newspapers were validating their worst fears by saying that in the new army a horseman would be as incongruous as a buggy on a boulevard. Uneasily the Chief of Cavalry sought to pour oil on the troubled waters by explaining: "We see in the future we will have two types of cavalry, one with armored motor vehicles, giving speed, strategical mobility, and great fighting power of modern machines; the other with horses, armed with the latest automatic firearms for use in tactical roles and for operations in difficult terrain where the horse still gives us the greatest mobility." Likewise, the *Cavalry Journal* felt it necessary to state under MacArthur's announcement that the directive in no way "intends rendering inactive as mounted troops any number of cavalry regiments."

But the damage had already been done by the romantic accounts in the press, and horse cavalrymen were militantly on the defensive. Whenever Colonel Chaffee appeared in their midst, there were mutterings of "treachery" and "treason," while they bitterly decried the sensational headlines. When Lt. Colonel C. L. Scott remarked in a piece called "Rider and Driver" that "the majority of cavalrymen welcome the opportunity to develop the mechanized force and show what cavalry can do with it," illustrious Major General James Parker, retired cavalryman, incredulously asked, "Can this be so?" adding pontifically "We, in America, are too impressed by new things."

The remarks of articulate Brigadier General Hamilton S. Hawkins, Chaffee's former chief at Fort Myer, Virginia, perhaps best epitomized the attitude toward their mechanized stepchild of all cavalry reactionaries, who regarded the mechanized cavalry only as a rival to the horsed cavalry, and not as an extension of cavalry power. Instead of recognizing the potentialities of a tank force in cavalry roles, General Hawkins stressed its inherent weakness and disparaged its strength. "It is absurd to think of tanks and passenger trucks carrying machine gunners romping through woods and swamps, creeks and villages," he said. While he conceded that mechanized cavalry more nearly resembled horse cavalry than any other arm, and might, in suitable terrain, be able to take over a few of the smaller and less important missions, yet he declared that horse cavalry must still perform the most important cavalry missions. To substantiate his arguments, he compiled an impressive list of tank shortcomings. What good is speed, he demanded, if the force needs oil and gas that must be brought up on roads? What good is forty miles an hour way out in front of infantry? The force would only have to stop and wait for supporting troops. What good was fire from a tank when it was so inaccurate? How much more efficient was the automatic pistol, "principal weapon" of cavalry troopers, which could "be fired to the front or right or left front with astonishing accuracy."[2] The good general, in fact, held so low an opinion of a mechanized force and so high a one of the horse cavalry that he predicted, in an encounter between the two, provided the cavalry was properly equipped, the horsemen could very well take care of themselves. Here one is reminded of the fate of the Polish cavalry before the German tanks. The true role which Hawkins envisioned for a mechanized force was to support horse cavalry and not to operate as a separate force at all.

And so began a controversy over horse versus tank which split the ranks of cavalry as long as the tank force remained under its control. Though Chaffee had expected some opposition from his fellow cavalrymen, he was not prepared for the bitterly obstructive tactics of his opponents, which dogged the development of the mechanized cavalry for the next nine years. It was difficult for him to understand such conduct on the part of the very men he had expected to be his allies, but he did not swerve from his plans for the future. When it was announced in the May 30, 1931, *Army-Navy Journal* that "Colonel A. R. Chaffee, who has played a leading part in the G-3 studies on the subject of mechanization," would join the force on June 15th, no one in the War Department was surprised. They considered it the natural assignment for the man who had been espousing a tank force for the past four years. Upon Chaffee's arrival at Eustis, he became the Regimental Executive of the Mechanized Cavalry Detachment and second in command of the handful of troops that remained of the original force.

The War Department had stated that a horse mounted regiment would be mechanized some time in the fall. Until this occurred, activity of the force was almost at a standstill, except for its preparations to move to a new post. Chaffee and Van Voorhis had long agreed that the Virginia fort was too small and flat to provide the proper training area for speedy, mobile troops, and too near Washington to escape interference from the chiefs of the branches, and for many months they had been busy finding a more suitable station for the armored unit. The Chief of Cavalry and the Cavalry School wanted to station it near the horsed regiments on the border, where the two cavalries could train together, while the two mechanized officers argued for Camp Knox, Kentucky. In the Kentucky reservation there were 33,000 acres of the rugged terrain needed for testing, training, and experimenting with mechanized vehicles and troops. Furthermore, the camp's proximity to the nation's large industrial centers made supply less of a problem than if the mechanized regiment were stationed at some far-away Texas outpost. In the end they won the approval of the War Department for Knox, and overnight the theme song of the mechanized men changed from "Carry Me Back to Ole Virginny" to "My Old Kentucky Home."

III

Hibernating in the rolling hills of northern Kentucky, thirty-five miles from Louisville, nearest large city, lay the future armored station, bedraggled relic in 1931 of what had been a busy World War training center in 1918. After the war, the camp had been discontinued as a permanent army post, although the Fifth Corps Area was then still using it as a summer training camp for the R.O.T.C. and National Guard, and in winter it was garrisoned by two companies of infantry. Named after Henry Knox, Revolutionary War general, who was Chief of Artillery for the American Army from 1776 to 1782, Commander-in-Chief of the Army from 1783 to 1784, and first Secretary of War under President Washington, Camp Knox was re-established as a permanent army post on January 1st, 1932, and redesignated "Fort Knox."

Hub of the camp was the former sleepy, country town of Stithten. Through its center ran the Dixie Highway, U.S. 31-W, main thoroughfare to Louisville, a narrow, winding road far removed from the stream-lined, four-lane highway that today carries Fort Knox soldiers to Broadway and Fourth Street.

Frame houses, erstwhile residences of Stithten citizens converted into military quarters, dejectedly overlooked the road,
while a small bank, a country school, a gloomy brick church, a
forlorn hospital, a Central Mess, a Hostess House, a barnlike Illinois Central Railroad station, a Post Exchange "no larger than a
good-sized living-room," according to Mrs. Chaffee, and row
upon row of dilapidated, green, World War barracks completed
the unimpressive army establishment. There were no paved
walks, no miles of winding, paved roads—nothing but acres of
oozy, red mud, which, in summer, turned to suffocating clouds
of dust. There was then nothing to indicate that ten years hence
Fort Knox would be one of the largest, busiest Army posts in the
United States, and Kentucky's second largest "city."

A wet autumn in 1931 added no cheer to the dreary Fort
Knox landscape that greeted the tired little mechanized convoy arriving at their new home in November after a perilous
trip over the mountains from Eustis. "But," recalled Mrs. Chaffee, "every one was happy. They didn't care how much mud
there was or how dismal the place looked. They just wanted to
get things started."

Colonel Chaffee had charge of the housing of the personnel. Before he left Eustis, he had secured a blue print of
dwellings available and had assigned the houses according to
rank: Van Voorhis the best, himself the second best, and so on
down the line. Corps area headquarters had provided a modest
sum of money for rehabilitating the quarters, and the quartermaster had been dispatched to Knox to prepare the houses for
the incoming troops. The job he had done was surprising. "He
had gone into the houses with a spray gun and covered all the
walls, floors, and windows. When the Eustis people arrived,
they had to find some more money to clean up the mess,"
recalled Mrs. Chaffee. All the houses and barracks leaked; all
needed repairs; all lacked adequate heating facilities. Until
they could be made more habitable, the enlisted men and
their families lived at the Hostess House; the officers and their

families at the Central Mess on "B" Street. When the men were not busy churning the first exploratory tank trails up and down the muddy slopes of the reservation, they were mending roofs and weatherstripping paper-thin barrack walls, and there was scarcely enough time left in the day to perform the routine duties of a military post. The discovery of a rock quarry and rock crushing machine hidden away in the southeast corner of the post was the occasion of as much rejoicing as if the quarry had been a gold mine. It meant stones for walks and roads, and one Sunday afternoon the Chaffees set an example of industry for the rest of the post when the entire family laid a flagstone walk before their house.

The plethora of mud and the lack of even the barest comforts were a constant worry to every one, and a cold winter and a rainy spring were no help. But one day the clouds went away, the sun dried up the red puddles, and the full beauty of spring in Kentucky at last appeared. The hills were lacy with dogwood and redbud trees. Mockingbirds sang incessantly in hedges of wild honeysuckle. Carpets of violets and mayflowers burgeoned along the tank trails. The inhabitants of Knox threw wide their doors and windows, and for the first time since they had left Virginia they felt warm and comfortable.

Not all the troubles that beset the small mechanized detachment at Knox, however, disappeared with the balmy breath of spring. The long-awaited cavalry regiment to be mechanized had not yet arrived, nor were there any indications that one had even been selected. In March, 1932, Fort Knox officially became the 7th Cavalry (Mechanized) Brigade post. The new commander, Brigadier General Julian R. Lindsey arrived, but no new troops. Spring passed, and still no word from the War Department. To the handful of men at Knox, the delay was ominous, and inquiries in Washington revealed their fears were well founded. In official Army conference rooms there was vocal and highly placed opposition to the unhorsing of even one regiment. "Get new recruits for the great experiment," they said.

"Don't rob the already too small horsed cavalry of any of its troops."

Reassurance came from Chief of Cavalry Henry, however, that the project was far from dead. Not only was one regiment to be mechanized, but, when that was properly organized and equipped, another regiment was to be unhorsed—the two to comprise the first mechanized brigade. Rumors began to fly thick and fast that the one-hundred-year-old 1st Cavalry Regiment at Fort D. A. Russell at Marfa, Texas, was soon to arrive at Knox. And when, on June 25th, 1932, orders were issued by the War Department transferring officers from the Mechanized Cavalry Regiment at Knox to the Detachment, 1st Cavalry (Mechanized) same station, effective July 1st, the transfer of the 1st Cavalry troops from Marfa seemed imminent. With revived hopes, all summer long the men at Knox awaited the coming of the men from Texas. But the only troops that materialized were the Fifth Corps Area summer reserve officers, who swarmed over the post like schoolboys on a picnic.

By the end of September, it was apparent that plans to move the 1st Cavalry Regiment to Knox had struck a serious snag. The howls of the opposition against the transfer had finally reached the ears of Texas Congressmen, and, since 1932 was an election year, political issue was being made of the loss of the cavalry at Marfa. Again the old argument of stationing the mechanized troops on the border instead of at Knox was revived. Immediately Kentucky Congressmen were up in arms. They wanted to keep the mechanized cavalry at Knox. In the middle of the dispute sat the harassed War Department. They could not afford to make enemies in the body that held their pursestrings and were hesitating to go through with the original project. Watching anxiously from the sidelines were Van Voohis and Chaffee. They knew the infantry still coveted their force and might offer to settle the problem for the War Department by offering a home for the "combat cars" at Benning. And if the dispute became too hot, the War Department might accept the offer. Finally Chaffee could restrain himself no longer, and he flew to Washington to secure first-hand information. The results of his trip are contained in a letter written on October 5th, 1932:

"Last week when I was in Washington, I talked to several Generals. . . . These are the three men whose views finally control in the matter of the solution of the problem in detail. I was given to understand by all three, independently, that the War Department would take up, following a political promise that had been made, a proposition to furnish the personnel of this regiment (mechanized) by abandoning D. A. Russell after the election; and they were hoping that this would be organized by the 1st of January. Failing that, they all spoke in an indefinite way of sending this detachment elsewhere and mechanizing a regiment. In a general way, they indicated the border, but I hope they will not do this because it would be a poor move from the point of distance and cost which would be involved in the matter of maintenance so far from the automotive centers of the army and country . . . and from the point of view that I do not believe that the mechanized unit will team up well as an integral unit in the cavalry division, its characteristics being complementary of mounted cavalry rather than identical. However, the solution may transpire that way. . . .

"It may transpire within the next two months that the cavalry cannot carry out its plans to mechanize a regiment, and that the army will either have to abandon such plans or revamp its ideas entirely. . . ."

While the whole future of the mechanized force was in this uncertain state, Brigadier General Walter C. Short, then commanding officer of the 1st Cavalry Division at Fort Bliss, Texas, tendered to Chaffee the post of chief of staff of the division. This was the opportunity, if Chaffee wanted it, to rid himself of the whole thankless business of mechanization, adjudged to be "so destroying professionally." His job on the border would be staff work, in which he had already earned much professional distinction. He had only to say yes, and an easy, comfortable life would be his. No more shabby quarters, no scoffers to convince, no disheartening uncertainty for the future. He would be welcomed back to the horsed cavalry service like a lost thoroughbred strayed from the stables. The offer was tempting, but Col. Chaffee refused, saying, "I think it is probably one of the best positions that an officer of my rank in the Army could occupy, and one of the best opportunities he could have. However, I have been associated with mobile mechanization in the Army since its inception. Quite involuntarily I was called upon by the War Department General Staff to foster this idea and to do everything to forward it. . . . The War Department has not yet been able to go through with its plans, and it seems a little doubtful whether it will do so in the end, but I feel I should stay with it until the War Department makes a decision in the matter. . . ."

The question was still undecided when the tanks and armored cars from Knox marched jauntily in their first Armistice Day parade in Louisville. Then one day early in December, with elections safely over, the War Depart approved the abandonment of Fort D. A. Russell at Marfa, and ordered the 1st Cavalry to Knox as soon after January 1st as practicable. "I received an order from the Commanding General, 5th Corps Area, Hugh Drum," wrote Colonel Van Voorhis, "to proceed at once to Marfa, Texas, with enough motor equipment to return the regiment to Knox." The colonel wasted no time in getting together a convoy of trucks, and on December 17th, even though it meant missing Christmas at home, he and his vehicles headed south. "We left with the temperature 10 degrees below zero," recalled Van Voorhis in a letter to the author, "and encountered cold weather through Tennessee and Arkansas. We arrived at Camp Marfa, where we found winter weather, with ice."

The weather, however, was warm in comparison with the iciness of the reception accorded the invading convoy. Organized nearly one hundred years before, in 1833 to be exact, for the Black Hawk War, the 1st Cavalry Regiment was the "oldest and best-known regiment of horsemen in America," and proud of its traditions. To most of its men and officers, the surrender of their horses for tanks was cause for the deepest mourning, which even the cheer of the Christmas season failed to mitigate. A ceremony tantamount to funeral services marked their departure from the garrison on January 1st, 1933.

At Knox, meanwhile, Chaffee was again grappling with the problem of housing the incoming troops and endeavoring, by feats of financial legerdemain, to make each dollar spent for repairs do the work of two. One of the coldest winters on record further added to his difficulties. In a letter to G-3 in Washington, Chaffee wrote: "Some of that weatherstripping money would come in pretty good right now. The water is freezing on the floor of my office, with the steam on. Water froze in the bathroom of my house last night, and I live in one of the warmest houses on the post . . ." To a friend he described his troubles in settling the families of the 1st Cavalrymen who were daily arriving by train. "Things are bad," he said. "I am having Lt. White or the chaplain call at every house every day to see if they can be of service to the women. Married enlisted men are beginning to appear in force and are rapidly filling up the Hostess House. The band leader with seven children does quite some filling by himself."

For Lieutenant White, such duties were a far cry from his job twelve years later, when he was a major general in command of the 2d Armored Division of Simpson's 9th Army in Germany in the closing days of the war.

Out of the jumble, however, order finally emerged, and with a sigh of relief Chaffee saw each family and soldier fitted neatly into place like the proper part of a jigsaw puzzle. There was an organization ceremony for the 1st Cavalry Regiment soon after its arrival at Knox, "partly to offset the funeral ceremonies held at Marfa, and partly to let every one concerned know that the old order has changed and is not going back. This is permanent, and they might as well make up their minds to it," declared Chaffee in a letter to Van Voorhis.

Though the inhabitants of Knox had been far too absorbed in their own affairs to pay much attention when Roosevelt entered the White House on March 4th, 1933, it was not long before they began to feel the impact of his New Deal measures. On March 5th, the new President declared a bank holiday, which left the entire post stranded with only a few nickels and dimes saved in piggy banks as ready cash. It became a period of "enforced semi-mourning": no invitations extended, no invitations received. This was their first encounter with the new administration. The following month CCC boys began to pour in upon the camp at the rate of 1,500 a day. Under the provisions of the New Deal law, it was the duty of the already over-worked post officers to house and organize them. Most far-reaching in its consequences to the struggling Kentucky post of all the Roosevelt legislation, however, was the PWA and WPA, which resulted in millions of dollars worth of military construction at Army posts throughout America.

Late in the summer of 1933, there came the first good news from Washington of a large sum of money available for building at Knox. Two and a half million dollars had been allotted for new construction, and $360,000 for reconditioning and utilities. Included in the list of items to be built were a hospital, barracks, NCO quarters, field officers' quarters and company officers' quarters, gas mains, telephones, a new headquarters building, and a radio station—only the merest beginning of the huge army camp Knox later became. On September 8th, Chaffee requisitioned an item even more urgently needed for the approaching winter—278 stoves for barracks and latrines.

Before the year's end, one more welcome bit of news came the way of the mechanized cavalry when it was intimated that two batteries of field artillery might soon be ordered to Knox.

IV

During 1933, the 1st Cavalry (Mechanized) Regiment confined its activities to exercises on the Knox reservation. Organizing and training absorbed the energies of every one from the commanding officer down to the lowest private intent on learning how to ride, feed, and care for his new "mount". There were three, later four, men on each iron horse, which did not jump fences like the cavalry horses they had turned out to pasture, but which crunched them to matchsticks beneath steel treads. Though the cavalrymen were mechanized, they still clung to the expressions of their horsy days, and continued to wear breeches and shining boots. Officers of the mechanized regiment habitually carried riding crops. The insigne of the 1st Cavalry (Horsed) was retained for the 1st Cavalry (Mechanized), and the crossed sabers and the Black Hawk were painted on tanks and trucks. But despite these few nostalgic touches, the work was unfamiliar and exacting, requiring day after day of relentless practice. When, early in 1933, the War Department suggested that a detachment of the mechanized cavalry participate in spring maneuvers with other military forces in the South, Chaffee wrote, protesting, "We have too big a job in front of us to get the regiment organized and trained in a basic way to be able to afford to go out and show it off. There is no use making concert engagements until you can play the piano. A year from now I hope this regiment will be able to be a combat team."

When a proposal was again made to include the regiment in maneuvers at Fort Riley in the spring of 1934, however, the reply was entirely different. A year of intensive training had elapsed, and the mechanized officers felt ready to put their little blitzkrieg force to its first public test. Although Van Voorhis and Chaffee pushed the idea vigorously, whether the Knox force would go to Riley was, for several months, extremely doubtful. Two obstacles stood in the way: first, the ever present problem of securing funds to pay for the trip, and second, the

question of who would take care of the CCC boys at Knox while
the 1st Cavalry was absent. The matter of money was solved with
the same ingenuity and resourcefulness that had accomplished
the rehabilitation of Knox. Of the second, somewhat impatient
with what he must have considered a petty hindrance, Chaffee
wrote: "I think the CCC itself might swing in and help manage
its own conditioning camp to an extent that would enable us to
get along without the 1st Cavalry. (Van Voorhis was to command the regiment at the maneuvers, while Chaffee, as Executive Officer of the post—an assignment which he had acquired
when Knox had become a brigade post—was to remain at
home.) General Lindsey has taken the position that it should
not be canceled. The maneuvers are too important to the
future of the Army."

Opposition soon wilted before such blunt reasoning, and
immediately the 1st Cavalry began a period of training which
made the previous months' work seem like mere warming-up
exercises. That the thermometer stood at zero and snowdrifts
were piled high did not curtail the regiment's activities a single
day or night. "In February the night exercises began at 11
o'clock at night and ended at 8 o'clock in the morning. The
troops got a taste of soldiering all right. In the morning a fried
egg froze while it was dropping from the pan to the plate."
March brought heavy rains and mud, but no slackening of the
pace.

Then, at daybreak, April 19, 1934, the "Iron Horse Cavalry"
roared out of Knox on the road to Owensboro, Kentucky, the
first leg of its 750-mile journey to Fort Riley, Kansas. In the
8-mile-long column (one mile in close formation) were 189
vehicles, 587 men, and 37 officers. It was organized into a long
distance reconnaissance unit—the armored car troop; a close-
in reconnaissance and security unit—the scout troop; an
assault unit—the combat car squadron of 24 combat cars; and
a holding unit—the machine gun troop. Actually, there were
only six combat cars in the column. One-and-a-half-ton trucks,
painted with yellow bands to indicate that they were supposed

to be combat cars, made up the deficiency. "We have never waited for full complements of equipment in order to develop tactics," explained Chaffee regarding the improvisation in the force.

Past startled cows and gaping farmers they sped—a cavalry in which there was not a single horse. In command was, not Colonel Van Voorhis, but Adna R. Chaffee—a circumstance brought about a short time before when Van Voorhis had been ordered to the Hawaiian Department and Chaffee assigned to the command of the 1st Cavalry (Mecz.) Regiment.

Reckoned by the enthusiasm of the public along the way, from Knox to Kansas, the "newest fighting service" was a definite success. Cheering crowds lined the walks of each midwestern town through which it passed. Business was virtually suspended; schools were dismissed; and every night the camp site of the troops was filled with curious spectators. "A civic-military delegation from Mt. Vernon, Indiana, including Col. Merle A. Wissinger and the President of the Chamber of Commerce, contacted Col. Chaffee and secured the passing of the regiment through Mt. Vernon instead of its movement directly from Evansville to New Harmony."[3] Mr. and Mrs. Citizen and their children, seeing tanks for the first time in their lives, were impressed. Not so Mr. Thomas Coyne, Kansas City Water Department clerk, however, who had been a trooper fifty years before in the 1st Cavalry when it had ridden the plains fighting Indians. "I guess it is all right," he said dryly, looking at a steel-turreted monster. "But I like a good horse. You haven't anything left of the old days but the bugle."[4]

Watching the strange military procession roar through its city, the *Kansas City Times* wondered editorially: "Was it indicative of the army of the future? Would whole divisions be similarly mechanized? Would all the troops—infantry and field artillery, as well as cavalry—ride to battle in machines and even fight from armored vehicles?"

On hand to greet the tanned, khaki-clad troops from Knox when they roared into Riley was a distinguished gathering of

brass hats—General Abraham Lott and Col. Bruce Palmer
from the Cavalry School, Major General Leon Kromer from
Washington, Lt. Col. Chas. L. Scott, Lt. Col. George S. Patton,
Lt. Col. Jonathan Wainwright. More important to the immediate future of the mechanized cavalry than any public acclaim
was what these assembled military men would think of it. In
their minds were quite different questions to be answered by
the maneuvers than those propounded by the editors of the
Kansas City Times.

In the three years that had elapsed since the organization
of the mechanized cavalry there had emerged in the cavalry
branch two opposing schools of thought on its employment:
one which took the view that mechanized and horsed cavalry
should be combined in combat; the other which maintained
that machines and horses would not mix and should be used
separately. In the former camp, stamped by their own public
utterances, squarely stood the majority of the high-ranking cavalry officers and the Cavalry School, where there had been an
intensive study during the year preceding the maneuvers on
"how horsed and mechanized cavalry can work in conjunction
with each other."

The War Department directive which had created the
mechanized cavalry was interpreted by the then Chief of Cavalry, General Kromer, to "visualize the combined action of
horsed and mechanized cavalry," while early in 1934, the distinguished cavalryman, Gen. Guy V. Henry, had testified before a
Congressional committee that "both (mechanized and horsed
cavalry) are needed in proper proportions and both must be
used in cooperation and coordination with each other." Perhaps the most interesting outburst of all came from Colonel
George Patton, at that time second in command of the cavalry
post at Fort Myer, Virginia, when he wrote in the September-
October, 1933, *Cavalry Journal,* "It is my opinion that such operations (the use of the mechanized cavalry independently) will
be the exception rather than the rule and that, in general,
mechanized and horsed cavalry will operate together . . . Think,

for example, of the possibilities of a combat car charge instantly exploited by horsemen. Or a pivot of maneuver, formed by portee troops, while the combat cars and horsemen move out rapidly to clinch the victory by a flank attack. . . . For night marches, machines will *always* be preceded by horsemen, or else become victims of ambush." If this greatest American pactitioner of armored warfare had followed his own advice ten years later, it is doubtful that he would ever have reached Metz.

Under this doctrine, the tank was shackled to the horse just as tightly as the infantry tank was tied to the soldier on foot. There was evidenced no inclination on the part of these dyed-in-the-wool horsed cavalrymen to explore seriously the possibilities of an independent tank force. A strong argument for their contentions, they felt, were British experiments with cavalry brigades composed of two horsed regiments and one armored regiment (containing light tanks, armored cars, and 6-wheelers), a combination which a British general had pronounced "ideal". "It is surprising," he declared, "how long it took us to realize the power of the combination of tanks and horsemen. We tried tanks and infantry. That was no good because of the difference in pace. Then we tried complete armored brigades and found that their operations degenerated into mere raids. Now you see the ideal—the horseman and the machine combined." Proponents of such a thesis were determined to fit mechanized cavalry characteristics to the shape of the horse cavalry pattern, no matter how incongruous the result might be. To them, the maneuvers at Riley were merely expected to "afford an unusual opportunity to develop the combined use of the two types of cavalry."

Almost alone defending the other side of the argument was Colonel Chaffee. The pre-maneuver training of his troops had been designed to fulfill the normal cavalry role, but substituting the vehicle for the horse. It was his belief that motorized infantry, rather than cavalry, would be used in combination with the combat car, and in the maneuvers at Riley he hoped to demonstrate politely but firmly his side of the argument.

The maneuvers were divided into three phases: one to acquaint the students and instructors with the horsed cavalry brigade participating and with the 1st Cavalry Mechanized Regiment from Knox; one in which horsed and mechanized cavalry were opposed to each other while both were employed on cavalry missions; and one where they worked in conjunction with each other on regular cavalry missions.

No one knew better than the men of the mechanized regiment the limitations of their little force as it was then constituted. It was badly equipped, inadequate in strength, and lacking the necessary components to make it an independent unit. The attachment of an air squadron and artillery troops for the duration of the maneuvers, however, filled some of the gaps. But when, in the fourth exercise, the horsed cavalry, operating against the mechanized cavalry, by using scout cars, *not horses*, with demolition personnel, destroyed bridges for such a distance that the mechanized cavalry was compelled to cover almost the whole state of Kansas and part of Nebraska to cross the Big Blue River, the need for specially equipped and specially trained engineers was abundantly clear. Five years later, in September, 1939, two weeks after the fall of Poland, the mechanized cavalry was still lacking this engineer component.

In the second exercise, both forces, again operating against each other, were ordered to seize and hold the same position. Before the horsed cavalry could reach the spot, however, the mechanized cavalry had taken the position and formidably entrenched themselves to defend it. The third exercise started out in the same manner, with the horsed cavalry again losing the race for the commanding position. This time, however, the horsed cavalry went into concealment until dark, and then proceeded to surround the mechanized enemy with artillery and cavalry which attacked at daylight. This demonstrated an already known weakness of the mechanized cavalry, as it was then organized without the necessary supporting troops, to hold a position at night after a day of fighting. In the sixth exercise, where the two operated together, the mechanized cavalry was bivouacked about three times farther away from the enemy than the horsed cavalry to ensure the arrival of both at the designated area at the same time.

Though the superior speed of the mechanized cavalry was demonstrated time after time in the maneuvers, advocates of mixed cavalries concluded that "the combination of horsed and mechanized cavalry gives us versatility in assuring continuity of action night and day, and the greatest application of force when and where needed." To Chaffee, this statement was so at variance with the obvious facts, that he found it difficult to restrain his temper. With ill concealed impatience, he indicted his colleagues in blunt language. "They seemed blind to the possibilities of a mechanized cavalry," he said. "I believe that mechanization and horses will not greatly mix within the cavalry division. I believe we have a place for cavalry divisions, and I believe we have a place for mechanized cavalry brigades, and that they must develop each along its own line to carry out the mobile mission of the army rather than the more narrow view of the horse mission of the army."

"Those fellows at Riley ought to understand that the definition of cavalry now includes troops of any kind equipped for highly mobile combat and not just mounted on horses. The motto of the School says, 'Through Mobility We Conquer'. It does not say, 'Through Mobility on Horses Alone We Conquer'."

CHAPTER FOUR

The Tortoise and the Hare

I

The triumph of the cavalry in securing control of the Mechanized Force in 1931 brought gloom to the hearts of a small group of infantrymen who had been enthusiastic proponents of the General Staff's mechanized experiments. They had been vigorous advocates of a re-examination of infantry tank doctrines and lively protestants against using the fast, light tank being developed by their colleagues solely for the narrow role of fighting in close support of the foot soldier. Their controversial ideas had been argued strenuously in and out of infantry conference rooms and discussed lengthily in the columns of service journals. Though they would have preferred the mechanized experiments to have occurred under infantry auspices, nevertheless their support of the project had been ungrudging. In thus advancing a new role for the infantry tank, they had experienced no sensation of treason or disloyalty to their parent organization. Any action which eased the advance of the doughboy, whether a cavalry charge, an artillery barrage, or a tank force blitz, they claimed was of first moment to the Queen of Battle. And since the tank was infantry property by an Act of Congress, it was their military duty to utilize all of its powers, no matter how unorthodox the result might be. With the stark pronouncement of the Chief of Staff, however, they saw themselves divorced from further participation in the development of a mechanized force, and their work with the Great Experiment effectively ended. The barriers between interbranch service in times of peace were as wide as the Atlantic Ocean and as impenetrable as a London fog.

One of the chief victims of the action was Major Ralph E. Jones, Tactical Instructor in the Infantry Tank School, whose vociferations on the subject of tanks filled the *Infantry Journal* during 1928 to 1931, and whose proposals to create an independent tank force plunged the faculty of the school into endless dispute. "We must recognize the facts . . ." he told his associates. "Tanks have been radically improved, and the improvements demand corresponding modifications in tactics." Though his proposals differed in certain outward aspects from the plan evolved by Chaffee, by and large the underlying principles were the same. The brass hats of the infantry were still arguing the merits of such a force, however, when the cavalry walked off with it. A few months later, Major Jones found himself relegated to the Siberia of infantry outposts at Fort Crook, Nebraska.

Another infantry exponent of an independent tank force was Major Sereno Brett, also at one time an infantry tank school instructor, in 1929 commander of the 2d Battalion, 1st Tank Regiment at Benning, later Executive Officer of the Eustis Mechanized Force. Early in 1930, he publicly advocated the inclusion of artillery, antitank, antiaircraft, communications, reconnaissance, command, and supply in existing infantry tank organizations to produce a balanced, self-sustaining outfit such as the General Staff had been experimenting with. It was his belief that the "existing infantry tank setup would produce little but grief for tank commanders and embarrassment for the high command" when confronted with modern antitank means. When the Mechanized Force at Eustis was disbanded, Major Brett returned to infantry tank service. In 1936, he succeeded Colonel Allen Kingman as Tank Instructor at the Command and General Staff School at Fort Leavenworth, where once again his voice was heard advocating a "powerful mobile force, strong in fire-power and armor, for use in the rapid attack against hostile rear areas."

It was during the period that the cavalry and infantry were occupied within themselves by dissensions over the proper uses of tanks that officers and instructors of the Command and General Staff School emerged as exponents of the gospel of armor. "Their opinions and ideas," said Hechler, historian of the Armored Force, "had a great deal to do with laying the foundation for later conceptions of the armored division." Included in the course of the school was an interesting study on tanks made in 1930 by another infantryman, Colonel James K. Parsons, inspired by observing the Mechanized Force at Eustis. Then commandant of the Tank School, this officer proposed that six tank divisions be organized in the Army. His plan was rejected by the Chief of Staff, but his study, which proved rudimentary in some respects and amazingly up to date in others in the light of future developments, became a part of the Leavenworth curriculum for some years.

While mechanized-minded infantry zealots mourned the passing of the Mechanized Force to cavalry control because it meant their exclusion from future experiments, a greater number of infantry men mourned the event simply because it meant their exclusive right to tanks had been infringed upon. Actually, they were a little bewildered by the tempest fomented by the appearance of the new tanks, which had induced hitherto sensible officers to espouse a crazy, new idea, and they were secretly relieved to have the responsibility for the development of a new kind of a fighting force placed squarely upon cavalry shoulders. To them, the new tank was merely a modern replacement for the old Marks and Six Tons, which would insure more efficient performance of the old infantry tank roles. They visualized it bounding out ahead of the doughboys crouching in trenches with fixed bayonets, knocking out machine guns right and left, and thereby saving more lives than the old tanks that could not get around so fast. Consequently, when MacArthur declared, "The infantry mission is to close with the enemy . . . Its success is a prerequisite to army success; hence its efforts must not be dispersed in the performance of auxiliary and supporting missions that can be carried out by other arms," they were slyly gleeful of the reproving slap which the Chief of Staff had administered to their starry-eyed colleagues who had been dallying with a mechanized force. When MacArthur further declared: "As one of the principal duties of the tank will be to support infantry, it should be trained with it to develop the most efficient types of machine and most applicable methods of tank support for infantry units," they were pleased to be embarked upon so clear and so comfortable a course.

Such an attitude of resistance to change, however, was in no way peculiar to the men of the infantry. For every foot soldier who refused to be beguiled by the experiment that might prove to be a mere Rube Goldberg phantasmagoria of wheels and levers, there was a military man in every other branch who persisted in the same outlook toward anything new. It was in 1930 that two young lieutenants, one in the air force and one in the navy, crashed head-on against this stone wall of conservatism and complacency predominating the military caste. These men, well known today for their vigor and far-sightedness, were Lt. Alford T. Williams and Lt. James Doolittle. The same sort of military cerebration that coolly disdained the blitz force as a rowdy stranger of questionable habits in a polite crowd of old friends happily accepted the resignation of these two stormy petrels from the service.

Perhaps one of the most unfortunate aspects of the assignment of the Mechanized Force to cavalry control was the resultant separation of effort of the small group of exponents of blitzkrieg in the two branches of cavalry and infantry at a time when the fledgling outfit needed every ounce of support it could possibly marshal, no matter where in the army it might happen to be. Representatives of both had cooperated to create the first organization at Meade in 1928, and labored together to assemble the force at Eustis in 1930. Into both feeble bodies had been channeled some of the lifeblood of the two parent organizations. Observers had witnessed the salutary phenomenon of a Chief of Infantry urging the development of an

infantry carrier for use with a mechanized force commanded by
a cavalry officer, and precedence being given to equipment for
the experiment over every existing branch. Such a state of
affairs had been unique and wonderful, indeed, in the annals
of United States military history. When MacArthur saw fit to
split the development of mechanization, the association of the
two branches automatically resolved into an internecine competition for money, men, and equipment, while infantry
thought on the subject of an armored force was dispersed to
the four winds.

II

One tangible result of the new War Department policy on
mechanization was a thorough shake-up of the infantry tank
organization. The Tank School was removed from Fort George
G. Meade, where it had been since 1920, to Fort Benning,
Georgia, and given the name "Tank Section of the Infantry
School". Likewise, the Tank Board was transferred from Maryland to the Georgia infantry stronghold. The 1st Tank Regiment became the 66th Infantry (Light Tanks), while the 2d
Tank Regiment, of which only Company F was active, became
the 67th Infantry (Medium Tanks). The experimental motorized 34th Infantry, which had ridden with the tanks at Meade
and Eustis, was reconstituted at Benning, there to continue
experiments. Thus occurred a change of nomenclature and
stations which coordinated infantry and tank activities more
closely than ever before. And with the Tank Board and the
Tank School under the keen eye of Infantry School moguls,
there was less likelihood of tankmen straying from tried-and-
true infantry principles.

Of the 66th Infantry (Light Tank) Regiment, which was
entirely active, the Headquarters, Headquarters Company, the
Service Company, the 1st Battalion and Company I were stationed at Meade; the 2d Battalion at Fort Benning, the 3d Bat-

talion, less Company I, at Fort Devens, and the band at Fort
Hayes. Of the 67th Infantry (Medium Tank) Regiment, only
Company F was active, and it was stationed at Fort Benning. In
addition, there were six active tank companies scattered across
the country from Miller Field, Long Island, to Fort Lewis,
Washington, and one at Schofield Barracks in Hawaii.

While the number of tank companies was fairly impressive
on paper, they were too widely scattered and too poorly
equipped to be very effective in action. Only Company F at Benning possessed up-to-date equipment, and even some of these
machines were unsatisfactory and already obsolete. In the
hybrid mixture of vehicles which belonged to Company F were
Christie M 1931 tanks, light tanks of the T1 series, and four
medium tanks produced by the Ordnance Department during
the preceding ten years. The rest of the infantry tank companies were still equipped with the thousand or so Marks and
Renaults inherited from World War I, which had performed so
inadequately in the mechanized experiments.

Thus burdened with hundreds of over-age machines as the
infantry was, it was not surprising, therefore, when the new
Infantry Basic Field Manual, published in 1931 as the guide and
bible of the branch, in the tank section continued to stress for
infantry tanks the "accompanying" role, which had emerged
from World War I and which had determined tank tactics for
the decade just finished. In the performance of this duty, tanks
stayed close to the foot troops in the attack and sought to
demolish strong points of resistance that obstructed the doughboys' advance. Usually one platoon of tanks was considered the
proper dosage for one battalion of infantry, and the tankmen
operated under the command of the battalion leader.

This method of employment for tanks was likewise the
principal tank doctrine of the French military, who used for
this role their heavily armed, light but not speedy, World War
Renaults. Like the United States, after the war they were sad-
dled with thousands of these obsolete machines. Instead of
junking them, however, and embarking upon a modern tank

program, French military leaders decided that a wall between them and Germany was more important, and bled the country white to build the costly Maginot Line. As a result, not until well into the 30's could France afford to spend some money for new tanks. By this time, French military minds were well conditioned for a war of defense, in which they visualized great masses of infantry and artillery coming to grips. In such slow-moving action, the tank walking with the *poilu* across the battlefield was a good companion.

In England, though originally the accompanying role was highly esteemed by the Royal Tank Corps[1], by 1932 authorities on mechanization agreed that "there is little, if anything, to indicate Great Britain attaches much importance to it."[2] Nevertheless, the British Army possessed "close support" tanks for use with the infantry consisting of light tanks with 47mm guns or mortars, self-propelled mounts for 18-pounder guns, and a medium tank armed with a mortar.

A second and less important job for tanks mentioned in the Infantry Basic Manual of 1931 was the "leading" role. Tanks engaged in this duty were to advance in mass ahead of the main combat troops, hurling themselves against strong frontal or flank hostile positions. Upon vanquishing these, they were then to bludgeon onward to the rear against artillery in positions and troops in reserve to prevent an enemy counterattack. While "accompanying" tanks stayed close to the foot troops, no such restriction governed the "leading" tank. Unless it broke down or blew up, its position in battle was usually well in front of the infantry—an armored spearhead for the main attack. The fact that the "leading" tanks were to be under the command of the corps or army, instead of an infantry battalion commander, likewise permitted more latitude of maneuver. This secondary role for infantry tanks had been evolved after the close of the First World War; hence its worth still remained to be proven in actual combat. There were, however, both at home and abroad, supporters who pinned their hopes to this usage of tanks, and detractors who termed it tank suicide.

France recognized the "leading" tank idea, though with certain modifications. For this role she favored very large and heavy tanks called "breaking-through" tanks, with heavy armament, thick armor, and little mobility. Instead of allowing them to proceed to rear areas subsequent to the penetration of the enemy front, as was prescribed by U.S. tacticians, however, French doctrine required them to wait for the advancing foot troops.

The habit of English generals, whenever engaged in army maneuvers, of launching armored brigades, bull-like, against strong hostile positions unwittingly paralleled the American and French idea of "leading" tanks, and caused British proponents of blitzkrieg to quiver with anguish. Just as often on maneuvers, armored brigades were split up and employed piecemeal along a wide front. After one such demonstration on the Salisbury Plain, Captain Liddell-Hart bitterly declared in a published post-mortem, "We are left to reflect chiefly on examples of how armored forces should not be used, and the power of mobility abused." Thus though England had pioneered with an armored force and kept her Royal Tank Corps independent of infantry control, yet in actual practice her tanks were circumscribed by the same thought that had shackled tanks in the United States and France to the infantry advance.

While the Infantry Manual of 1931 did not entirely ignore the question of an armored force, but defined it and officially admitted its possible future existence in the American Army, the main concern of the tank section of the volume was infantry tanks on infantry missions. In the execution of these tasks, infantry regulations maintained two paramount principles governing the employment of the tank: simultaneously in large numbers, and with a maximum of surprise. These two maxims, however, had a strange way of contradicting actual results, for it seemed that the habit of assigning a tank platoon to an infantry battalion, in effect, spread the tanks out in such long thin lines that a decisive mass blow was impossible, while tying the tank to the foot soldier permitted surprise only to the degree that the general action was a surprise. Such anomalies of doctrine were productive of much confusion in the minds of serious-thinking tank men, with the result that throughout most of the 30's there existed as much controversy in the ranks of infantry as to the proper employment of tanks as was to be found in the cavalry branch.

Grappling with the many perplexing problems which beset the formulation of infantry tank dogma during these years were scores of infantry officers who later joined forces with the cavalry to produce the Armored Force. Among them were Lt. Colonel Alvan C. Gillem, Jr., later Major General and Chief of the Armored Command; Lt. Colonel Stephen G. Henry, later Major General and creator and first head of the Armored Force School; Major Robert G. Howie, later Colonel and Executive Officer of the Armored Force School; Captain Joseph A. Holly, later Brigadier General and Commandant of the school; Colonel Bruce Magruder, later Major General at the head of the 1st Armored Division; Captain Edwin K. Wright, later Colonel and Assistant Chief of Staff, G-3, Armored Force; Captain Ralph E. Tibbetts, later Colonel and Executive Officer, G-3, Armored Force, and a host of others.

Not the least of their headaches was the problem of fitting the fast, new tanks, with which they eventually expected to replace the old Marks and Renaults, to the infantry tank roles. To some, the task appeared in the same light as an attempt to hitch a tortoise to a hare.

III

The provisions of MacArthur's mechanization directive, whereby infantry tanks were assigned to cavalry under the guise of combat cars, quite unwittingly complicated an already well-tangled situation. From this act, which provided two different branches of the service with a similar vehicle, stemmed a confusion and "vagueness of thought as to the proper use of infantry and cavalry tanks, and a lack of understanding as to the use of the weapons,"[3] which persisted for seven years.

The issue was further beclouded by the fact that the light tank was still in the experimental stage, the controversy of the Christie vs. the Ordnance T-1 not yet having been settled. In May, 1931, however, Mr. Christie, after a series of disappointing demonstrations during which the vehicle had frequently broken down, finally satisfactorily completed the model light tank which had been ordered by the Chief of Ordnance, and over which there had occurred such a furore the year before. Both the mechanized cavalry and infantry agreed that they wanted the Christie tanks, whereupon seven more were ordered from Mr. Christie, four to go to Knox and three to go to Benning. Two additional tanks were also produced and sold to Russia with the blue prints. The Russians were so impressed by Mr. Christie's tanks that they offered him a job in the U.S.S.R., which he refused. Thousands of Christie type tanks later appeared in the Russian Army, and the Soviet T-34 model, backbone of Russian tank outfits, contained many of the Christie innovations. Likewise, British Cruiser tanks developed during World War II incorporated important Christie tank features.

Since the completed Christie machine, however, weighed 10.5 tons instead of the 7.5-ton limit for the light tank, the infantry proposed to adopt it as a medium tank, to be used for both the accompanying and leading role. (The War Department limitation of tanks and combat cars to 7.5 tons was imposed because it was the load limit of divisional engineer bridges. Irked by the rule, which was seriously handicapping proper light tank development, the Chief of Cavalry pointed out that he could find only one divisional engineer bridge in the U.S.—"designed in General Grant's directive for his advance on Richmond in 1864–65"—and that it was high time the engineers brought themselves up to date by building a new bridge for heavier equipment. "It is interesting to note" says Gen. C. L. Scott, "that a 40-ton bridge had to be provided eventually in World War II, and even heavier ones are needed now.")

Other features of the tank were a 40 mile an hour speed on tracks and a 70 mile an hour speed on wheels, a crew of two, and armor from 0.25 to 0.625 inches thick. The tanks destined for the infantry were armed with one 37mm gun and one cal. 30 machine gun, while those for the mechanized cavalry carried one cal. 50 machine gun and one cal. 30 machine gun.

Inasmuch as the infantry was still in the market for a light vehicle, they requested Mr. Christie to build for them a light machine that would come within the limits of light tank requirements; i.e., one "that carries two men and is transported by a tank carrier." Not many months later, the sprightly Mr. Christie turned up with a smart little tank weighing five tons, carrying armor 0.375 to 0.5 inches thick, with a crew of three, and possessing a speed of 60 miles an hour on tracks and 120 miles an hour on wheels. The unique feature of the new model, however, was to be its carrier. Infantrymen were amazed to discover that the 68-year-old inventor had produced a tank to be carried in a special airplane and later released close to the ground. Christie's airborne tank was not accepted by the Army, however, on the grounds that there was no need for such equipment. Ten years later the Germans stopped the initial Allied advance on Bizerte with 50 tanks flown to North Africa, and Allied spokesmen declared that "had an airborne tank battalion been available it would have been sufficient to turn the battle in favor of the Allies."

The burdens of America's struggling tankmen were not made any lighter by the fact that money for more tanks and further experimentation was becoming scarcer than ever. The withering hand of the depression upon the army budget all through the early 30's made it well nigh impossible to secure funds for even the barest necessities, let alone dollars for what many army people still considered flighty experiments with armor. "Our present problem," declared the Chief of Infantry somewhat wistfully, "is to secure enough Christie tanks to permit study of tank tactics. With the funds available, there is only enough to equip our smallest tank unit, the platoon (3 tanks)." Indeed, 1934 infantry tank appropriations were so restricted that the only movement permitted tanks was to and from firing ranges. In all other activities, they were represented by "light vehicles", which required less gas and oil and fewer repairs to run. Harassed tankmen paused to chuckle appreciatively, however, at a cartoon in the *Infantry Journal* satirizing their plight. Pictured was a soldier riding on a scooter on which was mounted a battered G. I. can labeled "1st Tank Company". Beneath was the caption, "Lost my gas and oil allowance for training, but thank God I still have the old initiative."

Meantime, at the behest of the cavalry, the Ordnance Department had begun to tinker with a convertible armored car for use as a combat car. The resulting machine was a radical departure from any light tank previously built by them, and embodied many of the features which had hitherto characterized the tanks built by Mr. Christie as to general arrangement of the engine, drive, guns, and tracks. The Ordnance retained these new ideas. The changed models interested the cavalry, and disconcerted Mr. Christie, who complained privately to Colonel Chaffee that the Ordnance was stealing his show.[4]

After several years of continuous work along the new lines, there was finally produced by the Ordnance Department in 1935 a tank, dubbed Experimental Type 5-Experimental Modification 2 (T5-E2) which the War Department allowed the mechanized cavalry to accept as its first standardized light tank. Its official title thenceforth became "Combat Car M-I." And its characteristics were: weight 9.7 tons, speed 50 miles an hour, a crew of 4, armor 0.25 to 0.625 inches, one cal. 50 machine gun and three cal. 30 machine guns. "Rubber block tracks and volute spring suspension on this vehicle are characteristics of American tanks today," said Col. Robert J. Icks in his description of the cavalry machine. "Agile, dependable, it taught the U.S. much about tactics."[5]

When the infantry, which was still looking for a satisfactory light tank, saw the new cavalry combat car, they forthwith ceased all negotiations for any other light tank and proceeded to adopt the cavalry tank for their own use as well. They even retained the light machine gun armament, instead of replacing it with the 37mm gun which they had hitherto required.

According to infantry teachings, these new, light, fast tanks were deemed suitable for the accompanying role, while the fast, 10.5-ton, 37mm-gun armed Christie was well fitted for both the leading role and accompanying role. Thus to infantry tankmen was bequeathed the well nigh impossible task of devising a method by which a 50-mile-an-hour tank could be held down to an 8-mile-an-hour advance, and by which a 37mm-gun armed, lightly armored tank could be effectively hurled against a strongly fortified enemy position of machine guns, antitank guns, and cannons.

To many officers the attempt to fit the new tanks to such tasks appeared as sheer waste of mobility and suicide for the Christies. To others, however, the plan seemed altogether feasible. An ingenious method was accordingly devised by which the light, fast tank could accomplish its accompanying role. Instead of advancing at a steady rate in front of the foot troops, as the old wartime tanks were wont to do, the platoon of tanks would bound ahead of the infantry battalion, pop at the enemy right and left, then bound off to a hiding place, until the battalion caught up with it. Then the platoon would bound away again, repeating the same maneuver until the objective was achieved. It was estimated by one observer that under such tactics the tanks would be in movement about five minutes and in place sixty, an eventuality which prompted him to inquire: "Where are the tanks to go and what are they to do during these long pauses?" Battlefields do not insure ready-made shelters or immunity from enemy guns; nor is there any finer target than a halted tank.

With such speedsters in their possession, more than one infantry tankman succumbed to the temptation to step on the gas and dash off on a miniature blitz. Thus strange events frequently occurred during slow-moving infantry maneuvers. "But with this identity in type of vehicle, it is not surprising," declared the Chief of Infantry some years later in the November-December 1939, *Infantry Journal*, "that the infantry and the cavalry arms overlapped each other in function. Thus we found infantry tank units employed on long distance missions after the manner of cavalry. And it is believed that there was ground for attributing a desire on the part of some of the mechanized cavalry to expand into tank corps including all types of tanks."

The story of the medium tank is inextricably interwoven with the development of the light tank. The tale has its beginnings in the early 20's, when the infantry first began its post-war tank development. After considerable discussion, it was decided to produce one tank which would combine in a happy "medium" all the necessary features of a 7-ton Mark V and the 40-ton Mark VIII. The War Department accordingly fixed the weight at fifteen tons and gave the project priority. By 1925, three experimental models, all weighing over twenty tons and all quite unsatisfactory in performance, had been completed by the Ordnance Department, when a new Chief of Infantry took office. He argued that a light tank would be much more appropriate for infantry purposes and should be given priority instead. He won his point; work on the Ordnance T-1 light tank series began; and further experimentation with a medium tank was shelved until 1930, when another medium tank model appeared. By this time, however the infantry and the cavalry were in full cry after a light tank, and no one, save a few distracted ordnancemen, was interested in pursuing a medium tank. Though the infantry did call the Christie vehicle a medium tank, actually it was too lightly armed and armored to truly fit into this category.

One of the results of the preoccupation of the infantry with the light tank was the tragic shortage of new medium machines in America at the beginning of World War II. Not until 1939 was another medium tank produced, and then it proved almost too late.

CHAPTER FIVE

Test-Tube Tactics

I

It was in 1933 that two visitors from abroad appeared at the gates of Fort Knox, Kentucky. They were military in bearing, Teutonic in aspect, and frankly curious about the mechanized cavalry. The credentials which they presented to Colonel Van Voorhis, commander of the Army post, were impeccable. "I had been advised by the War Department," said the colonel, "that two German officers would visit Knox to see what we were developing in the way of mechanization. They were not particularly interested in our equipment, which was certainly not formidable at that time, but were interested in our views on the proper tactical and strategical employment of mechanized forces . . ."

The visit of the two Germans to Knox was no mere personal caprice of a couple of tank-minded men. Rather, it was a very definite part of a carefully planned program. Hitler had risen to power; soon the Reich would begin to rearm; and all over the world German military men were gathering information on modern weapons of war to bring back to the Fatherland. Forbidden by the Treaty of Versailles to manufacture such materiel themselves, they were studying what was being developed in the armies of their former enemies. When the time was ripe to throw off their bonds, they intended to profit by the mistakes and successes of the nations that had vanquished them.

Throughout all their tours of observation, the absorption of the traveling Teutons in tanks was most apparent, but in no wise surprising. It was the weapon that had helped to defeat them in 1918, and they were alive to the possibility that it might be able to do so again. Since the time of its first appearance at the Somme, the powers of the new fighting machine had been all-engrossing to the German military command.

In 1919, the German General Staff had created a special section devoted to the study of armored combat, and for fourteen years this group functioned as an effective component of the Staff. Since they had no tanks to experiment with, they utilized the experiences of the war to evolve armored doctrines in theory. "Two main phases of armored action received unusual attention: one, the use of and defense against an armored action, and two, the fact that Germany had been uniformly successful in breaking her enemies' front position, but had also never been able to exploit the initial success. The solution to both these problems was eventually found in the armored force of combined arms."[1]

The first fruition of German tank studies was the secret organization in 1929 of the nucleus of an armored force at Doeberitz, near Berlin, where officers and men engaged in clandestine training in the art and principles of armored warfare. They were equipped with tanks and armored cars manufactured, unknown to the Allies, in a German-controlled factory in Sweden, and with a few armored cars built secretly in Germany. Additional armored cars were built and tested in a Russia still friendly to the German Republic that preceded the Hitler regime. In large scale army maneuvers, which were carefully concealed from foreign military observers, armored warfare was simulated by the use of passenger automobiles and armored, unarmed police cars disguised as tanks. Such resourceful improvisation taught the Germans much about the inherent possibilities of machines in armored warfare.

There was no more agreement on the proper role of the tank in German military circles, however, than in other armies of the world. As tank studies proceeded, opinions divided along the same lines that had split open the military ranks of every country, and Teuton temperatures waxed high as the air stirred with heated debate. There were those to whom Colonel General Heinz Guderian, German exponent of blitzkreig, was a god, and General J. F. C. Fuller, British expert of mechanized warfare, a prophet. They pinned their hopes of future German victories on the formation of an independent, armored force. There were those who argued that the tank was a mere appendage of infantry. There were even the same horse-minded cavalrymen, who angrily denounced the gasoline revolution. It was the old, familiar story of cautious traditionalists lined up against the unruly forces of progress, but with a difference. For the Germans the dispute was resolved long before the war began.

In the secret councils of war which followed Hitler's accession to power, army leaders stressed the necessity of organizing the Wehrmacht for a short war of decision. Because of its geographic and economic situation, time worked against Germany in war, and unless victory could be won quickly, defeat was reasonably certain. These arguments of Hitler's war chiefs induced him to include fast armored units in his new army of the future, and, at the signal from the dictator's hand, all opposition to a blitz force wilted and the creation of Germany's mighty armored force began.

To a large area of "extremely varied terrain" in northern Prussia, known as Luneberger Heide, went a trained group of mechanized men. Here they sedulously engaged in putting the German armored vehicles through their paces and in testing tactical ideas based on the information gathered abroad and on the studies of their own tank staff section. When they concluded their grim gymnastics, they had determined the manner in which the German armored units would be organized and the types of armored vehicles that would be put into mass production. Immediately the organization of three armored divisions was begun.

In March, 1935, Hitler officially abrogated the Treaty of Versailles and six months later there occurred the first public preview of the new armored elements. What foreign observers saw was exceedingly impressive. Here was no bumbling, slapstick, make-believe exhibition, but deadly efficient and serious business. In analyzing this new force in the Wehrmacht, America's Chaffee has written:

"Among the initial concepts with which the Germans began their armored divisional organization were the following:

    a. The armored division must utilize the combined arms in combat.

    b. Armored units must be used in sufficient mass to permit sustained driving power.

    c. Armored vehicles must be simple and rugged of construction and design and must be suitable for mass production.

    d. The mobility of all elements of the armored division must be such as to maintain a unity of action in all phases of open warfare.

    e. One hundred per cent replacement of tanks and tank crews must be available during periods of active operations."

Such principles bore a marked similarity to the ones he had often enunciated himself to govern America's mechanized force. It was therefore not surprising to find prominent among the sires of the German armored force one of the Teuton visitors who had stood at the gates of Knox two years before. His name was Colonel Adolph Von Schell. Of the first public appearance of the Panzer units in 1935, he declared, "The German General Staff is satisfied that they have developed an effective method of armored attack." In 1936, Von Schell revisited Knox, where he was the house guest of Colonel C. L. Scott. By then his fame as a tank expert was well known, and it was no surprise when eventually he became the Chief of Motorization of the German State under Hitler.

II

While the German armored divisions steadily waxed more, formidable under the generous hand of the Nazi government, America's feeble armored regiment at Fort Knox went begging for equipment and its commander, Adna Chaffee, the country's leading exponent of blitzkrieg warfare, was ordered from Knox to Washington, there to sit behind a desk in the War Department and juggle figures in the Army budget. His new, official title became "Chief of the Budget and Legislative Planning Branch in the Office of the Deputy Chief of Staff," an assignment which entailed management of the financial affairs of the whole army. His unofficial title, however, for his four-year tour of duty in this capacity might well have been "Liaison Officer and Representative of the Mechanized Cavalry in Washington," for in his position as War Department budgeteer he found himself strategically placed to "keep an active eye on affairs at Knox and to further its welfare."

His successor to the command of the 1st Cavalry Regiment (Mechanized) was Colonel Bruce Palmer, former Assistant Commandant of the Cavalry School, and pioneer designer of a cavalry armored car, while commander of the bridgade post was General Guy V. Henry. In 1936, however, Van Voorhis was made a general and returned to Knox to succeed General Henry. The changes in command brought attendant changes in the post roster, and more names began to appear which later studded the history of the Armored Force: Colonel Willis D. Crittenberger, in World War II a Lt. General and pioneer commander of the 3d Armored Corps; Major Geoffrey Keyes, later a Lt. General and Patton's Chief of Staff in Sicily, who accepted the surrender of Salerno; Colonel Henry Baird, and Colonel Jack Heard, both of whom became leaders of armored divisions. Between these men, who came to carry on the work begun by the mechanized pioneers of 1931, and Colonel Chaffee in Washington, there developed a close connection based on their mutual desire to advance the interests of the mechanized force. A thick sheaf of correspondence gives mute testimony of the amiability of their relations.

The office of the Chief of the Budget Branch was no War Department sinecure. Every year each branch of the Army submitted its requests for the money required to finance its activities during the forthcoming year, substantiating its demands by strong arguments in their behalf. From the resulting mountain of facts and figures, it was the duty of the Budget Chief and his helpers to decide which items to reject and which items to include in the War Department estimates which were yearly sent to Congress. His work entailed close association with top military men of every branch, the Chief of Staff, the Secretary of War, and finally with Congressmen. To utilize to the best advantage the all too meager funds allotted to the War Department required a wide and thorough knowledge of the Army. And to smooth the ruffled tempers and maintain the good-will of those whose requests had to be refused called for the finesse of a diplomat. During Chaffee's tenure of office, he discharged these duties so eminently that his superior declared him "fitted for the office of the Chief of Staff of the U.S. Army," an opinion with which the incumbent Chief of Staff concurred. Likewise, the aid which he was able to obtain for the mechanized cavalry at Knox prompted the historian of the Armored Force to state that during this period "he conducted a one-man campaign for mechanization in the War Department."

In the fall of 1934, following Chaffee's departure, the long-awaited battalion of Field Artillery, the 68th, arrived at Knox. To provide equipment for the new outfit, Chaffee persuaded the Chief of Cavalry to request funds for six self-propelled gun mounts. "I have told the office of the Chief of Cavalry," he wrote Colonel Palmer, "that they better get a good strong justification in for these on the basis of the need for self-propelled guns. After they get the money, it does not make any difference what they do with it. The guns could be mortars or anything else, and if they fail to prove their need for that purpose, then a tank house can be put on them, giving you six more combat cars." And when the President, late in 1934, unexpectedly presented the War Department with 45 million dollars over the previous budget, Chaffee promptly saw to it that 5 millions of the money were inserted in the estimates for "tanks and other mechanized vehicles and their accessories." The mechanized cavalry could not fail to profit from such resourceful behind-the-scenes manipulation.

Effecting the mechanization of a second regiment was high on Chaffee's agenda of Fort Knox business during his sojourn in Washington, and the achievement of this objective cost him many a weary and perplexing hour and not a little gumshoeing around the offices of the Chief of Cavalry and of the Chief of Staff, General Malin Craig, former Chief of Cavalry himself. The 1935 budget carried a provision for an increase in the Army, and the cavalry allotment from the increase was to be 400 men and $95,000 in grades and ratings. Armed with this information, Chaffee called upon the Chief of Cavalry to persuade him to agree to the mechanization of another horsed regiment. Since the loss of the mounted troops would be counterbalanced by the new troops provided in the budget, the Chief of Cavalry gave his consent to Chaffee's proposal, whereupon Chaffee tackled the Chief of Staff, who ordered a General Staff study of the matter. The upshot of Chaffee's intensive finagling was approval by the War Department of a plan submitted by G-3 to transfer the 4th Cavalry from Fort Meade to Knox. Just when fulfillment of his designs appeared imminent, however, unexpected opposition developed in another quarter. Chaffee summed up the situation for his friends in Knox when he wrote, "From a political point of view the plan has proved to be impractical and has had to be dropped."

Far from discouraged, Chaffee set about devising other ways and means of accomplishing his end. This time he emerged with a proposal to reactivate the 15th Cavalry Regiment with station at Knox, and he won the approval of the Chief of Cavalry to man the regiment with the 400 men to be secured under the army increase, and with 200 additional men to be obtained by reducing the overhead in mounted regiments. To Colonel Palmer, anxiously awaiting word at Knox, he wrote: "When such a plan comes up, I am sure it will be approved. Please keep it under your hat." Chaffee's optimism, however, proved to be unfounded. Cavalry brass hats who resented their mechanized branch appropriating the all-too-rare personnel increase won the day, and on May 8, 1936, the day after his return from a Derby weekend in Louisville, he dispatched the gloomy news to Knox. "I am sorry to tell you that after I got back I found that the Chief of Staff had disapproved the solution of reactivating the 15th Cavalry and has told G-3 to seek some other solution. It is possible that the opportunity will occur to re-open the subject, but am not at all sure. The opposition in the General Staff is very strong."

This eager champion of mechanization was not much longer to be denied, however, for late in 1936, the War Department agreed to mechanize the 13th Cavalry at Fort Riley and send it to Knox. This time nothing appeared to prevent the consummation of the project, and accordingly on September 5th nine officers and two hundred and twenty-nine enlisted men entrained in Kansas bound for Kentucky, the remainder of the regiment being retained by the 2d Cavalry at Riley. Commander of the new mechanized regiment was Colonel C. L. Scott (later a Major General and commander of the Armored Force), who developed into a master trainer of mechanized troops.

With the increase in personnel at Knox, there occurred another crisis in housing, and Van Voorhis, recently returned as commander of the post, dispatched frantic messages to Chaffee in Washington. "In adjusting to meet increases," he wrote, "I have had to move 21 third-grade men out of temporary buildings into revamped barracks, which certainly are not comparable to those vacated. You know what shacks they are. In addition to this, I have had to move 25 non-commissioned officers off the post. We will have to place some officers on commutation . . ." Though such a shortage seems as nothing to those who have gone through the crisis of wartime conditions, yet inability to accommodate military personnel at their post in times of peace was considered a most irregular and undesirable condition. To ease the situation, Van Voorhis was asking for $350,000. "I am unloading all of this on you," he told Chaffee, "as I know that you can get quicker action than would be possible through any other channels."

The state of mind in which Colonel Chaffee received the appeals from his old friend, however, was far from cheerful. The sad truth was that a plan whereby he had hoped to net four million dollars for construction at Knox had just met with disaster. The story, which bore all the earmarks of a first-class, backstage, political drama, had had its beginnings the previous fall, when he had chartered a special War Department airplane and personally conducted Congressional members of the House Appropriations Committee on a flying tour of Army posts. The outcome of his missionary work had been "Congressional interest" in obtaining 162 million dollars for War Department needs. Before he could begin to work on the bill, however, he had been informed that the figure was out, President Roosevelt having rejected the appropriation of such a large amount. Instead, his Congressional friends advised him to prepare a 50 million dollar bill, which they would try to rush through Congress without Presidential approval in the final flurry of business before the close of the session. Accordingly, Chaffee proceeded to write a bill containing five items, each containing expenditures for some ten million dollars. Included in the fifth item was the money for Knox. But when the bill was presented to the House Chairman, he balked at the plot and refused to sponsor a bill of such proportions without Presidential authorization. The matter was finally resolved by cutting the bill down to two items, in neither of which was Knox represented, the clamoring of Texas Congressmen having forced the selection of items benefiting Texas army installations instead.

The outlook, though bleak, left Chaffee undaunted. If the House could not give him the four million dollars, maybe the

Senate would give him a million dollars for housing at his
beloved Knox. Hopefully he approached the Senate Appropriations Committee, who listened sympathetically to his plea and
promised to do what they could. Meanwhile, Chaffee set out to
win Senatorial support for his project wherever he could find a
friendly ear. So diligent indeed were his efforts that Mrs. Chaffee tells of one worthy solon who arose on the floor one day to
inquire "who the gentleman from the War Department was who
was always trying to wangle things for Fort Knox and what his
special interest in the place was." Senatorial curiosity was not
the only reaction to Chaffee's exertions in behalf of the Kentucky post. "In fact," said he to Van Voorhis, "there is considerable sentiment in some quarters of the War Department that,
because of my known interest and the fortunate position I
occupy, the Mechanized Brigade has received far more than it
ought to have. I do not share those views, but they are held
around here in some high places. Anyway, my very dear old
friend, you can always count on my doing the best I can with
any degree of propriety, and the game is never over until the
whistle blows." When the whistle blew, however, Chaffee found
that he had been able to eke out only $66,000 for construction
and $25,000 for roads at Knox. Not until the following year was
he able to get his million dollars.

Though set back smartly in his quest for housing money,
Chaffee was more successful in obtaining funds to pay for aug-
menting Fort Knox's sparse water supply. The heat of Kentucky
summers, almost tropic in intensity, is relieved by little rain.
Each summer the water on the reservation dwindled while its
population swelled, until emergency measures had to be
adopted to insure even enough drinking water. A military order
prohibited the watering of lawns and gardens, and the sweating,
dusty men went "back to the Saturday night standard" of one
bath a week. One summer, when the drouth was worse than
usual—so the story goes—to save water an officer hit upon the
ingenious plan of turning on the fire hose and ordering his
men to run through the spray fast. This in lieu of the weekly

bath. Such a state of affairs was a constant threat to proper sanitation and cleanliness, and money to correct the condition had long and vainly been sought by Knox commanders.

One night, two years after Colonel Chaffee's arrival in Washington, he and Mrs. Chaffee were guests at a formal dinner party, in company with other army officers and their wives. In the course of a conversation, Chaffee learned that the Ordnance Department had $500,000 left over from its portion of the 1935 War Department appropriations, which it intended to return to the United States Treasury. "When we arrived home that night," recalled Mrs. Chaffee, "Adna was in a high state of excitement, and he said to me, 'By God, Ethel, I can hardly wait to get to the office tomorrow. I think we've got our water supply for Knox.'"

"Next morning the first thing, he went to General Craig's office and told him about the Ordnance money. 'Would you ask Secretary of War Woodring, sir, if we could have that money for Fort Knox water?' he inquired. The Chief of Staff replied in the negative. 'Then, sir,' said Adna, 'have I your permission to go in and talk to the Secretary?' Craig said yes, and in Adna went. When he came out of the Secretary's office, he had the money."

The next summer, when the population of Knox in Test-Tube Tactics increased to 25,000 with its temporary summer students, there was no water shortage. A new 70-horse-power Caterpillar diesel-powered pump delivered to the camp 720,000 gallons of water a day from a large clear spring some four miles distant.[2] Later, when Knox grew to be the second largest "city" in Kentucky, there was another water shortage, but by that time money was flowing freely for National Defense.

Though the new combat cars and money for necessities were arriving in the merest dribbles, the enthusiasm of the men and officers for service in the mechanized brigade continued unabated. Some measure of the zealous spirit pervading Knox may be gauged from a perusal of the names in the graduating classes of the Brigade Schools on June 11, 1937. On that day there were graduated from the Brigade Officers School 45

officers, with General Van Voorhis leading the list; from the
Brigade Motor Mechanical School 50 enlisted men; and from
the Brigade Radio School 39 enlisted men. Chaffee summed
up the picture when he remarked, "It is one of the attractions
of service with the brigade that change and improvement are
constantly taking place. Nothing is stable, and I hope nothing
will be until war starts. Only in that way can we go to war best
prepared, best equipped, and best trained."

Fort Knox was no haven for dullards and sloths. Fat, old
soldiers winced in their armchairs as they read accounts of
"Organizational Activities" at the Kentucky post. Month after
month record numbers of hours of duty for soldiers in garrison were reported by the mechanized regiments. There were
tactical demonstrations, ceremonies, road marches, night
problems, target practice—even an ice march, which was conducted by the fledgling 13th Cavalry Regiment under the
doughty Scott. "During the night of January 25th–26th," an
account of the march began, "a cold rain changed into sleet.
The road and countryside on January 26th were covered with
several inches of very slippery ice, the temperature was zero, all
traffic on Highway 31 from Louisville to the south had ceased
due to the dangerous slippery condition of the roads. However,
the 13th cavalry made a short march . . ." Combat cars with
and without grousers (attachments for the purpose of gaining
traction) and wheeled vehicles with chains on all four wheels
rolled along the highway at a pace of "10 to 15 miles an hour."
"The major difficulty occurred," said Scott, "when halted vehicles of any type had to resume march up any hills or on steep
grades," when they slipped and slid crazily over the ice into
roadside ditches. (In the icy weather accompanying the Battle
of the Bulge in 1945, it was reported that some of the tanks
behaved little better.) Horses, which accompanied the cavalry
on the march for test comparison purposes, performed no
more nimbly than the tanks. "It is pertinent to note," declared
the report with overtones of smugness, "that actual road test
showed that horses smooth shod could not stand up either on

the road or on the frozen surface covering the entire country off the roads. Calks were necessary to move at all." Cavalry officers fresh from such country club stations as Fort Myer, Fort Bliss, and Fort Riley regarded such pioneer proceedings with an admixture of awe and consternation. Here was no leisurely, gentleman's life of horseshows and glittering parades, but a rude, bouncing, frontier existence, which produced purple bruises and sore muscles for the uninitiated.

Up to 1936, activities of the mechanized cavalry had been confined to modest exercises at Knox against imaginary enemies or summer students, and small scale horse vs. mechanized cavalry maneuvers at Riley. In the summer of that year, however, the 1st Cavalry Regiment (Mecz.), supported by National Guard motorized infantry, two extra batteries of field artillery, observation airplanes, horse cavalry, and a QM regiment, engaged in Second Army Maneuvers in the V and VI Corps Areas as the mechanized Red Force against two divisions of unmechanized troops dubbed the Blue Force. Thus for the first time since its organization in 1931, the mechanized cavalry had a chance to test the doctrines of its founders against a large mass of army troops.

Under the leadership of Colonel Bruce Palmer, the mechanized cavalry, with its borrowed support, was deftly maneuvered against flanks and rear and marching columns. The mechanized combined arms proved irresistible. Time and again marching troops of the Blue Force, lacking mobile anti-tank guns, were panicked by the onslaught of the tanks. In one action, mechanized troops demonstrated their mastery of the field by maneuvering completely across the rear of the corps troops, marching from one flank to a favorable position to attack the other. "Primarily the tactical endeavor in the mechanized force was to place its diversified fighting powers in a position which offered a choice of a varied course of action . . ." explained Colonel Palmer. The fact that on every day of the maneuvers, which lasted six days, the mechanized force was able to place itself in such positions as many as three times a day, despite the enemy, difficult terrain, roads congested by observers, umpires' conferences, and extensive unleased parcels of land, all of which contrived to hamper its mobility, attested to the ease with which the force achieved its objectives. The "incident of the ford of Mill creek," where the mechanized column was delayed and extended through lack of bridging, however, demonstrated once again all too clearly its need for engineer troops.

Perhaps one of the most valuable aspects of the whole exercise was the opportunity of putting into practice doctrines regarding the employment of motorized infantry in support of mechanized cavalry that had been evolved in theory in map problems, tactical exercises, and classrooms the preceding four years. Though the National Guard motorized infantry arrived only four days before maneuvers and was indifferently mechanized, yet the test proved enlightening. In the mock war, Palmer used the infantry to take over holding missions, to support combat cars in varying missions, and to fight a delaying action in conjunction with artillery. "This type of motorized infantry was very useful," declared Palmer in the November-December, 1936 *Cavalry Journal,* "when the particular missions permit of their being brought into the fight; first, with no necessity of providing the truck column with special protection on the march or on its movement into position, and second, where the attachment of the truck column does not interfere with the tactical mobility of the mechanized elements." Thus once again mechanized leaders evidenced their belief that motorized infantry was destined to play a vital role in conjunction with mechanized troops. Though no suggestion was made by them to introduce such a component in large numbers in the mechanized cavalry regiment, the need was nevertheless pointed out for the inclusion of a mounted rifle troop, whose duties were to be: protection against flanks and rear from sorties of hostile cavalry, close-in protection for artillery in position, dismounted patrolling, and outpost duty. "In short," said Palmer, "to perform the many duties of combat best performed by riflemen."

Though attempts to secure such a unit received a cold response from Washington, requests for observation airplanes for the mechanized cavalry met with more favor. In 1937, as a direct outcome of the maneuvers, the 12th Observation Squadron (less one flight) was attached to the 7th Cavalry Brigade (Mechanized).

While the mechanized commander expressed himself well pleased by the performance of his miniature blitz on wheels, not all cavalry observers were similarly affected. When MacArthur had assigned the mechanized troops to the cavalry, he had decreed that it was to execute normal cavalry missions. But the bold circumgyrations of the Red Force, in the opinion of many, had exceeded what they considered the proper bounds of orthodox cavalry. Instead of being impressed by the potential power of the improvised force, they were affronted by its aggressive behavior. The conclusion of the maneuvers, therefore, was the signal for an attack against the organization at Knox by these vigilantes of cavalry dogma. They argued that the mechanized cavalry was getting away from its original role and that its powers must be reduced. Accordingly, they proposed a reduction of combat cars and their replacement by light scout cars, a change that would have turned the mechanized cavalry into a mere reconnaissance force. High ranking officers tacitly backed the plan by giving it wide publicity, while proponents of mixed cavalry, who saw their chance to profit by such a weakening of the force at Knox, happily joined the fray. Reports of tank performances in the civil war in Spain, moreover, lent credibility to their contentions against the value of an independent tank force.

III

The first real test of a tank force in war occurred in 1935, when the Italian Army used hundreds of CV 3/33 tanks in the conquest of Ethiopia. These tanks, copied after the light British Carden Loyd Mark VI by Fiat and Ansaldo, went 26 miles an hour, weighed 3.85 tons, carried a two-man crew, armor 0.2 to 0.51 inches thick, twin machine guns, and had a range of 68 miles. Diminutive though these machines were, they scored a smashing success against the Ethiops, who had nothing to oppose them except boulders which they dropped on protruding tank guns, and brush fires, which they built to singe the tankettes.

In the Spanish Civil War, which began in 1936, tanks again rolled into action. Germany made no secret of the fact that she intended to use the conflict as the test tube for her newly organized armored elements, and dispatched quantities of her newly manufactured two-man, six-ton tanks armed with twin machine guns to Franco's aid, while Italy also joined the Fascists by furnishing hundreds of the CV 3/33 tanks which had proved so effective in Ethopia. Arrayed on the side of the Republicans opposing the revolt of the Fascists was Russia, who hastily sent to the Spanish Front scores of her 9-ton British Vickers-type and 11-ton Christie-type tanks armed with 47mm cannon. England, France, and America remained nervously neutral while their tankmen watched the fight from the sidelines and scores of prescient Americans rushed off to join the prelude to World War II.

Both armies had been hastily organized and were rudely equipped. They were untrained in modern war and unacquainted with modern equipment. The performance of tanks in such hands was obviously destined to provide little clarification of the controversial tank issue. In the first year of the war, military observers watched the tanks in Iberia violate almost every rule that had ever been laid down to govern their employment. They were sent out against the enemy without reconnaissance and ambushed. They were launched against emplaced gun positions and battered to bits. They were sent forward without infantry and artillery support and riddled by antitank guns. They were employed in mountains and thick forests, and bogged down in ravines. They were used in too small numbers to effect decisive blows. When on one occasion the contrary was true, transgression of another rule brought about a resounding defeat. It was in March, 1937, that 200 Italian tanks of the Soria Division of Ethopian fame, in company with slower-moving infantry and artillery, set off toward Guadalajara to engage the Spanish Reds. What began as an impressive advance, however, soon degenerated into a happy procession of speeding tanks. Perhaps the tankmen were overconfident from their easy victories in Africa, or perhaps it was just a fine spring day conducive to Latin exuberance. In any case, the tank drivers stepped on the gas and bowled smartly over the highway, soon outstripping their less agile support. When they were spotted by enemy aviation and attacked, it was too late for the infantry and artillery to come to the rescue, and before the hostile guns they were as helpless as clay ducks in a shooting gallery. That the Guadalajara offensive became an Italian debacle was in good measure caused by the failure of its mechanized spearhead.

Such misadventures in Spain served to obscure the already-confused tank question even more. Reports of military observers emanating from the battlefield almost unanimously tended to belittle the value of tanks. There were those who claimed that the speed and armor of the tank had been completely nullified by the development of antitank defense. "Wherever tanks encountered special antitank guns (20mm and upwards) they were either destroyed or immoblized before they were able to attain their objectives. . . . It appears that the defense against tanks has developed more rapidly and effectively than the tank itself."[3] Thus the condition of battle was regarded as almost approximating the stalemate of World War I. More especially were light tanks discredited. "German tanks have proved to be mediocre, Italian tanks even worse," said General Temperly of the British Army. "The Russian tanks are superior." But even they had been riddled like sieves by the German 37mm antitank guns. Observers pointed to the disasters that had befallen both the Red and Fascist tanks to illustrate the need for thicker armor and bigger guns, and tended to argue that tanks should be tied down to the infantry and not

used for an independent force. "The obstruent will argue that
Spain is a 'bad tank country,'" taunted a British writer. "All this
constitutes no confutation of their belief in the armored vehicles' all-around efficiency. To which the reply must be that no
potential cockpits are 'good tank countries'; the Argonne and
Galilee, Flanders, the Masurian Marshes, the Chapei rice fields,
the snow plains of Poland are too wet, etc., etc., so what it
comes to is, if anybody wants to play around with tanks in mass,
he will have to wait until he can declare war on a nation possessing a really 'good tank country'."[4] It was such disputations
which earned the retort that tank experiences in Spain should
be taken with a grain of salt.

The accounts issuing from Spain were varying in their
effects upon the tank doctrines of the nations. Official tank
thought in France, however, remained smugly unaffected.
Brass hats interpreted the failures of the tanks as a justification
of their World War I doctrines of tying them down to the existing arms. "It has often been said that modern warfare may be
summed up in two words, 'speed and armor'," they declared.
"Up to last year, great hopes were placed in motorization, mass
aviation, and fast tanks—a thesis the Ethiopian war seemed to
confirm. Today, however, the Spanish conflict calls attention to
the lessons of past wars. Tanks and motorized weapons to a certain extent have failed, while the superiority of AA defense and
inviolability of fronts has been demonstrated." Thus saying,
they continued to contemplate their expensive Maginot Line
with even more complacency than before. General J. F. C.
Fuller has estimated that with the money spent on this fortifi-
cation, 6,000 medium tanks could have been built and 20
armored divisions equipped.

While British neutrality in the struggle permitted no material succor to either side, the effects of the war were reflected in
a strengthening of the army organization and the establishment
of a new type of armored unit in 1936 called the "mechanized
mobile division." This was composed of two brigades of mechanized cavalry containing three light tank regiments, and one

tank brigade containing one light battalion and three mixed battalions with light, medium, and close-in tanks. In 1937, the mechanized division was employed in army maneuvers at Aldershot against an unmechanized foe in an exercise based upon the Spanish war. Some indication of the unsatisfactory character of the results, however, was given by the declaration of the mechanized general at the close of maneuvers, who said, "Making due allowance for the artificiality of the maneuvers, I do not think I saw a single attack launched on a prepared position in daylight which could have succeeded," while Capt. Liddell Hart suggested in his comments in the *London Times* that "a complete revolution in military systems might be the only answer to the present dominating power of defense." The obvious preponderance of light tanks in the mechanized division was the object of much criticism by observers present at the war games, and as a result the organization of the division was changed to include a few more medium tanks in the tank regiment. Likewise, British tankmen, who had watched the German and Italian tanks in Spain, began to lay plans for the manufacture of more medium tanks and heavier light tanks. Difficulties with design, however, and lack of monetary support from the Government combined to delay the execution of the program until it was almost too late. Lack of medium tanks nearly caused the British defeat in Libya, a deficiency that was not corrected until the arrival of American General Grants, Lees, and Shermans in Africa in 1941 and 1942.

When the civil war focused the spotlight on light tank bungling in Spain, U.S. infantrymen uneasily began to scrutinize the cavalry combat car that they had adopted for standard infantry use. Though considerably heavier and larger and far more sturdy than its German and Italian counterpart, yet it was armed with the same machine guns which had proved so ineffectual compared to the 47mm cannon of the Russian tanks, and armored no more thickly than these same Russian tanks that had been a push-over for the German 37mm antitank guns. It did not take them long to realize that somewhere in their quest for a light infantry tank, they had been thrown off the track. What they had not remembered was that a tank that might be suitable for fast, light, mechanized cavalry would never do for the heavy assault jobs of the infantry. They now proposed to design a tank that would be more heavily armed and armored, and, like the British, to institute a new medium tank program. To Colonel Chaffee unwittingly was given the power to further their intentions. A cut in the 1938 budget forced a choice between light tanks for the cavalry or medium tanks for the infantry. His decision was revealed in a letter which he wrote to General Van Voorhis. "The mechanized program is represented in there (the budget) only by medium tanks," he said, "which are our most serious deficiency in mechanization at the present time."

Simultaneously, the War Department issued a restatement of its tank policy, and there was promulgated to the service "a clarified doctrine with respect to the definition between the roles of the infantry tank and the mobile mechanization—the limitation of mechanization to those two ideas primarily with the exception that there was to be no limitation on research and development of artillery material forming a part of the mechanized cavalry."[5]

By its declaration, the War Department sought to end the destroying rivalry between infantry and cavalry tankmen, and to draw a clean-cut line between the two arms. According to the restated policy, the infantry was to develop tanks solely as an additional weapon for infantry, without reconnaissance, security, or support elements, while the mechanized cavalry was to continue its operations along cavalry lines by substituting the machine for the horse and extending its traditional missions.

Far from being displeased by the restrictive pronouncement of the War Department, infantrymen were inclined to feel that they had scored a distinct triumph. From the accounts they had heard of tanks operating independently in Spain, it might well turn out that cavalry tankmen at Knox had been indulging in impossible daydreams all these years. "Great faith was placed in the mechanized force and mechanized weapons, and in some countries they were hailed as independent agencies which would reduce the mass armies of the past to utter impotency," said the Chief of Infantry. "Small, swiftly-moving forces were to be the order of the day. As usual, when excessive stress is placed upon either fire power or mobility, the event disproved the claims of the extremists. Reports from the Spanish war theatre indicate mechanized weapons have attained success only when used in close cooperation with infantry and artillery. They have failed in all cases where they have been employed independently." Nor were infantrymen the only ones who looked askance at the Knox force. Its detractors in the cavalry seized upon the Spanish failures as an opportunity to reiterate their arguments. "The war in Spain," said General Hawkins, "has shown conclusively that whenever tanks have met antitank guns, the tanks have been immobilized. They dare not go forward farther nor faster than the infantry. However, they remain of great help to the infantry if used in close conjunction with it. We might also add here that mechanized cavalry units, light machine gun units, have become an indispensible part of a large cavalry force."

While their work of years was thus impugned, mechanized cavalrymen remained sturdily convinced "of the soundness of the 7th Cavalry Brigade (Mechanized) organization and tactical doctrines, which were conceived long before the war in Spain started." They agreed that tanks would fail without infantry and artillery support, but while their critics meant infantry on foot and slow artillery, they referred to motorized infantry and mechanized artillery as mobile as tanks. Instead of interpreting events in Spain to indicate the failure of mechanized weapons, they laid the disasters to unsound organization and improper tactical doctrines for the armored units. "It is apparent," said Colonel Scott testily in the March–April, 1938, *Cavalry Journal*, "that World War tank tactics are being applied to modern tanks in Spain. . . . These old tactics are unquestionably doomed to failure since military history shows conclusively that new weapons and new equipment demand new methods, for their successful employment."

While the verbal battle raged unabated, Franco's forces in Spain were growing more powerful, and under the tutelage of the Germans, the Fascists became increasingly adept in the handling of their mechanized forces. It is now known that on the plains of the Catalan and the Basque Franco successfully employed in test tube proportions the blitzkrieg tactics that Germany used in full-scale war to conquer Poland. The tragedy was that only Germany and Russia profited from the laboratory demonstration. The attention of the rest of the world was transfixed by Hitler's European game of chess or still diverted by the disputes remaining from the Spanish War.

CHAPTER SIX

Growing Pains

I

"This is a good outfit, the only trouble being that there isn't enough of it."

Thus declared Adna R. Chaffee when, on November 1st, 1938, he became a brigadier general and commander of the 7th Cavalry Brigade (Mecz.). That such was the case, however, could be blamed on neither Chaffee nor his predecessor. As early as 1936, General Van Voorhis had begun to advocate that the brigade be expanded to a division, while Chaffee in Washington had sought to interest brass hats in the proposition. His efforts met with a measure of success on July 8th, 1937, when, on that date, Chief of Cavalry Kromer recommended to the War Department the formation of a mechanized cavalry division with a strength of 3,000. This was approved, but for planning purposes only—which meant, in effect, that the division was merely a paper organization. So matters stood when Chaffee returned to Knox to assume command of the mechanized troops, and one of his first moves was to attempt to translate this paper division in the files into a real one on the field, and to augment it by another thousand men.

In November, 1938, the mechanized brigade numbered some 150 officers and 2,500 men, and well over 500 vehicles. There was a brigade headquarters, though skeletal in numbers, and "such as it is," said Chaffee, "it must be taken from the regiments," which themselves could ill afford to spare the personnel. There were two mechanized regiments, the 1st and 13th, with 56 combat cars apiece, and each regiment contained a headquarters troop, with a troop headquarters, staff platoon, signal personnel and a mortar platoon of six 4.2 chemical mortars; a reconnaissance troop equipped with scout and armored cars; and a machine gun troop mounted on what were then considered obsolete half-tracks equipped with four 30 and 50 calibre machine guns. There were likewise in the brigade four batteries of field artillery with sixteen 75mm howitzers drawn by half-track, unarmored prime movers and 4-wheel-drive trucks; the 12th Observation Squadron (less one flight) consisting of five 0-47's and four 0-43's, with a BT-2 and two B-10's for training and administrative purposes; the 19th Ordnance Company, a self-contained, mobile, maintenance company with 33 trucks; and Company E, 5th Quartermaster Regiment, but lately come to Knox. Radio was the most important means of interbrigade communication, while 109 motorcycles served to carry messages between cars, and to scout and patrol.

"The brigade as it exists," said Chaffee, "is not the largest and most powerful striking force which can be controlled by one command." Accordingly, he proposed to increase it to 248 officers, 4,220 men, and 1,056 vehicles—the expansion to take the form of increased strength within each existing regiment rather than the addition of another cavalry regiment. Under his plan, an adequate division staff was to be provided, and the combat car strength of each regiment was to be raised by one squadron, resulting in 168 tanks for the brigade instead of 112. The howitzer strength was to be increased from 16 to 24, providing a 6-gun battery instead of a 4. Proportionate increases were to be embodied in the reconnaissance elements, motorcycle units, and machine gun, signal, supply, and staff outfits. Instead of one observation squadron less one flight, there was to be a full squadron. New troops Chaffee proposed to attach to the brigade to form the division would be riflemen mounted in armored scout cars, engineers, and a medical troop with "the special problem of evacuation of a force of this character, which has never been adequately studied, much less practiced."

"This new organization," declared Chaffee, "will vastly increase the fighting strength and maneuverability with a very, very low increase in overhead and train. We call it a division, but it might just as well be called a reinforced brigade since the number of regiments is not increased."

Not included in Chaffee's proposed mechanized cavalry division were medium tanks, intermediate antitank guns, or a large supporting group of motorized infantry. These had been rejected, for one reason, on the grounds that they were unwieldy and slow and would tend to immobilize the speedy, light, cavalry division. Thus was the influence of the cavalry doctrine of mobility clearly reflected. Moreover, Chaffee knew that any attempt on the part of the cavalry to annex any more such important infantry properties would have encountered the sternest resistance from that jealous arm, and he deemed the going rough enough as it was, without incurring further wrathy opposition. It was Chaffee's idea, rather, that mechanized cavalry, motorized infantry with antitank, and medium tank regiments be developed separately, later to be welded into a corps under one commander. "We have neither the law to incorporate such an organization," he wrote a friend on May 25, 1938, "nor up to now, have we had the funds to support it . . . but I hope some time to see it done. . . ."

Despite the fact that the war in Spain had discredited the lightly armored and armed tank, he proposed no increase in the calibre of the guns or in the strength of armor on the standardized cavalry combat car, adjudging that its maneuverability and proper handling would offset any lack in fire power or protection. Chaffee's reliance on the fast, light vehicle was another evidence of the influence of cavalry doctrine.

One of Chaffee's first acts upon assuming command of the mechanized brigade was to fly back to Washington for a three-day visit to confer with the Chief of Cavalry and the Chief of Staff regarding the proposed expansion. A new Chief of Cavalry, General John Herr, had recently taken over that office. He was an ardent horseman, fresh from command of horse troops on the border, and inclined to be suspicious of any expansion proposals of mechanized cavalry, lest they jeopardize the strength of his beloved mounted troops. Moreover, it was his firm conviction that the mechanized brigade should be stationed on the border in Texas instead of at Knox, and in a speech which he had just delivered before the Army War College he had bluntly advocated such a move. Chaffee resisted his proposals to change the mechanized station with the same arguments he had employed in 1931. He reassured Herr, however, that he did not intend to expand the brigade at the expense of the mounted troops, but planned to secure the new personnel from army increases instead. It was a tribute to Chaffee's tact and enthusiasm that when he departed from Washington he had won the support of the Chief of Cavalry for his expansion and had created a receptive attitude in the office of the Chief of Staff.

"It has been intimated," wrote a friend close to inner War Department councils on December 15, 1938, "that there is a general concurrence among all divisions of the General 'Staff on the proposed expansion of the mechanized cavalry brigade into a division. Your visit and General Herr's 100% support of your plans seem to have done the job. The totals of enlisted personnel proposed in your Tables of Organization apparently have been included in the initial plan for the augmentation of the Army. Today the indications are that these totals will go forward without much change . . ."

Spirits were high at Knox, and the Christmas of 1938 was the occasion of much military celebration, especially since Chaffee had returned from Washington also with $100,000 for equipment and repair in his pocket and promises for much more for Knox to be included in the forthcoming Army bill. The joy at the mechanized post was short-lived, however. Not long after the New Year reports began to drift back that all was not well with the proposed expansion. General Herr was growing perceptibly cooler, and the division plans lay carefully neglected on War Department desks. It was obvious that Chaffee's missionary work was being undone by the horse lovers in the cavalry. "I hope you will keep talking and pushing along," he wrote uneasily to Herr, "because that is the only way we ever get anything." Privately, however, he concluded that no active help would be forthcoming from that direction, because he knew that Herr still feared the expansion would utilize mounted troops. His opinion was based on a transcript of testimony given by Herr before the House Appropriations Committee which had recently come to his desk. The pages had made bitter reading for the mechanized chieftain, who saw that the Chief of Cavalry had stressed the limitations of the mechanized brigade in order to justify the need for more horsed troops. Chaffee was not proved wrong. Not many weeks later, he learned from the press and from communications from Washington that expansion of the brigade had been deferred and eliminated from the earlier phases of the War Department defense program. Seeking to salvage what he could from the wreckage of his plans, however, he immediately wrote to the Chief of Staff. "I am sorry to learn that expansion has been shelved," he said. "But I hope at least you will approve the tables of organization for the division. That will give us something to shoot at in the future."

During the next three months, the fortunes of Chaffee's proposed tables of organization fluctuated with every breeze that blew from the capital, and in the course of that time Chaffee flew twice again to Washington in an effort to bolster his wilting defenses. Early in March, word from the inner sanctum of the General Staff disclosed that the basic organization of the proposed division was undergoing drastic changes at the hands of G-3, all apparently prompted by a desire to economize. In Chaffee's proposed division, scout cars were designated for reconnaissance, as personnel carriers for the divisional semi-automatic rifle troop, and as a command and staff car. Next to the combat car, it was the brigade's principal vehicle. Manufactured by the White Company, the scout car was wheeled but equipped with puncture-sealing rubber tires, armored for protection all the way around but open at the top, and armed with

one .50 cal machine gun and two .30 cal machine guns plus one
.45 Thompson submachine gun. It weighed five tons and could
go 60 miles an hour on good roads. For this expensive but tactically important scout car, G-3 was proposing to substitute ordinary station wagons and passenger cars in which the command
and staff would ride until battle became imminent, when they
were to transfer into combat vehicles. It is difficult to conceive
of a way better calculated to throw the whole organization into
more confusion than the sight of its leaders scrambling madly
from vehicle to vehicle at its most critical moment. Likewise,
G-3 proposed to mount the supporting rifle troop on cheaper,
unarmored infantry carriers instead of on the scout cars designated by Chaffee, and suggested eliminating scout cars in the
combat car squadrons which provided for getting the first sergeant, the armorer, the clerk and like personnel on the battlefield where they could be used. G-3 pushed its economy
measures even farther by suggesting a reduction of regimental
reconnaissance, instead of an increase as proposed by Chaffee,
to compensate for the addition of divisional reconnaissance,
thereby robbing Peter to pay Paul.

Chaffee's consternation upon learning of G-3's proposed
surgery upon his tables of organization was revealed in a letter
that he wrote to a friend. "The division organization is in a
mess," he said. "Comments from G-3 indicate a totally different
conception on the part of some one and has animated Van
Voorhis, Palmer, Scott, and myself and every man who has had
a hand in building up this force in the field. Instead of a mechanized force under the definition of mechanization [the application of mechanics directly to the combat soldier on the
battlefield] approved by the Chief of Staff in 1928 or 1929—
and from which we have never deviated—in other words, a
conception of an armored force able to live and move despite
.30 calibre fire, a cavalry which cannot be stopped by .30 cal.
fire, we are being asked to accept commercial substitutes for
such things as command vehicles and for the important fire
support units of this outfit, which must move in the zone of fire

right on the heels of combat cars. In other words, they are changing it to a motorized [the substitition of the motor-propelled vehicle for the animal-drawn in the supply echelons of all branches of the Army and in providing strategical mobility for untis of all types through the carrying of men, animals, and equipment in motor vehicles over roads] force with some tanks, and that is not the conception that we have ever had of the mechanized cavalry . . . There isn't a scout car, a truck, or any other vehicle in the tables which we have proposed, the tactical need for which has not been most carefully considered and studied . . .

"As soon as I have the data assembled, I must come to Washington and see the Chief of Staff on this subject. It is too important to be allowed to be changed without his personal knowledge. With that end in view I am planning to be in Washington some time the latter part of this month."

Equally disturbed was General Van Voorhis, then Commanding General of the Fifth Corps Area, in which Fort Knox was located. "I certainly am unable to understand the mechanized cavalry situation as it is being handled in Washington," he wrote Chaffee. "I wouldn't concede a thing . . . and would insist that your view be accepted unless the War Department by personal investigation and study on the ground could convince you to the contrary. I thoroughly understand how you feel about people acting on matters of this kind who have never seen your command."

Thus it was that on March 23rd, Chaffee was again winging his way to Washington to confer with the Chief of Staff. It was his intention to go directly over the Chief of Cavalry's head in order to be certain that his arguments reached the ears of the Army's highest officer. He found, however, that the big guns of infantry had also joined the attack. The men from Benning had informed the Chief that mechanized cavalry had strayed far away from its original conception; that it stressed reconnaissance and mobility too much. The situation topside was even more complicated by the fact that the selection of a new

Chief of Staff was impending, and the incumbent in that office appeared reluctant to commit his successor to any far reaching policy on which there existed so much controversy. Ironically, one of the three leading candidates, and the man backed for the job by the Secretary of War, was none other than Chaffee himself. (Gen. Hugh Drum, and Gen. George Marshall were the other two candidates.) In view of his anomalous position, Chaffee could do little more than once again state his arguments and retire to Knox.

In April, a report came to Knox that G-3 was recommending the creation of another cavalry brigade similar to the 7th for station in New England. This was a move to which Chaffee was irrevocably opposed as he considered it folly to perpetuate the errors of the brigade as it was then constituted by organizing similar units. Though by now despairing of approval of his tables of organization, on May 21st he flew to Washington for the third time in six months. If he could not save the division, it was his intention to make sure that money in the forthcoming budget provided for additional combat cars and scout cars for the brigade. "The only thing we can do about the division is just to keep driving along until we get it," he said. "Take a reasonable plan of organization and equipment and get it approved so as to have something concrete upon which to hang on, continuing demands for men and materiel. That is the line of progress we can take at present. If the European situation keeps hot, we will probably get the additional next year. If it cools off, we won't get it for many years perhaps, but our demands for materiel should go forward anyhow because it takes a long time to make it."

Hardly had Chaffee's plane cleared the ground on its return to Knox than the announcement was issued from the office of the Chief of Staff which officially disapproved Chaffee's tables of organization for a mechanized division. Close on the heels of this statement came another one that declared the organization of another mechanized brigade had been deferred. "As experience mounts with this yet incompletely war-tested mechanized force," said the Chief of Staff, "our training indicates too great emphasis on detached and independent missions with a consequent disregard of hard-hitting supporting missions which have a direct influence on battle. There should be available for those missions a powerful mechanized organization to be used, when opportunity offers, as a decisive attack element. Tendencies to date are leading toward a dispersion of effort with a consequent loss of equipment and a probable absence of this arm from the field at critical times. Present tactical doctrines should receive intensive study from this viewpoint."

With the statement of the Chief of Staff that mechanized cavalry was being frittered away on independent missions, Chaffee offered emphatic disagreement. "The idea of us leading the brigade has never been to waste it on detached and independent missions, but to use it on those missions for the army as a whole where a hard-hitting blow struck in a decisive direction will produce the greatest results. . . . But we have had to operate in the field with what we had—a small and incomplete brigade. . . . I am perfectly in agreement with the thought that a more powerful and a more numerous mobile mechanization should be built up in our Army."

Though Chaffee's private gloom was intense at the abortive outcome of his efforts, nevertheless he maintained an undiscouraged mien before his officers and men. From Van Voorhis, brooding in Columbus, came consolatory words. "I know what you are up against," he said. "The only consolation that I have ever received is from the thought that never in the history of the Army has the introduction of anything new been accepted without a long, vigorous fight . . ."

Agitating Chaffee simultaneously was a practically complete turn-over of the key personnel in the brigade. Instead of receiving the increases he had hoped for, he found that he was losing his best leaders, among them the executive officer, the training and operations officer, the brigade S-4, the post signal officer, and the commander of Company E of the quartermaster regiment. Though the transfers "damned near ruined me" said Chaffee, two incoming "green" officers in a measure offset the loss of his trained men. One was Lt. Colonel Alexander Surles, later a major general and army public relations officer; the other, Major Ernest N. Harmon, who wrote: "I don't know very much about the tactics and employment of the mechanized cavalry, so will not be much good at first. However, I come anxious to learn and willing to work, so hope to develop to be of some use." So well did this officer learn his lessons that four years later he was a major general, had earned the nickname "Hardboiled" Harmon, and was in command of the 1st Armored Division when it "was credited with the success" of the final offensive drive in the Tunisian Campaign and "the taking of 38,000 German prisoners."[1]

Unique in the Chaffee files is correspondence concerning another officer, Lt. Colonel Terry de la Mesa Allen, a rakish, hard-riding horse cavalryman on the border. Ordinarily when Chaffee offered a post with the 7th Cavalry Brigade (Mechanized) to an officer, he accepted with alacrity. Not so Colonel Allen. When Chaffee attempted to interest him in coming to Knox, Allen elected to remain where he was, refusing the offer in no uncertain terms. "I am sorry," said Chaffee of Allen's action, "because my only thought was to extend his knowledge of cavalry so as to make him more useful in the future." He termed Allen a "one-sided cavalryman" and relegated him to the limbo of the unprogressives in the cavalry branch. Such epithets could hardly be applied to the spectacular Allen, however. While he was at the staff school at Leavenworth, a colleague asked him: "Why in hell are we training cavalry officers in peacetime when they won't use them in wartime?" to which Allen retorted, "Because they make the best infantry division commanders in wartime."[2] In 1943 Allen proved his statement, when he led the crack 1st Infantry Division to victory in North Africa, and again in Europe, when he commanded the incomparable 104th "Timberwolf" Division.

II

Had Chaffee been a vacuum cleaner salesman, it is quite likely he would have been a blue-ribbon success, for he was a firm believer in the principle of persuasion by demonstration, and adept at its practice. Of its efficacy he had experienced tangible proof during his tour of duty in Washington, when his flying junket to army posts with Congressmen had paid such generous dividends. And he saw the principle magnificently at work in the public response to the sight of his marching tank force. He gave frequent expression to this view in letters, usually with reference to some particularly uncooperative staff member in Washington, by saying, "Why doesn't that fellow get some orders and come out here to see what it's all about?" It was not surprising, therefore, when his difficulties with Washington began to mount, that he should hit upon the idea of bringing an assortment of dignitaries to Knox to observe the mechanized cavalry in action. The guestbook at Fort Knox during the spring and summer of 1939 read like the program of a star-spangled revue.

First to arrive was General Lesley J. McNair, Chief of Staff, General Headquarters. He came on March 12th and stayed only four hours, but, chortled Chaffee, "we crowded a good deal into that time. I think he went away with a good taste in his mouth."

General H. H. Arnold, Chief of the Air Corps, in Louisville to make the Defense Day dinner speech on April 6th, was the next object of Chaffee's solicitous attentions. Motorcycle escorts screamed; tanks roared and clanked in review; the 12th Observation Squadron turned itself inside out, and Arnold saw not only the still-unfinished Godman Field but everything else at Knox.

"Fort Knox," declared the Air Chief, thoroughly impressed, "is one of the finest posts I have ever visited."

A few weeks later the Air Corps office dispatched $25,000 to Knox to assist in the work on the airfield. More than that was needed to finish the job, but Chaffee did not complain. $25,000 was good pay for a day's entertainment.

On April 10th came General Van Voorhis for a tour of inspection. Chaffee had no need to worry about his opinion of the mechanized cavalry; he knew where the General stood on the subject. When Van Voorhis returned to Fort Hayes, he wrote, "As I stated to you, I did not feel that I was making an inspection. The entire party who made the visit is still talking about what a wonderful time they had and what a wonderful command you have. To me it was just a visit, and one of the most pleasant and satisfactory ones I have ever had. Everything I saw was pleasing to the eye. There was not a thing I found that could be in any way criticized or improved upon. What gave me the most satisfaction was the feeling that, from you down to the last private, it was a pleasure to play your parts in the wonderful show you put on."

Scheduled to arrive at Knox on April 20th were the new Chief of Staff, General Marshall, Congressman A. J. May, Chairman of the powerful Military Affairs Committee, and ten of the Committee members. For them Chaffee had prepared a spectacular show. When, on the appointed day, however, only Congressman May appeared, though Chaffee was disappointed, he "nevertheless gave him escorts, a review, a thorough inspection of the post and a luncheon . . ." Bill HR 5735 was then before Congress. It was an authorization to purchase 51,342 additional acres for the Fort Knox military reservation, the culmination of three years of effort in which petty politics and personal interest had played a retarding role. The influence that Congressman May would have in securing passage of the bill was considerable. Chaffee's show proved not to have been wasted, when, three months after May's visit, HR 5735 became a law.

Chief of Cavalry, Major General John Herr, was next on the guest list. His visit "can't do any harm, and may do some good," opined Chaffee somewhat quizzically. Herr stayed from April 27th to May 8th, and it was no accident that Kentucky's most splendid entertainment, Derby Day, was included in the general's visit. Under the tactful ministrations of the residents of Knox, the cavalry chief visibly mellowed. "I really believe he is enjoying his visit," reported Chaffee. "I hope it will continue that way. It amused me a little bit yesterday morning to find that when he went riding, there wasn't a horse left in our stable. Lee (Chaffee's aide and pilot) flew to St. Louis, and as he passed over the reservation he noted that it was dotted with horses." General Herr returned to Washington from his "very profitable visit" at Knox, "in high spirits and much impressed over his marvelous reception," came word from the cavalry office.

Then came a host of other "visiting firemen," including Messrs. Harley and Davidson of motorcycle fame, Capt. G. Allen King of the South African Army, General Julian Lindsey, even Westbrook Pegler. "In one month alone," recalled Mrs. Chaffee, "we had fifty house guests."

By the time Maj. Gen. Aurelio de Goes Monteiro, Chief of Staff of the Brazilian Army, sometimes called "The General Grant of Brazil," arrived on July 4th, the "blitz boys" had learned their roles perfectly, and Knox was putting on the best show in the army. The tank demonstration so impressed the South American that he was still talking about it when he reached the New York World's Fair several days later. At a luncheon given for the general by Grover Whalen, Chaffee's "name was prominently mentioned" by General Monteiro, "in illustration of how well acquainted he is with our military lore. He commented on your following in your illustrious father's footsteps."

The outstanding entertainment of Monteiro at Knox brought a glowing letter of commendation from Chief of Staff Marshall to General Chaffee, which Chaffee acknowledged with an invitation to Marshall to visit Knox.

Although the fame of the tank show was spreading, not all comments were complimentary. There were some who claimed that the mechanized force was becoming the "leading spit, polish and parade demonstration outfit of the Army." Chaffee ignored the accusation. He knew his methods were producing results. All such activities, however, were but mere warming-up exercises for the biggest "show" of the brigade's entire career.

III

The fall of Barcelona to the Franco Fascists in January, 1939, marked the first tragic date in the world's blackest year since 1914. Two months later, Germany, breaking her promise at Munich, overran the rest of helpless Czechoslovakia. In April, Mussolini seized Albania.

With Europe tense and poised for war, the United States Army prepared to mobilize the greatest number of troops in its peace-time history. For two weeks in August, more than 50,000 officers and men of the Regular Army, National Guard, and Organized Reserves were to be assembled under the command of Lt. General H. A. Drum, for First Army maneuvers in the Lake Champlain region of New York State. Army units from the Northeastern and Central Atlantic States were to comprise the force, the largest any general had commanded in the field since World War I, and the 7th Cavalry Brigade (Mechanized), although located in Second Army territory, was invited to attend.

Nothing could have afforded more pleasure to General Chaffee than to lead his tanks to New York; but the invitation, coming early in 1939, found him embroiled in a controversy with G-3 in Washington over a reduction of brigade maintenance funds which seemed likely to preclude any trips to army maneuvers anywhere that year. The cost of marching the brigade's vehicles and men to Plattsburg would be $290,432.07; $93,000 of it would be forthcoming from First Army maneuver funds; the remainder—$197,000—would have to be wrung from the reluctant coffers of the War Department. From his budgetary experience, no one realized better than Chaffee the difficulties he would encounter in securing the money from the watch-dogs of the Army treasury; nevertheless, he determined that somehow he would find a way to get his troops to New York.

Early in February, the General Staff in Washington replied to Chaffee's figures by suggesting that the maneuver cost be cut by shipment to Plattsburg by rail of all full track and half track vehicles in the brigade, since the greatest maintenance expense was in track replacements. Chaffee was opposed to the idea for two reasons. In the first place, he wanted to show his tanks to John Q. Public in the northeastern states, and secondly, he wanted to give the tank drivers experience in long-distance operation. But after some serious thought, Chaffee decided to capitulate. "I rushed off rail estimates for the First Army maneuvers late yesterday afternoon [February 9, 1939] without further comment," he informed Van Voorhis, "feeling that perhaps additional protest against rail movement would militate against our going at all." Three trains of 83 flat cars, which it would take the railroads three weeks to assemble, would be required to move the machines.

While the General Staff pondered the new expense figures, Chaffee decided to take steps of his own to acquire the money by resorting to an old budget trick. In a personal and confidential letter to Senator Henry Cabot Lodge, who was "a captain in this outfit and very much interested in showing it to the people near his home town," Chaffee sought to persuade the youthful legislator to introduce a special item providing for the money in the pending Appropriations Bill.

"All winter long," he told Senator Lodge, "we have been batting back and forth between here, the War Department, and General Drum, an official proposal to include the Seventh Cavalry Brigade (Mechanized) in the maneuvers of the First Army near Plattsburg or Pine Camp, N. Y., this coming August.

"The real difficulty is money. . . . While we might get there and back on the allotment they will be able to make us, I am sure we will have used up our whole year's maintenance by the end of maneuvers.

"I think if you will talk to General Craig, he will admit he needs money in order to get this Brigade to those maneuvers, and I think he will admit that it is highly desirable that the Brigade go to maneuvers. . . .

"My suggestion would be that when the Army Appropriation Bill comes up to the Senate Committee you insert in Project 3 of the appropriation 'Ordnance Service and Supplies' an additional amount of $100,000 and state in the record that it is to meet the expenses involved in the march of the Mechanized Cavalry Brigade to the maneuvers of the First Army."

As Senator Lodge unfortunately belonged to the minority side of the Senate Committee, and was a new member to boot, he could not comply with the request, and so Chaffee's plotting came to naught.

Thanks to Chaffee's energetic efforts, however, by the end of March only $30,000 was lacking of the money needed to take the brigade to maneuvers, a mere drop in the bucket by wartime standards but then a formidable amount. When the suggestion came from Washington that this shortage be eliminated by sending only a part of the brigade to New York, it was met with a flat, unequivocal "No" from Drum, Van Voorhis, and Chaffee. "It was refreshing to see," said Van Voorhis of the complete accord on this point. On March 29th, Chaffee's executive officer wrote to G-3 in Washington, "By this time you have probably gotten our last effort on the First Army maneuvers . . . I hope it answers your questions, and if not, that it is sufficiently confusing so that you will give up figuring and just give us the total amount we ask for." Although G-3 may have been confused, it did not produce the money. But despite the shortage, Chaffee and First Army Headquarters proceeded with preparations as if the question of the brigade's participation were already settled.

"Every one seems interested . . . in the brigade," came word from a former Knox officer, then stationed at First Army Headquarters, "and needless to say, they are out to stop you."

Observed another mechanized cavalryman, "It is interesting to see how little even the higher-ups know about its operation." A colonel at headquarters advanced the opinion that it would take only one piece of artillery in the advance guard of the opposing force to pile up the whole brigade. Generals who were designated to lead troops in the mimic war at Plattsburg wrote to the Knox chief, asking for information "as regards the proper tactics of the mechanized force at the present moment." The umpires of the war games were frankly confused, "and we admit," they told Chaffee "that we have very little to go on where your vehicles are concerned." They requested him to send a "draft of what you consider the best data and rules to use in umpiring your operations, including weapons opposing you." A bulletin on "means" and "methods" to defeat the brigade was prepared by army engineers. "A means" suggested was the erection of road blocks for the mechanized force at places where the army did not have trespass rights on either side of the road. Said Chaffee, "I wrote a note to General Drum and said I didn't think very much of that army engineer bulletin and its subterfuges . . ." With so much ignorance and misunderstanding beclouding military minds regarding his blitz force, no wonder Chaffee was so eager to show what it could do.

Early in June Chaffee and his pilot flew to Plattsburg to reconnoiter the maneuver area. That 400 square miles of countryside contained forests, mountains, rivers, farmland, lakes, bog, almost everything, in fact, but desert; and Chaffee saw that the terrain would be a difficult test for the brigade even without any engineers' tricks. From Plattsburg he flew to Governor's Island to confer at First Army Headquarters, and from there to Washington.

The $30,000 was still lacking, and Chaffee, getting more nervous as time grew short, intended to confer with G-3 on the matter. He found the War Department without funds, but willing to authorize the First Army to give him the money, with the War Department, in turn, guaranteeing to make up the deficit

to them from 1940 funds. On June 23rd, the First Army agreed
to the proposal, and so, at last, the presence of the brigade at
the maneuvers was assured.

That is, it would have been assured had not a mistake in
figuring freight expenses suddenly been discovered the last of
June, and estimates on the cost of sending the brigade to
Plattsburg shown to be short by $8,000. This was how it hap-
pened. Back in March, when the cost of shipping track vehicles
had been figured, "we obtained through the railroad authorities here and in Chicago," explained Chaffee, "a Class 6 rate on
combat cars to Plattsburg at approximately 41c a hundred
weight. Then we sent a radio to the Quartermaster General to
confirm this rate, and it was confirmed. However, the Illinois
Central, who wanted us to load here (Knox) instead of in
Louisville, pointed out later that there was no such rate north
of the Ohio, and when we re-investigated the matter we found
such was correct, and they quoted us a Class 40 rate at something like 79c. The net result was a difference of some $8,000
in shipping our combat cars to and from Plattsburg, which was
never in our estimates and which has not been supplied, of
course."

The general's office was in an uproar the day the mistake
was verified, but Chaffee was determined that no such picayune
would stand in his way. "Please don't count me out of maneuvers," he wrote to First Army Headquarters, "For I shall be there
if I have to walk. P. S. It's a damned long walk." As a last resort,
if he could find the money nowhere else, he decided to use his
regular training funds, then after maneuvers, fly to Washington
to pry loose the money needed to keep the brigade moving the
rest of the year. Cancellation of Third Corps Area air maneuvers, which released $10,000 in training funds to the War
Department, however, made such a move unnecessary, and
through the good offices of Colonel R. R. Allen (later a major
general and himself commander of an armored division in
France) the money was assigned to the 7th Cavalry Brigade

(Mechanized). No more obstacles now stood in the way of the brigade's trek to Plattsburg.

IV

[T]he maneuvers was a repetition of the brigade's trips in the Midwest, and Chaffee found that Ohio, [Pennsylvania] and New York liked his outfit as much as had [Kentucky], Indiana, Missouri, and Kansas. Indeed, the heady cheers of the crowds that lined the streets of every town and hamlet through which the mechanized troops passed were in shameful contrast to the suspicions and jealousies with which many military men were wont to greet the brigade. Throughout all those struggling years if its destiny had been placed in civilian instead of military hands, perhaps the story might have been different.

Arriving at Plattsburg on August 8th, Chaffee took time to write a continuous letter to his wife on the backs of seven postcards covered with scenes of the maneuver area. "We came in right on schedule day before yesterday," he said. "A very successful march. One man hurt—no sick—no A.W.O.L. A remarkable record for the Brigade. Unloaded our combat cars and drew heavy tentage. Pitched permanent camp yesterday morning in the rain, but the afternoon dried us out and now we are snug and comfortable. Have wool clothes on. I wish you could see the lovely sight of this camp from my tent, with the Adirondacks in the background.

"We will finish straightening up the camp today, and then start on regimental problems. There is so much interest in the Brigade that we are bound to have visitors of all ranks by the score. Jack Davis and Twigg came for dinner last night, and the Generals have started visiting around. Suppose I'll have to go return some calls this afternoon. We are 25 miles from the nearest unit. Suits me fine.

"The Brigade attracted lots of interest on the march east. Rochester and Erie almost overwhelmed us with kindness. Front and middle pages of papers covered. I broadcast four times, flying out of the way to Syracuse for one."

At the huge army maneuver area, the ugly duckling of the Cavalry stole the show from the other more pedestrian performers. Its detractors sulked on the sidelines, while around its embattled head raged a violent controversy. "Is it a valuable army unit or a pretty toy?" asked the International News Service[3] summarizing the debate for its readers. "It is agreed by the entire Army that the mechanized cavalry puts on a dashing and impressive show with its hundreds of motor units," said the article, "but agreement ends there . . . Mounted cavalry would as soon discuss the devil as its rival on wheels, and the infantry has a low opinion of the mechanized brigade, which it terms 'the men from Mars'." But whatever disputes the brigade might engender or whatever honors it might win in the mock war, Chaffee was determined to prove one thing: that Craig, the late Chief of Staff, had been wrong when he had accused the brigade of wasting itself on independent missions with a blithe disregard for the main action. Before the brigade departed from Plattsburg, it was Chaffee's intention to strike a blow with his troops which would turn the tide of battle for the entire army and force General Craig to retract his words.

The Army Exercise was preceded by two distinctly separate Corps Exercises held simultaneously on August 21 and 22, one exercise being confined to the western half of the area, the other to the eastern half. The mechanized brigade was divided, and detachments participated in both problems. When the battle grew hot, corps leaders again divided the mechanized detachment to protect both flanks of a sorely beset infantry brigade, leaving remnants of the mechanized brigade so weakened that it was able to operate ineffectively against the heads of enemy columns only. Such tactics were contrary to every principle that had ever been taught by mechanized cavalry leaders, and time after time they warned against this practice on the grounds that it was destroying to mechanized effectiveness. "It was a mistake to split up the Brigade," said Chaffee of the exercise, "and it was a greater mistake to split up the regiment." Clearly the Corps Exercise demonstrated nothing except how to reduce the mechanized brigade to impotency.

The Army Exercise that followed, however, was more propitious for Chaffee's designs. In this phase of the maneuvers, the mechanized brigade was used intact as a part of the Blue Force opposing a numerically greater, but ground-bound Black Army, and it was on the third day of the exercise that the tactical situation played into Chaffee's hands. The previous night orders had been received at the brigade bivouac area to march south eleven miles, cross the Saranac River, and from the west attack the Black Army which was pressing heavily the Blue troops. By 2 A.M. advance units of the brigade were on the move, and the rest of the action proceeded with such dispatch that not many hours later the mechanized cavalry streamed across the communications and lines of supply of the whole Black Army, and was preparing to attack the enemy rear, engaged in front with the Blue Force, when the umpires, eager to save the problem from ruination, set the mechanized brigade back.[4] "In my opinion," said Chaffee, "the greatest assistance possible was rendered to the Blue Corps by this action of the mechanized cavalry brigade . . ."

Had the troops of the Black Army been properly equipped with antitank defenses, however, it is possible that the outcome might have been somewhat different. As it was, the rear areas had no antitank protection, while the front line troops were inadequately supplied. Moreover, there existed no clear ideas as to the most effective usage of the scanty antitank weapons that they possessed. Time and again throughout the maneuvers, front line artillery was detached and concentrated in the rear against expected tank attacks, leaving the infantry without sufficient gun support and dangerously weakened. One division even went so far as to use a 155mm howitzer as a road block to guard its rear area. Other road blocks used by the

Blacks were nothing more than temporary annoyances to the mechanized troops, and demolitions were piecemeal and proved no obstacle to the tanks. It was evident that the Black Army, as it was then equipped, could produce nothing to stop the mechanized cavalrymen.

Such weakness in antitank defense combined with flagrant misuse of the means at hand served to magnify the strength of the brigade in the minds of the troops out of all proportion to its actual power, and, said Chaffee, "they spent all their time hanging around the crossroads waiting for us to show up." Even the press was carried away with enthusiasm for the "dust eaters" and "yellow legs," as they fondly nicknamed them. Whole news dispatches were devoted to their activities to the exclusion of the other 48,000 soldiers who were battling it out at Plattsburg. And in his critique on the final night of the maneuvers, General Drum singled out the brigade to pay it a handsome compliment. "As the battle progressed," he told the listening officers and newsmen, "my troops first called the Seventh the 'mosquitoes,' then the 'hornets,' then the 'devils,' and finally a name I dare not mention." If the heads of the blitz boys were not turned by so much flattering attention, it was because their leaders knew the truth. What was a pitiful handful of mechanized troops when what the country needed were powerful divisions?

Then, on August 25th, in the midst of a drenching rain, the mimic war was declared over, and the weary, sodden troops dispersed to their homes. That is, all but the 7th Cavalry Brigade (Mecz.). For full two weeks rumors had persisted that the brigade was going to New York to be exhibited at the World's Fair instead of going directly back to Knox, and Chaffee had been delighted with the idea of showing off his troops to more of the public. "I think the Brigade would make an excellent impression for the Army as a whole," he had said. Not until August 23rd, however, was the rumor made definite, when orders were received directing Chaffee and his men to proceed to New York with the War Department footing all the bills for the excursion. For three days after the end of maneuvers, the men of the Seventh labored light-heartedly to rehabilitate their machines, for every vehicle in the outfit, tanks and half tracks included, was going to make the march.

At last, with every machine in order down to the last bolt, and with military critic Hanson W. Baldwin of the New York Times, aboard, the iron cavalry struck southward through the mountain country of the Adirondacks en route to its first lay-over city, Albany. The journey was not without mishap, however. Misdirected by state troopers, the brigade took a wrong turn in the highway, traveling miles out of its way through that bleak region. While caustic commentator Westbrook Pegler sneered publicly at the "dashing brigade of farm implements which got itself lost like any other holiday tourist on well posted highways," the Seventh collectively blushed. Not long delayed by their mistake, however, the mechanized troops poured into Albany at 2 P.M., covering in a few hours substantially the same route that it had taken British General Burgoyne weeks to travel. At the state capital, Chaffee was entertained by Governor Herbert Lehman at dinner in the Executive Mansion, and the next morning, when the brigade departed, it had taken on a new passenger, the Governor's son John.

Two events made the trip to the Fair unforgettable for Chaffee. The first of these occurred when he led his brigade through the north gate of the United States Military Academy the next afternoon. It was a proud occasion for the General when his men passed in review before West Point's Superintendent and the Cadet Corps. Perhaps the mechanized men sensed their Old Man's feelings, for they seemed to give just a little more than the best they had to offer, and the cadets reciprocated with a full-dress parade in honor of their visitors. That night the Seventh bivouacked in the Cadet Camp, a spot filled with memories for former West Point Cadet Adna Chaffee. "I hope our occupation did no damage," he said to the Superintendent, who replied, "The organization and materiel of the Brigade was most impressive. Even more impressive was the outstanding evidence of the efficiency of its officers and men and of their military bearing, exemplary conduct, and high morale. I consider it indeed fortunate that the Corps of Cadets has been permitted to observe an organization of such a high character."

The German attack on Poland, September 1, 1939, the day after the brigade's arrival in Flushing Meadows, New York, was the second memorable event. It marked the vindication of all of Chaffee's preachings for which he had been termed "visionary" and "crazy." So closely were his ideas of mechanized warfare followed by the German Panzer Divisions that it was almost as if he had written the blueprint of Hitler's attack.

Gen. John Pershing, commander of the American Expeditionary Force in World War I, played an important role in the early stages of the American armored force. The M26 tank is named for him.

Lt. Gen. George S. Patton, pictured in March 1943. Serving under Pershing in World War I, the young Patton developed the U.S. Tank Center in France and later commanded a tank brigade at St. Mihiel. He gained more lasting fame during World War II as commander of the 3rd Army.

A soldier stalks a tank while training with the 2nd Army in Tennessee in 1942.
LIBRARY OF CONGRESS

An M3 crew at the ready, Fort Knox, Kentucky, June 1942.
LIBRARY OF CONGRESS

M3 tanks in action at Fort Knox, June 1942.
LIBRARY OF CONGRESS

Line of M4s at Fort Knox, June 1942.

An M4 crew takes a break from training at Fort Knox, June 1942.

A tanker poses with the 75mm cannon of an M3 tank at Fort Knox, June 1942.

A tank commander
on the course at Fort
Knox, June 1942.
LIBRARY OF CONGRESS

Light tanks at Fort
Knox, June 1942.
LIBRARY OF CONGRESS

Light tanks training
at Fort Knox,
June 1942.
LIBRARY OF CONGRESS

An M3 tank kicking
up some dust at Fort
Knox, June 1942.

Tanks maneuvering
in a mountain
pass in Alaska,
summer 1942.

American tanks
thunder down an
English plain
during group
maneuvers, 1942.

The crew of an M3 tank of the 2nd Battalion, 12th Armored Regiment, 1st Armored Division, takes advantage of a break at Souk el Arba, Tunisia, to shave, clean kits, and review maps, November 1942.
NATIONAL ARCHIVES

An M3 tank crew of of the 2nd Battalion, 12th Armored Regiment, 1st Armored Division, poses with shells for the tank's 75mm gun, Souk el Arba, Tunisia, November 1942. NATIONAL ARCHIVES

Tanks on maneuver in England, 1942.
LIBRARY OF CONGRESS

Using an M3 tank instead of a sleigh, soldiers of the 1st Tank Group distribute gifts to children in England, December 1942.
NATIONAL ARCHIVES

One of the Army's most effective land combat weapons, the M10 tank destroyer was speedy and maneuverable and packed a fierce punch.
LIBRARY OF CONGRESS

A tank, nicknamed "Eternity," lands at Red Beach 2 on Sicily, July 10, 1943.
NATIONAL ARCHIVES

Troops of the 24th Infantry, attached to the Americal Division, participate in a tank assault against the Japanese on Bougainville, 1944.
NATIONAL ARCHIVES

During the Battle of the Bulge, tankers of the 5th Armored Regiment, 1st Army, gather round a fire on the snow-covered ground near Eupen, Belgium, opening their Christmas packages, December 30, 1944.
NATIONAL ARCHIVES

Americans mop up on Bougainville. Here, a tank—"Lucky Legs II"—crawls forward, infantrymen following in its cover. NATIONAL ARCHIVES

American troops of the 60th Infantry Regiment advance into a Belgian town under the protection of a heavy tank, September 9, 1944.

Crews of U.S. light tanks wait for the call to clean out enemy machine-gun nests in Coburg, Germany, April 25, 1945. NATIONAL ARCHIVES

Soldiers of the 55th Armored Infantry Battalion and a tank of the 22nd Tank Battalion rush through a smoke-filled street in Wernberg, Germany, April 1945. NATIONAL ARCHIVES

CHAPTER SEVEN

Blueprint for Blitzkrieg

I

At 5:30 A.M. on September 1, 1939, while American tankmen were sleepily recovering from a strenuous first day at the Fair, the first bomb of World War II fell on the Polish fishing village of Puck. It was the calling card of the mighty German Army of a million men that was moving inexorably toward the borders of Poland. All that day bombers and fighters droned overhead in the skies, destroying bridges, railroads, airfields, and shooting down Poland's tiny air force. When the first German troops appeared simultaneously from the east, the southwest, the northwest and the south, intent upon a gigantic pincers squeeze, already the hapless country was bleeding internally, though her front line forces still remained intact. Thirty crack Polish infantry and cavalry divisions strategically manned the borders. Thirty reserve divisions were assembling to join their comrades at the front. Though they had no tanks, no antitank guns, and nothing left of their air force, Polish leaders knew their soldiers were brave and well-trained and their horse cavalry the most dashing in Europe. Military miracles had been managed with less.

What happened to the stalwart Poles in the next two weeks will not soon be forgotten in history. Before the onslaught of the German mass, the front lines wavered and broke. Through the gaps roared the mighty Panzer Divisions. It was the formal debut of the fearful blitz troops, which shocked the world and brought to bitter fulfillment Chaffee's prediction of 1930 that an armored force would constitute "a great part of the highly mobile combat troops of the next war."

The strategic plan of the Poles had been to retire slowly to positions in the rear in order to conserve manpower and shorten their lines. They would then be in a position to counterattack after the Germans had extended their lines of communication. The speed and power of the pincer-like German advance, however, were totally unexpected. Lacking mobile mechanized and motorized units, tank mines, and antitank guns with which to stop these lightning thrusts, the Poles found themselves continually outflanked. When they sought to retreat, they found the railroads and bridges in the rear areas already destroyed by German planes. The reserve troops in the rear were unable to proceed to the front. As the German tanks advanced, infantry in trucks, antitank guns, and artillery took over the captured ground. At the end of seven days they had driven 200 miles into Polish territory. On the eighth day they arrived at the Polish defenses near Warsaw. One-third of the Polish Army had been entrapped between the steel claws of the Germans and gobbled up by the slower-moving foot troops. By September 17th, organized Polish resistance had ceased.

When Germany attacked Poland, she possessed ten full-fledged armored divisions, and more in the making. Each division, 15,000 strong, consisted of reconnaissance mounted in light tanks and armored cars, a tank brigade of two regiments—each equipped with 158 light tanks and 36 mediums—a motorized infantry brigade made up of two motorized rifle regiments and one motorcycle rifle battalion, an artillery regiment with thirty-six 105mm howitzers, and supply and service echelons. Each division was manned with 66 antitank guns.

Compared to such mechanized might, British armor was less than impressive. The outbreak of the war found Great Britain's tank outfits still recovering from the most recent of a long series of paralyzing reorganizations that had afflicted their career. Early in 1939 England abolished the Royal Tank Corps and the Mobile Mechanized Division and assembled her tank

Blueprint for Blitzkrieg 135

units into an Armored Corps. Eighteen mechanized cavalry regiments mounted in light tanks and armored cars formed the bulk of the new arm, which also included two motorized infantry battalions, two artillery regiments, and a mixed anti-tank-antiaircraft regiment. The sum total constituted two armored divisions, or one-fifth of Germany's armored strength. In January, 1940, the Armored Corps was abandoned. Thus we behold the nation that invented the tank and created the first armored force caught short in war with an embryonic tank organization, confused as to its proper operational role, and unappreciative of its importance. Five months later the tanks and equipment of one British armored division and one tank brigade lay strewn along the highways of the Lowlands and on the beach of Dunkerque.

Bad as the British plight was, the French armored situation was even worse. When the war began, France had two light mechanized divisions organized to act as a part of a cavalry corps, and eleven tank regiments within the infantry arm. The mechanized cavalry was designed to be launched through a gap against a limited objective, where it would stop and the advance would again be taken up by the infantry, while the tank regiments were used to support assaulting infantry. No attempt had been made to coordinate the tactics of the cavalry and infantry tanks, and no independent mobile units, such as the Germans employed in Poland, had ever been contemplated as a part of the French Army. Though the organization of armored divisions was begun in February, 1940, highly specialized, mechanized troops are not equipped and trained overnight. Moreover, French chiefs displayed no intention of aping the German blitzkrieg tactics with their new armored troops. In March, 1940, two months before the German offensive against the Lowlands and France, General Gamelin declared: "Generally speaking, a large armored unit cannot cover its own movement nor carry out the reconnaissance of an insufficiently determined enemy. It must always act within the cadre of a corps or of a mechanized groupment under the orders of a cavalry or motorized corps commander." It was obvious that French military leaders believed the Panzer Divisions that had slashed so quickly through ill-defended Poland would be powerless before their magnificent Maginot Line.

If the British and French had no armored might worth thumping their chests about, the United States had even less, with its puny 7th Cavalry Brigade (Mechanized) and few scattered infantry tank outfits. A study of the American situation revealed the startling fact, however, that the proposed mechanized cavalry division, which had been rejected the previous spring, contained all the basically essential elements of the Panzer Division. To produce an American counterpart, albeit somewhat lighter in weight, required merely the attachment of a force of motorized infantry and of medium tanks. Even more significant was the fact that time after time, on exercise and maneuver fields, cavalry leaders of the American mechanized brigade, reinforced by infantry units, had employed, on a small scale, tactics identical to those used by the Germans in Poland. Here, then, was the proof General Chaffee felt he needed to convince the War Department of the soundness of using his mechanized organization as the foundation upon which to build a true armored force.

With the headlines ablaze with the feats of the Panzer troops in Poland and with a substantial increase in the Army almost a certainty, the opportunistic Chaffee, therefore, deemed the time ripe to revive the issue of mechanized expansion. Two days after his return to Knox from the New York Fair—and two days before the end of the Polish campaign—he dispatched to the Adjutant General in Washington "Some Observations and Recommendations Pertinent to Any Future Expansion and Development of Mechanized Cavalry Which May Be Contemplated by the War Department." Pointing to German successes with mobile armored troops, he silenced the skeptics who had said, "It might be done in maneuvers, but how about war?" and proceeded to state once more the need for expansion, this time, however, recommending, instead of one division, four mechanized divisions—one for each of the four American field armies.

In his memorandum, Chaffee struck boldly in other directions. He used the lessons of the Polish campaign to advocate officially for the first time what hitherto he had dared to discuss only privately: that is, the inclusion in the American armies also of highly mobile infantry units and medium tanks. It is interesting to note that even then, despite the auspiciousness of the moment, he did not recommend the immediate formation of a corps of the three elements under one command. "At the moment," he said, as he had also declared the previous spring, "we should continue to develop them separately." He may have taken this course with the thought of achieving the quickest assemblage of the three elements of an armored division with the least possible amount of friction. Mobile infantry and medium tanks belonged to the infantry over the fence, where no cavalryman had a right to trespass. By the same token, the cavalry branch was a jealous watchdog of its own mechanized forces. Such was the bitterness of the rivalry between the branches that no union of these three elements seemed likely without prolonged bickering and endless delay. Moreover, tortuous Congressional proceedings would then be required to make the step legal. If, however, they could be assembled under an army commander as a component of his army, it would constitute the same thing as an armored division and no one would complain.

In the first days after the fall of Poland, Chaffee's ideas seemed to fall on receptive ears in Washington. "The War Department General Staff is hot on the subject of mechanization," wrote a staff officer to Chaffee, "and the proposed mechanized cavalry division appears to be on its way to approval as an item in the proposed expansion of the Army to 280,000. Conferences on mechanization are coming thick and fast . . ." Chaffee was optimistic when he wrote George H. Goodman,

Kentucky WPA Administrator, and said, "We already have indications that there will be an immediate increase in this garrison, and further information leads me to believe that the
garrison may be greatly increased in the near future. When this
takes place, I will call on you for further help . . ." That his high
hopes were tempered with a caution born of long acquaintance
with War Department vacillation, however, was made clear in
his closing statement, when he requested Mr. Goodman "to
treat this matter in strictest confidence as it would be very
embarrassing to have the press publish this information prema-
turely." It was a request that proved to be shrewd in the light of
subsequent events.

A letter to Chaffee, dated September 16th, from the Chief
of Cavalry, indicated his support of Chaffee's expansion proposals, though with the proviso that the expanded brigade or division be merely a part of a cavalry corps of at least two horsed
divisions. An illuminating postscript appended to the letter
stated Herr's opinion that the two of them should try to clarify
their respective views on the use of the mechanized cavalry:
whether it should be used separately from horse cavalry, "as I
suspect you (Chaffee) believe," or together with horse cavalry,
as Herr had long advocated. At this time, both men were still
talking in terms of an organization of 3,000 to 4,000, as outlined by Chaffee in November, 1938, and there was no question
that Herr desired to reconcile their differences in order to present a united front in War Department councils.

Three days later, on September 19th, Herr utilized the
occasion of his talk to the Army War College to press Chaffee's
plans for expansion of mechanized cavalry, to advocate stationing one of the mechanized contingents on the border (a project long near and dear to him because of the opportunities it
afforded for the training of horse and mechanized cavalry
together), and to stress the need for ever more horsed cavalry.
Thus, though it is obvious that both men were heartily agreed
on the necessity to expand the mechanized cavalry, it is equally
evident that they were still as far apart as the poles on the man-

ner of its employment. Then, suddenly, overnight, Herr introduced a change into the picture.

The press was still screaming the powers of the mighty Panzers that had overrun poor Poland. In comparison with such
armored might, the cavalry proposals for mechanized expansion were regarded in certain quarters as pretty puny, and
doubts as to the efficacy of Chaffee's small mechanized division
resolved themselves into such pertinent questions as: "Was the
cavalry equipped to organize a division that could compare with
the German's armored division?" "Would the cavalry employ
medium tanks (strictly infantry property) in such a division if
necessary?" Scenting the challenge to cavalry control of mechanization, General Herr replied: "Yes, the cavalry would employ
medium tanks and any other equipment needed to execute
normal cavalry missions," and he immediately determined to
pick up the gauge by proposing an American mechanized division of some 8,000 men. His decision was communicated to
Chaffee on the day following his speech before the War College
in a letter in which he said, "I am going to submit right now a
project for a division of about 8,000 men . . . I have had numerous conferences with Andrews on the whole subject, and he is
favorable to us.

"I hope you will be able to come here at least a day or so
before you speak at the War College (Sept. 29) in order to confer with us about these urgent matters. I feel confident that if
we all pull together for a common objective we will be able to
balk the buzzards who would now like to steal from us control
of mobile mechanization."

Chaffee's reaction to Herr's proposal for a stronger division was one of hearty accord—though privately he expressed
skepticism that such a large increase would be granted—and in
his lecture before the War College on the subject of "Mechanized Cavalry," he indicated the outcome of his conferences
with Herr. "I am only too happy to say," he declared, "that the
Chief of Cavalry has, on the date of this lecture, agreed to recommend the organization" of a mechanized division compara-

ble in strength and materiel to the strength of the German Armored Division, "but organized as we have done with our smaller divisions, along well understood American principles for the decentralization of command." Four such divisions would be advocated, and before his interested listeners Chaffee proceeded to outline the steps by which he would utilize the brigade, then the division, to produce such a force.

"If expansion were to start tomorrow, this is what I would recommend," he said.

1. That the tables submitted for a Mechanized Cavalry Division be approved without delay. If peace remains, changes will naturally appear with further experience but they do give us something to go on and to procure on.

2. That all materiel included in the fiscal year 1939 and 1940 appropriations applicable for mechanized cavalry be expedited and concentrated and be assigned for this purpose and the balance needed for the equipment of the initial division be supplied from early emergency appropriations. If any light tanks are surplus to the infantry, through its trend towards the medium tank, they also might be used.

3. That a full officer and enlisted complement, together with a 50% surplus in both, be supplied at the expense of our present quotas of horse cavalry and possibly some infantry, if it is not practicable to obtain this personnel from an immediately available increment to the Regular Army. (On this point, Chaffee and Herr, who refused to consider expanding the mechanized cavalry at the expense of the horse cavalry, were also in hot dispute.)

4. That Regular cavalry and field artillery officers, particularly of command rank and capabilities, be withdrawn from existing units and assigned as above and their places be filled by Reserve officers on extended active duty who have had horse cavalry and field artillery training. (Chaffee wanted no lame ducks in his higher echelons of command—posts which he deemed more exacting in requirements in mechanized cavalry than in any other branch of the service). That a proper pro-

portion of the junior officers needed as in paragraph 3 above be Reserve officers on extended active duty.

5. Expand our existing Brigade schools at Knox for the intensive training of radio personnel, mechanics, and other specialists.

In this manner we could quickly form, equip, and train the 1st Cavalry Division (Mechanized); operate it with a portion of motorized infantry and medium tanks: continue our study of organization; and at the same time train intensively on the same materiel the officer and enlisted cadres of two other mechanized divisions until their own equipment could be manufactured.

Out of the confusion prevailing in the War Department, Chaffee's calm, clear statements emerged like beacons in a fog. But instead of ready acceptance of his ideas, there were, instead, foolish arguments and objections. When he returned to Knox from Washington, his earlier optimism was tinged with gloom. To Mrs. George Patton, who, with her husband, had entertained him at dinner at Fort Myer during his stay in the capital, he wrote, "Every time I get a good chance to sit down and talk to George, it is always just as refreshing as a sea breeze. He always thinks in very straight and clear terms, and I had just come from three days of talking to people who did anything else but that."

The official presentation of Herr's proposals for an 8,000-man mechanized division in no wise lightened Chaffee's pessimism, for he knew how weighted down it must have been with representations for enhanced horse cavalry divisions. Developments in Europe had precipitated a kind of free-for-all in the Army family for control of the military plum of mechanization, and although Chaffee had attempted to prove that the mechanized cavalry brigade was the logical nucleus for quick expansion—"the nearest thing to it being only a battalion of infantry tanks"—nevertheless, "there are too many individuals who are not ready to let the cavalry absorb such a large mechanized expansion as proposed." It was obvious, therefore, that what mechanization needed was a strong, 100 percent booster in War Department councils. Instead, it had a man of partisan loyalties, whose case was weakened by his persistent espousals in favor of the horse. Such branch quarrels and intra-branch misunderstandings were the evil that Chaffee had feared, for it meant mountains of talk and hundreds of memoranda, while mechanization languished pending the outcome. Day by day, it was becoming more apparent that, until mechanized cavalry threw off the shackles of any branch control, no real progress was possible.

Discouraging news continued to come out of Washington. Toward the end of November, a General Staff officer gloomily reported to Chaffee: "There is nothing new on the proposed mechanized cavalry divisions. It is my belief that the whole subject of mechanization will be brought up for restudy." To Chaffee it seemed like pure folly to waste time in going back over the whole question of mechanization, especially when American military observers reporting back from German Panzer operations in Europe "so confirm the views of the usage of highly mobile mechanization that my predecessors and I (Chaffee) have held that the answers might just as well have been written at Fort Knox." Undismayed by the turn of events, however, Chaffee prepared to force the issue in the War Department from another angle—through Congressmen. To numerous Senators and Representatives he sent mimeographed copies of his War College speech for the express purpose of arousing discussion "around the Committee tables in Congress this year . . . Then maybe the War Department will conclude that it is best to arrive at a definite policy and we will have some action." Only in a letter to John Pugh, enclosed with his speech, was his bitterness discernible. "Since the Polish campaign," he wrote to the secretary of the Appropriations Committee, "there has been a very live interest in this subject on the part of the public and the press. From a distance it would seem that the interest is greater in those quarters, perhaps, than it is in the Army."

Although expansion of the 7th Cavalry Brigade, Mechanized, was deadlocked in the War Department, mechanization-conscious generals of the Second, Third and Fourth United States Field Armies were clamoring for its services in forthcoming maneuvers. Word came to Chaffee that his brigade was wanted for Army games at Benning, Bliss, and San Antonio, and for more maneuvers in Louisiana, Wisconsin, and Minnesota. But Army plans were changing so fast during the late months of 1939 that it was impossible to predict just what would happen to Chaffee and his tanks. "Out of it all," wrote an officer of the inner circle in Washington, "the one thing that seems to be definite is that your command is going to cover considerable ground during the next six months. I need not tell you that whenever possible discreetly to say so, I suggest that every effort should be made to hold the mechanized brigade together." Participation of the brigade in such war games was exactly what Chaffee wanted. If he could not get a mechanized division through routine channels, perhaps he would be allowed to organize one on the testing ground of maneuvers.

According to the plans that finally took shape early in the new year, the brigade was first to go to Third Army maneuvers in the Sabine River area of Louisiana early in May. Fortunately for Chaffee, the Commanding General of the Third Army was Stanley D. Embick, his former superior in the Budget Branch and the officer who had declared his fitness for the office of Chief of Staff. Fortunate also was the fact that Embick's Chief of Staff was Lt. Colonel John S. Wood, later a major general in command of the 4th Armored Division in the American drive across France. Here, then, were the good men into whose hands was placed the power to shape the immediate destiny of the mechanized brigade.

On January 24th, 1940, General Embick and Colonel Wood appeared in Washington to confer with the General Staff on the maneuvers. Chaffee had been apprised of the conference beforehand, and though not invited to attend, his ideas were very much in evidence when it came to discussions of the 7th

Cavalry Brigade, Mechanized. His behind-the-scenes activity in
this direction had been astute. Previously he had dispatched a
strongly worded memorandum to G-3 of the General Staff, recommending that the brigade at once be constituted a "tentative
divisional organization" by the addition of a regiment of motorized infantry, a battalion of light motorized field artillery, a division headquarters, and expanded services, "in order to take
maximum advantage of coming extended field exercises." Powerful friends in Washington had promised to push the recommendations, while General Embick and Colonel Wood were not
unprepared to listen. When, therefore, the question of rein-
forcing the brigade was presented at the meeting, the result was
"that favorable consideration is now being given to the project
of attaching the 6th Infantry Regiment to your command," and
that "yes, a mechanized division would probably be formed at
maneuvers." This news was relayed via "confidential" letter to
Chaffee at Knox. "Wood agreed with the necessity of giving you
some time, if you are to organize and command such a division," continued Chaffee's informant, "and readily saw that the
actual organization should not be left to chance; nor should
actual consideration of it be deferred any longer . . . So the
whole thing was discussed in this morning's conference, and
apparently you are going to be allowed to write your own
ticket—at least insofar as a supporting infantry (motorized)
regiment is concerned."

The upshot of Chaffee's "missionary" work was that,
although he did not get his "tentative divisional organization"
before the maneuvers, he did secure the 6th Infantry Regiment, which was directed to report at Knox on March 1st,
1940. When orders also came through for the organization of
an engineer troop on February 1st, and soon thereafter of a
medical troop, Chaffee consoled himself by saying, "So little by
little we are getting the troops, if not the name and dignity, of
a mechanized division . . ." With this he had to be content until
the month of May.

II

While great events disturbed the peace of the world, the home front at Knox was far from quiet. Flying circuses, 17 below zero weather, a near-epidemic of influenza, and fires distracted the busy mechanized commander.

On November 9th, a party of fifteen Congressmen were entertained at Knox. Then came General Van Voorhis on a farewell tour of inspection. He was leaving to take over command of the Panama Canal Zone, and before going to that far-off post he wanted one more "looksee" at the brigade, his last in an official capacity.

At the end of his visit, Chaffee flew to Columbus to "continue the motion" of farewell by attending receptions and parties for the departing general. Mechanization was losing a good friend.

On December 8th, the post restaurant, run by Chinaman Lee Dot, burned to the ground. "It happened in the middle of the night, which was bitterly cold," recalled Mrs. Chaffee. "We were in bed, and when we first saw it we thought it was the Fort Knox studio burning. Then we decided it looked like the PX. Adna was dressed and tearing off to the fire in a minute, with me at his heels. When we got there, every one was screaming because Lee Dot was inside and he wouldn't come out. So Adna went inside to get him. He found Lee Dot trying to save his safe and the Christmas present he had bought for Adna and me. For two hours Adna stood out in the cold and directed the firemen. Only the one building was lost, although only inches separated it from other frame buildings. The fire happened at a time, though, when we couldn't afford to lose anything at Knox." In less than two months General Chaffee had secured the money for a new restaurant, however, and soon the steam shovel was at work on a "maison for Lee Dot, which I have no doubt," he said, "will compare favorably with the Cafe de Paris."

A few days after the fire, Mr. Banks' Post Tailor Shop burned. "I certainly think," wrote Chaffee in a letter to Geoffrey

Keyes in Washington, "that we have a fire bug out here, but I haven't been able to find him yet, and neither has Mr. J. Edgar Hoover and Company."

The holidays brought a gentle, sifting snow that buried the reservation under a soft, white cover, while the thermometer stood near zero. It was real Christmas weather, and "we will have a little letdown during the holiday week," declared Chaffee. "I have always believed in the adage that 'all work and no play makes Jack a dull boy,' and this command has been going at top speed since last Christmas." Chaffee enjoyed nothing more than a good party, and a festive holiday week was climaxed on New Year's Day by a party which he and Mrs. Chaffee gave for five hundred guests at the Officer's Club.

Shortly after the holidays came another influx of visitors, this time officers of the General Staff in Washington, headed by dynamic, air-minded General Frank Andrews, a former classmate of Chaffee's at West Point and newly appointed Assistant Chief of Staff G-3. "There is some missionary work that might well be done with three of them," came a tip from Washington, "and I don't mean the QM or the pilot." Quite unnecessary was the reminder to the Commanding General of Knox that his guests needed some eye-opening. His program included a tour of the post and a battle demonstration of the brigade. The thank-you letters he received from Andrews and the others revealed that his efforts had not been wasted.

"All were enthusiastic about the energy and resourcefulness being displayed at Camp (sic) Knox," wrote General Andrews, "and I am confident their interest and enthusiasm will be reflected in better support in the War Department than you have sometimes had in the past, though I cannot say at the moment what concrete form it will take.

". . . I suggested to Marshall that he see the demonstration you pulled for us. He said he did not want to see anything all cut and dried. I told him I though it was the only way to get a quick realization of the technique and fire power possibilities of the Mechanized Brigade . . . but if he gets there, I suggest that you offer him the demonstration. He will get a lot out of it."

Zero weather contrived to keep the Chief of Staff from coming to Knox, but Andrew's visit resulted in his active support in the Third Army maneuver conferences of the proposal to send the 6th Infantry Regiment to that post.

The infantry member of the "flying circus" was no less impressed. His message to Chaffee verged on treason to his branch when he wrote, "The demonstration was one of the most impressive that I have ever seen, and I was at Benning five years . . ."

Fort Knox, in January, 1940, was crowded to its capacity, and more. Besides the officers and men of the brigade and of the Post Detachments, approximately 3,000, there were also now stationed at the Kentucky post two artillery regiments and the 48th Quartermaster Regiment, totaling some 2,000. With this military strength, plus families and resident WPA laborers, the population of Knox amounted to about 7,000, and every building was full.

Likewise, the 33,000-acre reservation, while larger than most, was "cramped with all the activities that are thrown on it." Not only was it the training area for the most mobile command in the army, but three regiments of field artillery were also firing on it—"probably," said Chaffee, "more firing than goes on at Sill," a field artillery post. When the summer reserve troops arrived, "it is just like a pocket handkerchief. Every brigade problem for the Seventh Cavalry has to terminate, of necessity, in one locality, and when several artillery regiments, together with Organized Reserves and R.O.T.C. are firing, and other troops are trying to maneuver, the need of additional land is badly felt."

According to the provisions of the Land Act (Bill HR 5735) passed by Congress in 1939, five millions of dollars had been voted for the purchase of military acreage, with land for Fort Bliss given first priority in Section I, the money to become

available in appropriations for the fiscal year 1941, and the
land for Fort Knox given second priority in Section II, the
money to be forthcoming in 1942. With the future expansion
of the brigade very much on his mind, Chaffee was frantic at
the prospect of such delay in securing the money to enlarge
his post. If the reservation was too small then, what would it be
if the mechanized force should suddenly be increased. Moreover, he knew that, even after the money had been appropriated, the actual acquisition of the land would involve long
drawn-out legal proceedings, and more delay. It was not surprising, therefore, when he determined, by resorting to his old
tricks, to take matters into his own hands and, despite Section
II and the War Department, to attempt to secure the money
for Knox in the 1941 budget after it had reached Congress
early in 1940.

In his efforts he shrewdly enlisted the aid of influential Ken-
tuckians who were his friends, among them Mark Etheridge,
Barry Bingham, and George Chescheir. They, in turn, communicated with Kentucky legislators in Washington regarding the
matter. A letter to Mr. Chescheir throws light upon the manner
of Chaffee's scheming. "Any attempt to have the Knox land substituted in first priority for the Bliss land will meet with determined opposition both in the Senate and in the House," he
wrote, "since Senator Sheppard, Chairman of the Military
Affairs Committee, is on the one side, and Mr. Thomason is a
very influential member of the Military Affairs Committee on
the other side. Therefore, the only course of practical politics is
to secure the simultaneous or previous modification, or revoca-
tion, of Section II of the act. If Senator Barkley would introduce
a little bill, saying in substance—'Section II of the act approved
July 26, 1939, is hereby rescinded,' and get it favorably reported
out of the Senate Committee, it could then be tacked on as an
amendment to any bill that was before the Senate, with Mr.
Barkley's explanation that he desired its passage to permit the
Appropriations Committee to consider at the proper time an

appropriation for Fort Knox land in the fiscal year 1941 instead of the fiscal year 1942. Then the Appropriations Committees on each side would be authorized to consider adding the Knox land to the bill.

"If the above is not successful in the end, Mr. Barkley or Mr. O'Neal (Kentucky Congressman) might endeavor to get the appropriation for the Knox land added to the other items in the War Department bill, the provisions of Section II of the Act notwithstanding. This procedure, however, in my judgment, would be subject to a point of order if originated in the House." That Chaffee realized the value of his remaining in the background as the arch conspirator, while his friends did the work, is evidenced in the closing line of his letter, which read: "It is much better that I do not appear in the picture at all." But he nevertheless did take advantage of the visits to Knox of the fifteen Congressmen and of General Andrews to stress the immediate need for a larger reservation.

His carefully laid plans went awry in the House, however, thanks to the opposition of Congressmen Robsion and Creal, the latter representing citizens of the Kentucky counties affected by the transaction, who did not like the idea. In the budget bill hearings before the House Appropriations Committee, Kentucky Congressman A. J. May had succeeded in inserting an extra million dollars in the bill for the purpose of purchasing land for Knox. When the bill reached the floor of the House, however, the Knox provision was furiously assailed by Congressman Robsion. "This item," he cried, "was not recommended by the Bureau of the Budget or by the President. The gentleman from Kentucky (Mr. Creal) has pointed out to me that this will take up perhaps 25 to 30 per cent of the acreage of Meade County, many churches, schools, villages, highways, nearly 500 farms, the R.E.A. electric lines, and cut off the people of other parts of Meade County and other sections from the bridge or bridges on the Ohio River. No hearings were held on this item and, so far as I can see, no one has appeared and justified the acquisition of this large acreage and the expenditure of this large sum of money."[1]

Although May attempted to defend the measure, when Robsion demanded, "Why did not the Army ask for it, and why did not the Budget ask for it, and why did not the President ask for it?" May could give no adequate answer without involving his friend Chaffee, and he knew the general desired to remain behind the scenes. The item was consequently lost from the bill. Mr. Robsion's speech had cost Knox exactly one million dollars.

This did not end the affair for Chaffee, however. The week following the disaster in the House, he invited to a conference at Knox political representatives of the counties in the purchase area, and the leading bankers and principal landowners of that community. A compromise agreement was reached, and "the contemplated acquisition of land to enlarge the Fort Knox training area was definitely and amicably settled." A delegation of citizens from the affected purchase territory then went to Washington, where they called upon "Mr. Barkley, Mr. Chandler, and Mr. Taft, all of whom stated they will do all they can to get the item back in the Senate bill. They had a conference with Mr. O'Neal and Mr. Creal. Mr. Creal will withdraw his objections, I understand, and go along with the proposition, and I am sure that he will ask Mr. Robsion to do likewise." The outcome of the machinations was that. Chaffee secured, not one million dollars, but $650,000 in the 1941 budget with which to initiate his land purchases.

Thus the toilsome road on which Chaffee inched forward toward his objectives.

Yet not all matters pertaining to the improvement of Knox gave headaches to the General. Early 1940 saw the completion of the colonial-style, red-brick Commanding General's quarters, and for the third time in two years at Knox, the Chaffees moved. "The garden intrigued Adna," recalled Mrs. Chaffee, "especially the rock garden, made of old, old stones brought from Dripping Springs on the reservation. We also had a gold fish pond, and one day he brought home a dozen gold fish that he had bought in the five and ten in Louisville. In a few months there were thirty-five fish in the pond, and every one of them a pet of Adna's."

Nothing, however, brought the General quite as much pleasure as the remodeled, red-brick Post Chapel, which had begun its existence on the Dixie Highway years before as the Catholic Church of the town of Stithten. During the early days of the mechanized troops at Knox, it had served both as a church and movie, and its interior had become dirty and dark from the smoke of two, big, old-fashioned stoves that were used to heat it. By 1938, when the Chaffees returned to Knox, a new theatre had been built, the money for which he had secured while he was on the Budget Staff, and the church was then being used only for religious services. Although Van Voorhis had replaced the unsightly stoves with a furnace, the building still bore the evidence of its rigorous years of double life and, said Mrs. Chaffee, "a dignified place of worship was badly needed for the post. I was the President of the Chaplain's Auxiliary, and Adna promised me he would paint, remodel, and provide the aisle carpet, if the ladies of the Auxiliary would provide everything else. This we did." The pews were built from specifications of the pews in the chapel at West Point by the Post cabinetmaker out of wood cut on the reservation. The stained glass windows were purchased with money donated by the organizations at Knox in early 1940: the 1st Cavalry Regiment (Mechanized), the 13th Cavalry Regiment (Mechanized), the 68th Field Artillery, the 12th Observation Squadron, the Ordnance, Finance, Signal, Medical, and Quartermaster Corps. Since there were nine organizations and only eight windows, the two smallest outfits, Finance and Signal, were combined, and each window bears an inscription showing the name of the donor. The result of this joined effort of many willing hands stands today as a beautiful monument of Chaffee's love for Knox.

III

Relegating all else to the background that cold winter of 1940 however, were preparations for the great Army war games in Louisiana. But on February 5th, just when Chaffee received summons to his first conference with General Embick in Atlanta, Georgia, on plans for the Brigade's participation in the maneuvers, he was confined to bed with influenza, his second attack that winter. Sick though he was, it took strict orders from the doctor and firmness on the part of his wife to keep him from making the trip anyway. He compromised by writing a letter to General Embick, which he dictated in bed. "I have hopes that by the first of next week they will have my illness cleared up," he said. "There are many matters concerning the Brigade and its participation in these maneuvers, especially matters of its probable reinforcement, the preliminary training of these reinforcements, and matters of supply, which I should like to talk over with you and your staff, and the earlier I can understand your views on these subjects, the better the Brigade will be prepared." A choice report of a "high-powered conference on the maneuvers" in Washington indicated that many meetings were likely to be necessary to clear up misconceptions regarding the mechanized force. At the meeting one of the problems discussed was the supply of gasoline that would be needed by the Brigade during the war games, and 5,000 gallons had been mentioned as the required amount. Actually, 5,000 gallons was not enough gasoline to get ten tanks to the maneuver area and back again.

On February 14th, just six days after dictating his letter to Embick and still weak from his illness, Chaffee flew to Atlanta. Following lengthy conferences there, he pushed on to Monroe, Louisiana, where he reconnoitered the maneuver area. On his return trip, he planned to stop at Jefferson Barracks, Missouri, to confer with the commander of the 6th Infantry, scheduled soon to report at Knox, but bad weather dogged his flight, and he was grounded at Memphis. "So I passed up St. Louis," he said, "and came home, having been gone seven days when I expected to be gone only three."

A letter written at the conclusion of his trip to an officer in Washington described the proceedings at the conference at Atlanta. "They were all very cordial and just as helpful as they could be under the circumstances," he said of Embick, Wood, and the Third Army Staff. "A good many of their plans for these maneuvers apparently have not yet crystallized into detail. In some respects they are still drawing large goose eggs on the map. But I got a good deal out of it.

"In the matter of the infantry regiment . . . there are two flies in the ointment. First, General Embick was quite set on the regiment being utilized during the middle of April in Fourth Corps Area maneuvers in Georgia." This meant the infantry regiment would have only the month of March for training at Knox in mechanized tactics before the maneuvers in Louisiana. And "second, the 6th Infantry has to be mounted in cast-off trucks, which will be available at Benning only after the three divisions have received their new equipment." Thus, not until some time in April would the regiment have its own trucks, and then only well-worn ones at that.

Chaffee tackled the "two flies" with characteristic energy and resourcefulness. What he really wanted, of course, was a motorized infantry regiment with permanent station at Knox, but for the time being he would be satisfied to keep the 6th until the end of the maneuvers. It was the middle of March when his vigorous representations in G-3 on the importance of the 6th's remaining at Knox finally had their effect. The War Department issued orders for the 34th Infantry to replace the 6th in the Georgia exercises, and the 6th was allowed to remain with the brigade.

The problem of providing trucks for the infantry regiment during March, in order that they might train with the mechanized brigade, was solved "by taking all the trucks away from the Brigade trains and mounting two or three companies at a

time." In April, when the castoff trucks became available at
Benning, a convoy of drivers was dispatched to Georgia to pick
up the transportation and bring it up to Knox. As for the badly
needed new trucks to replace worn-out vehicles of the brigade,
"it is going to be touch and go," said Chaffee. "Some of them
are almost going to have to make a direct march from the factory door at Detroit to Louisiana in order to get there in time."

Chaffee outlined his plans for training the 6th Infantry in a
letter to Fifth Corps Area Headquarters, which read: "The early
part of March I will work on the 6th Infantry to provide it with
drivers, motorcyclists, maintenance specialists, and some details
of its motorized tactics. The latter part of March I want to have
several brigade exercises with the 6th Infantry, and also employ
the newly organized Engineer Troop and Medical Troop."

His schedule for April was even more crowded. And when
he learned that after Third Army maneuvers in May the
brigade would go to Fourth Army maneuvers in Minnesota in
July, and to Second Army maneuvers in Wisconsin in August,
he knew that he and his men would not be able to slacken
their pace for many months to come. The "tall trees" around
them, however, did not prevent him from seeing the "black for-
est." "I am beginning to think," he said reflectively to a friend,
"that all of this is small change, and we had better study a little
world geography, because who knows where we are going?"
This long view, however, did not keep him from being a little
touchy on the subject of his tank force when Maj. General
William H. Wilson wrote to him from Hawaii and said, "Come
to Hawaii and I'll give you a brigade and you can be a *real* soldier." To this somewhat tactless remark, Chaffee replied, "The
garrison here now numbers some 6,000 men, and according to
present plans, by the end of August I will have taken the 7th
Cavalry Brigade through maneuvers with all four of our Field
Armies and marched it some 7,500 miles in the space of thirteen months, so I believe I am doing a little 'real soldiering' of
my own."

No doubt General Wilson's invitation had been prompted by the knowledge that, according to Army regulations, a change of station was imminent for Chaffee. "They tell me in Washington," he said early in April, "that I am due for foreign service soon." He had information, however, that it was to the Philippines, not to Hawaii, that he was to be ordered. The thought of leaving Knox at such a critical time must have affected him deeply, but there were no signs of any inner disturbance when he wrote to Colonel Scott, "If they would make you a brigadier general, I should be glad to turn over to you a damn big post when I leave. I don't know when that will be, but I know I can't stay here forever."

On April 1st Chaffee flew to San Antonio to confer with Generals Herbert J. Brees and Walter Krueger, commanders of the Eighth and Ninth Corps Areas respectively, with whose troops the mechanized brigade was to operate in the Louisiana maneuvers. By April 6th, he was back in Louisville to take part in the Louisville Army Day Program and to entertain Maj. General David Stone, successor to Van Voorhis in the Fifth Corps Area command. From April 21st to April 25th, he observed Fourth Corps Area maneuvers at Fort Benning, Georgia. And on April 27th, he staged a review of the entire brigade at Knox for the Governor of Kentucky.

The training and preparation of the brigade to go south were in themselves enough to task the full energies of the Knox chief, without his also running a cross-country race with time. Small wonder, then, that in the midst of so much feverish activity the illness, from which he had not allowed himself to recover properly in February, recurred, and once more sent him to bed with a high temperature. For several days, not nearly long enough, the General stayed confined, then back to work he went. "Was sorry to hear you say you had been laid up," wrote a friend, "but haven't you been riding a free horse rather carelessly? I don't know how to tell you to do it, but can't you slow down to a pace for which the human machine was made?"

Such friendly warnings might as well have been left unsaid, for all they were heeded by the busy mechanized general. The great test lay immediately ahead, and now was no time to coddle oneself. On the morning of May 2, 1940, the general led his troops off to Louisiana.

CHAPTER EIGHT

One Sunday in June

I

Assembled in Louisiana for maneuvers under Major General Stanley Embick in May of 1940 were nearly 100,000 Regulars and Reserves, and, for the first time in history, all the tanks the United States Army possessed, both infantry and cavalry, except for two infantry tank companies in the far west. Chaffee's 7th Cavalry Brigade (Mechanized), reinforced, and a recently organized Infantry Provisional Tank Brigade, commanded by Brigadier General Bruce Magruder and including one full regiment and two separate battalions of light tanks and one company of old medium tanks, "twin-turreted crocks," comprised the total mechanized force. These mechanized troops, according to Hechler, historian of the Armored Force, were the heart of the maneuvers, and "were used in many combinations and changed from one side to another as the exercises progressed."

In the second phase of the maneuvers, the 7th Cavalry Brigade (Mechanized) and the Infantry Tank Brigade were combined into one fighting force. No practice training of the two brigades together was allowed, and they were given forty-eight hours to organize and to move seventy-five miles into an offensive action.[1] Captain Gustavus West, then General Chaffee's aide, described his chief's activity during this period as "terrific." For two days, recounted Captain West, Chaffee went without sleep or the proper food. "One morning we were driving along the road," said his aide, "when we had to pull over and stop to let some troops go by. I saw a kitchen in the troop train and jumped out to get him a cup of coffee to drink while we waited. Before I could get back, the general had driven off, leaving me standing in the road with the cup of coffee in my hand. He was so wrapped up in the exercise that he didn't even know I wasn't in the car.

Among the observers who had witnessed the demonstration of the mechanized men was General Frank Andrews of the War Department General Staff. In fact, it was on one of those hot May afternoons during maneuvers that he, General Chaffee, and Colonel Gillem, then Magruder's Executive and three years later Chief of the Armored Force at Knox, "sat together under a tree and discussed"[2] the formation of an armored force. Events in the Lowlands and in France lent a particular urgency to their informal talk, for on May 10th the "sitzkrieg" had ended and the German blitzkrieg had struck again. Even then Allied armies in Flanders were falling back before the onslaught of the German war machine, which was moving toward the French frontiers. On May 25th, the final day of the maneuvers, another impromptu conference on mechanization occurred in the basement of the Alexandria, Louisiana, High School. Present were the leading officers of the two brigades, as well as General Andrews, his Executive Lt. Colonel T. J. Camp, and Colonel George S. Patton, Jr., who was still with the horsed cavalry at Fort Myer, Virginia, but highly interested in mechanization. Pointed was the exclusion from the meeting of the Chief of Cavalry and the Chief of Infantry, both of whom were also in Louisiana attending the maneuvers. Cavalry and infantry connections were forgotten, when the officers at the meeting unanimously concluded that development of mechanized units could no longer be delayed, and that such units must be removed from the control of the traditional branches to become a separate organization. Too long had mechanization played second fiddle in equipment and personnel to foot and horsed troops.

When the basement meeting adjourned, General Andrews flew back to Washington, and the next day Chaffee, pushing the matter while Army interest was still high, wrote him a letter from 7th Brigade Headquarters in the Field at Monroe, Louisiana, giving "my views on a method of obtaining two armored divisions promptly. I believe," he told General Andrews, ". . . that we must do away with our present policy and utilize the means which both the infantry and cavalry have." To form two armored divisions, it was Chaffee's plan to take the 7th Cavalry Brigade (Mechanized) and add to it medium tanks, carrier-transported infantry with supporting artillery—including a battalion of 105mm howitzers—a division staff, and military police, to comprise one division to be stationed at Knox; and to take infantry light and medium tanks and give them reconnaissance, communications, machine gun units, engineers, and other supporting troops comparable to 7th Cavalry Brigade (Mechanized) units, carrier-transported infantry with artillery, a division staff, and military police for a second armored division at Benning.

In his letter, Chaffee purposely used the term "armored division" instead of "mechanized" or "tank" in a deliberate attempt to get away from infantry and cavalry terminology. If the new divisions were thus named, "then no branch can kick," he said. "We must do away with present restrictions of branch responsibility. To do this, the wording of the National Defense Act—'Tanks will be operated by Infantry'—must be repealed. This will do away with the fictional name 'combat car,' which was invented to get around the legal restriction. . . . For the later divisions, when you get the law changed, you can raise armored regiments outright."

As the brigade sped northward the following day on the first leg of its journey back to Knox, although Chaffee's keen eyes were on the roaring column of machines, his thoughts must have been in Washington. Was he at last going to have his mechanized division, perhaps even an armored corps—or would he be disappointed again as he had been only nine months before, when he had believed success was certain? Andrews might agree with his fine plans, but would the Chief of Staff—and the others in the War Department? He was doubly cautious this time about allowing his optimism to play him any more sad tricks.

But Chaffee need not have worried. In Washington, the recommendations of Andrews, the spokesman of the mechanized men, were receiving close attention. German successes with just such divisions as were being proposed were too frightening to be ignored. Belgium had surrendered even while Chaffee was marching back to Knox, and already Nazi Panzer Divisions were turned toward Paris. The Chief of Staff delayed no longer, but ordered G-3, of which Andrews was head, to draw up plans immediately to organize at least two armored divisions at once, and to consider the requirement of GHQ armored troops.

On June 10th, a "full-dress" conference of officers representing the War Department and every branch of the service was held in Washington to discuss Marshall's directive, as well as a change, or broadening, of the War Department policy on mechanization-implying a move to create a separate force. Present were Andrews, Chaffee, Magruder, C. L. Scott, Sereno Brett, Charles L. Unger, the Chiefs of Infantry, Cavalry and Field Artillery, officers from G-1, G-3 and G-4, and members of the coast artillery, engineers, air corps, ordnance, signal corps, chemical warfare, and quartermaster.

The meeting revealed powerful opposition to removal of mechanized units from control of the branches despite the slow progress that had been made under such an arrangement in the past. The creation of a separate armored corps was termed fantastic, and the whole plan denounced as a conspiracy to grab power. Where quick action and concerted efforts were needed, spurious objections and branch animosity prevailed. It was "the old order in military circles holding out to the bitter, reactionary end."[3]

For ten typewritten pages they talked, these stiff-necked men who refused to budge from their one-sided branch loyalties. The atmosphere of the smoke-filled conference room was tense; faces were flushed with ill-concealed bad feeling. So far, Chaffee had said nothing, but his eyes twinkled like blue electric lights. "He was in a very good mood that day,"[4] because even then he must have known that nothing these men said or did could now prevent the formation of an armored force. He was happy, too, because he had just been told he was not going to be ordered to the Philippines. His friend General "Skinny" Wainwright was being sent instead.

Then, on page 10 of the transcribed report of the conference, Chaffee spoke his first words, cutting straight through the confused jungle of talk with a clean stroke "We have a directive to consider the organization of two armored divisions and how we can get them . . . and speed is essential. We have got to do it now. That means that we must make use, in starting the organization of these two divisions, of what we have and go forward from that as the material comes in. Cavalry contributes everything it has; infantry everything it has. We must not stop and haggle over a lot of detail and figure out a lot of things that have been studied over by boards and by commanding officers in the field and tested in maneuvers time and time again . . ."

By the time the meeting was ended, Chaffee's ideas had won the day, and a five-man board was created to make recommendations for the development of equipment for the proposed armored divisions. General Chaffee, General Charles L. Scott, Colonel Gladeon Barnes, Colonel Sereno E. Brett, and Major Ingomar M. Oseth comprised the committee.

Who would command the contemplated armored organization was still unknown to Chaffee; but he received an indication when General Andrews asked him to "submit his recommendations for the principal command positions of the Armored Corps" before he returned to Knox. These recommendations, together with the equipment report of the board, he delivered to Lt. Colonel W. M. Grimes of G-3 on June 19, the same day he left for home. His growing tension on the subject of the top command, however, was expressed in a letter which he wrote the following day to Andrews. "I think those are decisions (regarding equipment and commands) which the Chief of Staff should make promptly," he said, "and until he has made them I don't see how I can go farther than I have. I did prepare a complete personnel chart and a memorandum for G-1 on the subject of personnel, but until I am told definitely that I am to command this Corps, this I do not feel I should submit.

"If I am to command the Corps, then I should like to go to Benning, or whatever station is selected for the other division, with the authority to reconnoiter the situation there physically, and then come to Washington for final instructions and conferences. I think we should get going very promptly."

Apparently the War Department agreed that there was no time to lose, for on June 24th he was ordered to return to Washington for further discussions. It was then that he was informed that he was to be the first Chief of the Armored Force.

Sunday morning newspapers on June 30th carried the official War Department announcement of the creation of "PANZERS FOR THE U.S." and the selection of General Adna Romanza Chaffee as their "Papa." While a sleepy American public was reading the details of the news over their breakfast tables, Chaffee was playing golf on the Fort Knox course. His elation must have affected his game, for he ended with a score somewhat higher than usual. It was still early in the day, and a Sunday at that. But instead of going home and relaxing as he should have done, he went to the office of the Post Quartermaster and summoned him and the Post Engineer by telephone. When they arrived, they found him standing before a huge map of the Fort Knox reservation pinned on the wall. It was in the Quartermaster's office on that June day, that Chaffee planned the whole of Knox as it stands today.

On July 10th, the War Department issued the official directive stating: "For the purposes of service test an Armored Force

is created", and with these words Fort Knox was formally graduated from being known as "That place in Kentucky where Roosevelt has buried practically all the gold in the world" to "The
home of the Armored Force". The term "service test" was used
to circumvent the National Defense Act, which made no provision for a separate armored branch, and which further specifically prohibited the creation of a new branch of the Army
without the authorization of Congress. By the simple expedient
of using these two words, the War Department could immediately raise and organize the necessary troops for the armored
divisions without waiting for the long, tedious process of getting
a new law through Congress and an old one repealed. When,
however, an attempt was made five months later to establish the
Armored Force legally as a separate arm of the service, the
move was defeated by the sharp opposition of the Chief of
Infantry and the Chief of Cavalry.

The structure of the Armored Force followed the lines suggested by Chaffee in Louisiana. The backbone of the new
organization was the 7th Cavalry Brigade (Mechanized) and
the Infantry Provisional Tank Brigade. Out of these units were
formed the basic components of the I Armored Corps, the 1st
Armored Division, the 2d Armored Division, and the 70th
GHQ Reserve Tank Battalion. To lead the new troops, from
Fort Benning, Georgia, came infantryman General Bruce
Magruder to command the 1st Armored Division at Knox, the
nucleus of which was the 7th Cavalry Brigade. To the infantry
stronghold at Benning went cavalryman Brigadier General
Charles L. Scott, to command the 2d Armored Division made
up of the infantry tanks. On the Corps General Staff were
Colonel Sereno Brett, Chief of Staff; Lt. Colonel Madison Pear-
son, G-1; Lt. Colonel Percy Black, G-2; Lt. Colonel Charles
Unger, G-3; Lt. Colonel Ernest Harmon, G-4. Chief of Staff of
the 1st Armored Division was capable Lt. Colonel W. D. Crittenberger; of the 2d, Lt. Colonel Geoffrey Keyes. En route to a
foreign assignment, Lt. Colonel Robert W. Grow "was practically taken off the boat at the last minute" to fill another post

on the 2d Armored Division staff. Listed also on the early roster of the Armored Force were Colonel Hugh J. Gaffey, an artillery specialist, later a major general commanding the 2d Armored Division in North Africa, and Colonels Alvan Gillem, Jr., Jack Heard, and William Grimes. But perhaps the most significant assignment of all, in the light of later history, was the command of the 2d Armored Brigade at Benning, which was given to Colonel George S. Patton, Jr.

This peppery cavalryman had been on the list of officers that Chaffee had recommended to Andrews for the principal command positions of the force, and on June 26th Patton had addressed the following letter to Chaffee:

"My dear General (Adna): I was unfortunate in being unable to connect with you for any meal while you were here. I did see Scott, who told me that you were good enough to mention me in connection with a command in mechanization. I certainly appreciate your kindness and want to assure you, if it is necessary, which, knowing me, it probably is not, that I am always willing to fight and am enthusiastic in whatever job I have. I will always do my best to give satisfaction should I be fortunate enough to be selected." To this surprisingly humble missive, Chaffee replied, "I put you on my preferred list as a brigade commander for an armored brigade. I think it is a job which you can do to the queen's taste . . . I hope things work out favorably for you. I shall always be happy to know that you are around close in any capacity when there is fighting to be done."

And so the clan of master tank tacticians was gathering for the portending battle.

Insigne for the Armored Force was a triangular shoulder patch divided into three equal segments of yellow for cavalry, blue for infantry, and red for field artillery—symbolizing the union of the branches into one. In the center of the patch was the outline of a tank track on which were superimposed cannon and a bolt of lightning, representing respectively mobility and armor protection, fire power, and shock action. At the top were black numerals: the black signifying a general's command,

the numerals designating the number of the armored division.
Collar insigne of the force was a miniature Mark VIII tank, the
slow, 44-ton monster built in America in 1919.

Thus was forged the thunderbolt which was the Armored
Force.

II

The new member of the service was clearly the product of its
first chief, and, at an early meeting of the officers he had chosen to help him to build the Armored Force, he outlined the
nature of the future organization he planned and the principles underlying its employment.

"The role of the armored division," said Chaffee, "is the
conduct of highly mobile ground warfare, primarily offensive
in character, by a self-sustaining unit of great power and mobility, composed of specially equipped troops of the required arms
and services." Speed, surprise, and teamwork were the keynote
of its being.

"Armored divisions were not created to win skirmishes or to
fool around on outpost duty. The strength of the armored divisions should be conserved for missions, either strategical or tactical, whose accomplishment will affect to the maximum the
total destruction of the enemy. However, don't get the idea," he
cautioned, "that armored divisions will win the war by themselves. The greatest benefits will accrue from the close cooperation between armored divisions and combat aviation, supported
by other large bodies of normal troops.

"The form of action of the armored division," he declared,
"is offense and aggression. It constantly seeks to attack through
hostile weakness. It creates surprise, which is essential to successful combat, by the sustained celerity and power of its tactical movement. It uses its mobility to choose the most favorable
direction for attack to reach vital enemy rear areas. Its defense
is elastic and mobile and characterized by the counterattack.
This applies to even the platoon. Never attack an enemy where

he is strong. Put your strength in the weakest place and break through. Use your mobility to find the weak place and to get there. Then give your attack a direction that will be vital—cut his heart out!"

It was with these words that the new armored chief sought to instruct the future leaders of the Armored Force. Many were new to the service. Many had been a part of the tank outfits at Knox and Benning. But all of them listened with the same eager attention. "Those of us who have had the pleasure of serving under him count it a privilege without equal," wrote one of his Armored Force officers[5] some months later. "We had the occasion to see the sincerity of purpose in his sharp, searching eyes. We were allowed to hear his earnest voice as he spoke about the Armored Force. We were given the chance to carry out in practice the principles that he evolved in theory. We snapped to attention rigidly when he came around on an inspection tour of our outfit. We knew that he knew what the score was. We believed in him . . . His spirit is the spirit of his 'baby', the Armored Force."

To those scattered few who had been in the Mechanized Force that had assembled at Fort Eustis, Virginia, ten years before, his words had a familiar sound. They were the same rules that had guided those first rude experiments. Then the whole idea had been deemed fanciful and foolish by high military experts. Now it had become a fearsome weapon in the hands of the enemy. Then the Mechanized Force had been a handful of obsolete tanks and trucks and a few thousand untrained men. Now divisions—even corps—of armor were being readied for battle. But the principles had remained the same; only the size had been increased.

Substance of the new division was five echelons: command—to direct the troops; reconnaissance—to find the enemy; striking—to hit the enemy; support—to hold the enemy and assist the striking force; and service—to minister to its well-being. Even so had the Eustis force been conceived ten years before, though in test tube proportions.

Command echelon of the Mechanized Force at Eustis had included a headquarters platoon to direct operations and a signal platoon to transmit orders and information. It was a miniature of the command echelon of the new armored division, composed of a division headquarters, a headquarters company, and a signal company, which were charged with the same duties.

To overcome the blindness of tanks, reconnaissance had been provided for the Eustis force in the form of ten armored cars—the only wheeled reconnaissance the army possessed in 1930. In the powerful armored division, eyes of the tanks had grown into a far-seeing squadron of airplanes, two companies of scout cars and a company of light tanks, supported by a company of mounted infantry and engineers.

Striking echelon of the Eustis men had been fifteen tanks—all that could be spared by the War Department for the dubious mechanized experiment—and a detachment of chemical warfare troops equipped with three guns to lay down smoke to protect the tank attack. Striking echelon of the armored division of 1940 was an armored brigade, composed of two light tank regiments, one medium tank regiment, and a field artillery regiment. In effect, the tank strength had been increased more than 27 times.

A company of motorized infantry machine gunners to hold and protect, a battery of field artillery to provide close supporting fire, and a company of engineers to bridge streams and demolish obstacles had comprised the supporting echelon of the Eustis troops. The new armored division contained a supporting element of a motorized infantry regiment, a field artillery battalion, and an engineer battalion. Not only were the elements the same as those of the experimental force, but they were also charged with almost identical duties.

An ordnance company and a quartermaster unit had furnished supplies and repairs for the Eustis troops. The new division incorporated the same units in its service echelon, though in strengthened numbers, as well as the medical troops.

Though considerably neglected by him in the early force, in 1940 General Chaffee was much concerned with the medical phase of armored service. Lack of such training had proven costly to the Allies in the Lowlands and France. "The whole question of medical service in the division needs very careful study and thought," he said, "both by the unit detachments and by the battalion. General Pratt's report of the British tank operations in Arras mentions, among other things, the difficulty of removing wounded men from tanks. He had to devise on the spot a sling and derrick in order to get the wounded out through the turret. Obviously, this was something that should have been taken care of during peacetime." And this Chaffee proposed to do in his new organization.

Thus, with only minor exceptions, the conception of five echelons and their duties was the same as ten years before, though the elements had changed and increased. During the years of war that followed, the elements were again shifted about to meet the exigencies of combat, but the original concepts of their duties survived throughout. And Chaffee was but stating the facts when he declared, "It is true that the organization of our armored division is very similar in principle to that of the German panzer division, but it is not a question of our blindly following the latter. Rather, it proves the soundness of our own development, since the Germans in general followed the principles of our own mechanized organization which existed prior to the development of the present German organization."

Tables of organization to implement the armored division called for 9,500 officers and men for peace, 11,200 for war; 287 light tanks, 120 medium tanks, 431 other armored vehicles, 148 armored carriers; 1,388 other vehicles including motorcycles; 2,184 rifles and automatic rifles; 1,172 machine guns; 26 37mm guns; 36 artillery pieces that were then 75mm but which were to be changed to 105mm as soon as available; eight other 75's for antitank defense; and 16 81mm and 21 60mm mortars.

Although the armored divisions looked impressive on paper, actually the existing organizations were only a feeble percentage of their required strength. To increase each armored division as quickly as possible from its strength of approximately 4,000 to the needed number, to secure weapons with which to equip them when industry had not yet begun to retool for war, and to train the men into a serviceable fighting organization of the most complex and specialized form was the formidable task confronting the armored chief.

In July, 1940, registration of the first conscripts was still three months distant. Not until these men were inducted into the Army would Chaffee have available the manpower he needed. In the meantime, he dispatched twenty-six recruiting parties from Knox to secure recruits, and requisitioned men from other branches of the service. A mere drop in the bucket were the nineteen men who had gone A.W.O.L. from other regiments and come to Knox to get into the Armored Force. "These will be tried here (at Knox). If found guilty, they will be imprisoned, then probably assigned to a mechanized unit— which is what they wanted in the first place."[6]

Equally difficult was the problem of officers for the expanding force. Though hundreds of letters came to Chaffee's desk from officers eager to serve in the Armored Force, it was another matter to secure their release from the chief of their branch. In the formation of the force, the Chief of Cavalry had been charged with supplying officers for the units at Knox, with the exception of the infantry regiment, and for the reconnaissance battalion at Benning, while the Chief of Infantry had been directed to supply officers for the Benning units, with the exception of the reconnaissance battalion, and for the medium tank regiment and the infantry at Knox. But too often when Chaffee requested a highly rated or mechanized-trained officer, he received what he called "a lame duck" instead. With the skill and energy of every officer at Knox and Benning being spread thin to cope with the growing organization, such an officer was

only an added burden. In view of the general expansion of the
army at this time, however, and the consequent pressing need
for top-grade officers in every branch, the reluctance of the
Chiefs to part with their most capable officers can be somewhat
understood.

Quarters for the incoming troops gave Chaffee "particular
concern". Six days after the creation of the Armored Force, he
voiced his anxiety in a letter to General Van Voorhis. "I expect
about 400 new officers within the next few weeks," he said. "You
well know the lack of adequate rental property here and in
Louisville. At the moment this is one of my greatest concerns,
for when the personnel is working hard, it is necessary that they
have a comfortable and satisfactory home life." Although
money for additional quarters had become available with the
creation of the force, yet such construction could not be finished overnight. In July, there had been 864 buildings at Knox.
Soon new ones were going up at the rate of 160 a month. "Con-
tractors are working all over the place," said Chaffee. "In addition I am working 2,500 WPA's. The place is a beehive . . ." At
Benning a similar scene was being enacted.

Most serious bottleneck confronting Chaffee was shortage
of equipment. The Armored Force fell heir, in July, 1940, to
some 400 light tanks, 18 antiquated medium tanks, and a handful of armored personnel and weapon carriers, the total, except
for the light tanks, being less than either division required.
While Chaffee anticipated little difficulty in securing non-com-
bat vehicles such as trucks and motorcycles, tanks, half-tracks,
scout cars and weapon carriers were a different story.

The gravest deficiency of equipment in the Armored Force
was modern medium tanks. The medium tank designed by the
infantry in 1939 as the immediate result of tank experiences in
Spain had been the M-2, in which many of the features of the
infantry light tank had purposely been incorporated for reasons
of economy and facility of production. It weighed 19 tons, went
30 miles an hour, and was armed with one 37mm gun and eight
.30 calibre machine guns. The use by the Germans of a medium

tank armed with a 75mm howitzer and carrying thicker armor in the battle of the Lowlands and France, however, indicated the need for a more powerful medium tank than the M-2. Accordingly, it was completely redesigned. Three weeks after the formation of the Armored Force, the pilot model of the new vehicle was started at the Rock Island Arsenal. The new tank was called the M-3, and it weighed 31 tons, carried a crew of four, went 25 miles an hour, and mounted a 75mm gun, which was its chief distinguishing feature. By the last of July, 1940, negotiations had begun with Chrysler Corporation to produce 1,500 of the M-3's. "It seems reasonable to expect," wrote an ordnanceman in Washington to Chaffee, "that within a year the Armored Force should have the bulk or all of this number." This optimistic prediction, however, went far astray. Not until the 24th of April, 1941, did the Chrysler people present the first M-3 to the Army, and in June, 1941, there were but 66 precious medium tanks in the whole Armored Force.

Not only difficulties of manufacture, but the requirements of Lend-Lease as well, contrived to prevent the armored organizations from receiving the required numbers of this tank. Medium tanks were the vehicle most urgently needed by the British in their North African war. Overburdened with light tanks themselves, and still seriously handicapped by the losses suffered in the battle of Flanders, they found themselves on the brink of defeat before the heavier German tanks. Quantities of the M-3 dubbed "General Lee" by the British, were consequently rushed to the rescue, while American industry concentrated on manufacturing a British version of the M-3, known as the "General Grant". According to Col. Icks in his book, Tanks, when these tanks reached the British in Africa, the soldiers literally shed tears of joy at having a machine that at last was a match for the 'Germans'. The deficiencies of the M-3 that appeared in combat were corrected in the M-4 Medium Tank, developed the following year. This tank was named the "General Sherman", and was considered "the best medium tank in the world."

Another vehicle vital to the efficiency of the armored division was the armored half-track. Developed originally by the cavalry as a cross country personnel carrier, it could negotiate with ease cross country terrain that would have bogged down most wheeled vehicles, including the armored, wheeled scout car, which it resembled except for the half-track feature. To enable supporting troops of the division to maintain the cross-country pace of the tank columns, Chaffee proposed to mount the infantry regiment, mortars, engineers, and artillery on this capable vehicle, and to switch the mount of the regimental reconnaissance and of the machine gun company to it instead of the scout car, which had hitherto been used for these troops. Later it served as a radio vehicle, ambulance, prime mover for antitank guns, antiaircraft automatic weapons mount, and as the first tank destroyer gun mount. Though desperately needed by the force, months elapsed, however, before they were being manufactured in adequate numbers.

The sole bright spot in the combat equipment outlook was the light tank, which formed the preponderance of the striking power of the armored division. To equip the light tank regiments of the Armored Force, it was decided to standardize the infantry light tank, which was a heavier armored and armed version of the cavalry combat car developed during the preceding five years. The rapidly changing design of the tank was thereupon frozen to facilitate speedy production, and soon light tanks were rolling out of the factory at the rate of three a day. By the summer of 1941, sufficient quantities of the vehicle were being produced.

The M-3 light tank weighed 14 tons, and had a speed of 35 miles an hour and a crew of four men. Armament consisted of a 37mm gun with a coaxial machine gun, a .30 calibre machine gun in the bow and another outside the turret on the antiaircraft bracket. Not only was this tank used to equip American light tank regiments, but it was also shipped under Lend-Lease terms to the Russians and British, who called it the "General

Stuart" after the South's immortal cavalryman, Jeb. They fought in large numbers in the British African campaign, where the speed and maneuverability of the tank made up for its light cannon and also earned for it the affectionate nickname "Honey", when its performance against the Germans was particularly sweet.

To private industry was entrusted the manufacture of these Armored Force weapons, and, at the behest of the Army, engineers and mechanics accustomed to building shiny, new automobiles and sleek locomotives turned their attention to warlike machines of olive drab and to conferences with military men. One of the first acts of the War Department after the creation of the Armored Force was to give General Chaffee a "brand new transport plane to get around in some degree of comfort instead of having to bundle myself into flying clothes and a heavy parachute" as he previously had had to do to ride in his small, uncomfortable plane. And less than a month after he became the armored chief, he was making a flying tour in his new plane of the industrial centers where his armored vehicles were abuilding. To newspaper reporters who interviewed him, he explained the reason for his trip. "When I was put at the head of the Armored Force," he said, "I decided to tour the manufacturing plants to educate myself so that I could talk sensibly with the Ordnance Department. I also thought it would be a good idea to get a picture of the manufacturing problems involved. Thus, when a change in equipment is suggested, we will be in a position to know whether it involves a comparatively minor adjustment or the tearing out and replacement of a whole set of tools and assembly line."

First stop of his itinerary was the Rock Island Arsenal, where the pilot model of the medium tank was being built. In Chicago he visited the Diamond T Truck Company, whose vehicles were being considered as equipment for the Armored Force, and the Buda Engine Company, which was engaged in making diesel engines for tanks. In Cleveland, he saw scout and reconnaissance cars being manufactured by the White Motor Company; in Berwick, Pennsylvania, the light tanks rolling out of the factory rooms of the American Car and Foundry Company. His trip ended in Washington, where, appropriately enough, he conferred with the Chief of Ordnance on what he had seen.

Despite superhuman efforts, however, it was not until 1943 that the difficulties of equipment were overcome.

III

Long before the organization of the Armored Force, Chaffee had recognized the need for a school to train highly skilled specialists to handle the complicated machines of mechanized warfare, and for years he had been annoying his cavalry and infantry colleagues with his immodest remarks that mechanized men needed more brains and education for their jobs than any other soldiers in the army. When, therefore, the War Department directive of July 10th authorized the establishment of a school at Fort Knox "at such time as the Chief of the Armored Force deems it necessary", Chaffee wasted no time initiating plans for an Armored Force School.

In the new armored division, 50 percent of all enlisted men were classified as occupational specialists in a dozen fields, and to instruct thousands upon thousands of green officers and men in the complicated arts of radio, tanks, engines and machinery of every kind was the tremendous job with which the school would be faced. Available at the outset were some of the literature and talent of the Tank School at Benning and of the Communications and Motor School formerly operated by the 7th Cavalry Brigade at Knox. With future expansion of the Armored Force inevitable, Chaffee's educational problem, therefore, was comparable to the task of organizing a great university out of a nucleus of a few, small, scattered schools. Cognizant of the magnitude of the undertaking, Chaffee determined to secure as head of his school system an officer who had earned considerable reputation as a tank instructor and technician at the Infantry Tank School. The protestations of the Chief of Infantry against the loss of this officer's services to his branch were loud and lively, but to no avail, for on July 25th, 1940, despite his objections, Lt. Colonel, now Major General, Stephen G. Henry was designated commandant of the as yet non-existent Armored Force School. Two days later, he was directed to "plan, organize and operate" the new institution. Second in command was Major Robert G. Howie, whom General Chaffee selected from the Infantry School at Benning to become executive officer of the new organization.

Together Henry and his school staff set about planning the huge educational plant at Fort Knox. The result of their work was the approval on September 19th by the Secretary of War of the establishment of an Armored Force School and Replacement Center. On October 1st, 1940, the Adjutant General affixed his official seal of approval to the organization, and soon bulldozers were chewing at the empty acres that became the site of the Armored Force School. Though original plans combined the School and Replacement Center, on October 25th, 1940, the Center was redesignated as a separate unit.

Meantime, unless precious time was to be wasted until the school was ready, educational facilities had to be found for the hundreds of troops daily joining the force. Since the schools inherited from the infantry and the cavalry were far too small to cope with such large numbers, one of Colonel Henry's first steps was to survey civilian trade schools within a radius of 400 miles of Knox with a view to utilizing their facilities until the Armored Force School was ready. Accordingly, 731 enlisted men from the 1st and 2d Armored Divisions were enrolled in five of these schools on October 9th, 1940, as automotive and diesel mechanics, radio electricians, welders, and machinists.

That the Armored Force School opened its doors to its first class of 200 officers and 2,000 enlisted men only one month later, while carpenters were still hammering on the walls, was

an indication of the killing pace which the new organization
had set for itself. Included in the Academic Division of the
School were these sections:

Tank Department, which was the largest in the school and
which taught the mechanics of the all-important light
and medium tanks.

Wheeled Vehicle Department, which trained its students in
automotive maintenance of the scarcely less important
wheeled motor vehicles and half tracks of the division.

Gunnery Department, which instructed in the care, operation, mechanical functioning, marksmanship, and combat firing of all the weapons in the Armored Force, not
the least of which was the most difficult art of learning
to shoot accurately from a moving tank.

Communication Department, for instruction in radio operation (early in May, 1943, this Department graduated
its 10,000th radio operator) and maintenance.

Tactics Department, which gave a basic course designed to
train platoon and command leaders, as well as an
advanced course for field officers of higher units.

Motorcycle Department, which trained men in the repair
and maintenance of motorcycles. With the declining
use of motorcycles and its replacement by the quarter-
ton "jeep" in the armored division, this department was
inactivated on July 26, 1943, and merged with the
Wheeled Vehicle Department.

Clerical Department, which produced the clerks and typists
for the Armored Force.

Later departments added to the curriculum of the school
were the Officer's Candidate School, established May 12, 1941,
and Teacher Training Department, February 6, 1942.

"Our plan for the School," said Chaffee, "contemplates
turning out 200 officers and 2,000 men every three months."
There was then no time to plant ivy for its walls or grass for its
lawns. It was considered enough that the School provided a
roof over the heads of its students. Not many months later, the

School was caught in another tidal wave of expansion, and, following the example set by the nation's industry, went on a two-shift day.

When the Replacement Center cut loose from the School and went on its own only a month after its creation, Brigadier General Jack W. Heard became its first commanding officer. The purpose of the Center, in the words of the Armored Chief, was to work "in conjunction with our schools," and to provide "a pool of trained replacements so that the divisions, particularly in the field, can be supplied with trained specialists and replacements, in order that their effectiveness can be maintained at a maximum."

"In our plans," continued Chaffee, "we have set aside 5,000 men for the Replacement Center. Until this personnel becomes available under the Selective Service Act, the War Department plans to give us an overstrength in the division of 2,500 men each."

In the meantime, the Armored Force Replacement Center chiefs were confronted with the same monumental task of building a huge training plant from scratch with which the school heads had struggled. Buildings, training areas, and drill fields had to be constructed, tables of organization and equipment prepared, and a training program mapped. Lack of trained personnel, equipment, and, alternately, Kentucky mud and dust conspired to hamper their efforts. Yet, less than three months later the Center was under way, and General Heard was supervising the education of 5,431 raw, unseasoned recruits for service in armored units.

The initial schedule of the Replacement Center called for a 12-week basic course (later extended to 13, then to 17, weeks). The first half of the period recruits sweated through infantry drill, calisthenics, tent pitching, and all the other fundamentals of military life. Midway through the cycle, they were introduced to specialized Armored Force routine, when they sweated even harder. Now the class was divided into three groups: In the first group were 10 light tank and 2 machine gun companies; in the second group, 4 medium tank, 2 reconnaissance, 5½ field artillery, and ½ field artillery (antitank) companies; in the third group, 4½ infantry (rifle), ½ infantry (antitank), 1 infantry (heavy weapons), 2 engineer, 1 signal, 1 ordnance, 1 quartermaster, and 1 medical companies. In the ensuing exercises, they learned the duties they would be expected to perform as a part of an armored division or battalion. On graduation day, however, not all recriuts went to a place in an armored unit. According to the aptitude they had shown, some went to Officer's Candidate School, some went to the Armored Force School for more specialized education; and some remained behind at the center as instructors to put new classes through their paces.

As military observers returned from abroad with firsthand reports of armored warfare, battle training technique at the Center became more and more realistic. In the exercises, whistle bombs, smoke and tear gas were launched at unsuspecting green troops, while bullets flew overhead and phonographs played records of machine gun fire to condition the men for the noises of battle. A platoon of soldiers, dressed in Nazi uniforms and led by German-speaking officers who shouted commands in German, made frequent day and night raids on bivouac areas and assembly points. Unwary recruits, who failed to step lively, were apt to be taken prisoner by the "Nazi" platoon and placed in its barbed wire "concentration" camp, a mortification which had a salubrious effect on their conduct in future raids. By 1943, the motto of the Armored Force Replacement Center—Kill Or Be Killed—was paying gratifying dividends in combat abroad.

"Brain trusters" of the new Armored Force were the officers who comprised the Armored Force Board. In the War Department directive of July 10, 1940, which created the Armored Force, was also contained the sentence: "The duties of the Chief of the Armored Force include the development of tactical and training doctrines for all units of the Armored Force, and research and advisory functions pertaining to development and procurement of all special transportation, armament and equipment used primarily by armored units." Since it was obviously impossible for the busy boss of the Armored Force to perform all these duties single-handed, an advisory group of specialists was appointed to assist him in carrying out the directive. All the work formerly belonging to the Mechanized Cavalry Board and the Infantry Tank Board passed over to the new board, and its scope was extended to include the needs of other branches represented in the Force as well. Likewise, it was charged with shaping tactical doctrines and technical improvement.[7] First head of this powerful, little group was Lt. Colonel C. C. Benson, a cavalry officer long associated with the equipment of the mechanized cavalry brigade.

Though originally designed to shoulder a wide variety of responsibilities, it soon became evident that the tactical section of the Armored Force Board was merely duplicating work being done by G-3 of the Armored Force Headquarters and by the Armored Force School. Gradually the board was stripped of these functions, and by June, 1941, its major job had become the "testing of equipment to determine whether it met the combat requirements of the force."[8] To its members goes much of the credit for the superior weapons with which American armored troops were eventually equipped.

To smooth the path of the Armored Force in the War Department and to insure protection of its interests, a liaison office was established in Washington, staffed by two officers "who can, and do, represent at a moment's notice by radio, telegraph, or telephone, the Chief of the Armored Force in the War Department." Yet despite their most strenuous endeavors, the difficulties which the new armored head encountered in Washington in those early days were both manifold and aggravating. "They have given me quite a job," he wrote to a friend. "And there are a great many trials and tribulations connected with it. As usual in such jobs, there is a lot of enthusiasm topside in the War Department at first when they all know the Chief of Staff has suggested the matter and has said it is hot and has got to get going. But after a little while, when they have passed the job out to the man in the field, and he begins to want men, equipment, instruction, and all that sort of thing, their stock answer is, 'Well, we didn't figure on that,' and 'we haven't got this' and 'we haven't got that.' So then the troubles begin, and there are a good many of them every day . . ."

One of his "tribulations" no doubt had been a set-to with G-4 in Washington on the subject of funds for fourteen additional school buildings. Anticipating a further increase in the Armored Force, and hence a need to enlarge the capacity of the school, Chaffee had telephoned the General Staff quartermaster officer and asked for $171,000 for the school construction. "Chamberlin told me this could not be done," he protested to General Richard C. Moore, Deputy Chief of Staff and the officer mainly concerned with Armored Force matters in the War Department, "and that the funds would have to be included in the estimates along with estimates for construction to house the draftees. I asked him then if he could give me half of that amount—$85,000—for material, and I would take the rest from WPA to build them. He said he couldn't do that. Then I got Harmon (Armored Force G-4) to telephone Eberle in G-3 and ask if it would be all right for me to use $85,000 which is available from my Special Field Exercise money. I received back the attached radio saying, 'G-4 advises details on project upon which to base action have not been submitted. Decision as to Field Exercise funds for this purpose is withheld pending receipt of information justifying subject construction and action thereon.' In order to get action and promptly meet the necessity, I think they could well leave the details to me," he concluded somewhat testily. Even his new, high-sounding title and the urgent demands of a grave emergency were no proof against the obstructive channels of routine War Department red tape.

It was Chaffee's "considered opinion" that in a year's time the strength of the Armored Force would be in the vicinity of 70,000 men, a nine-fold increase over the original force. Chaffee proved not to be mistaken in his anticipations, for the organization and training of the 1st and 2d Armored Divisions' had scarcely begun, when he was informed that the War Department desired to create two more armored divisions the following spring, with six more to come. This meant cadres for the new divisions would start arriving in December, with attendant increases in the number of trainees at the School and Replacement Center. "So it keeps me very busy with my nose to the grindstone," said Chaffee in a spectacular understatement of his activities.

When he learned, however, that G-3 proposed to station the two new divisions at Fort Knox and Fort Riley respectively, he immediately took issue on this point. "Riley is a comparatively small reservation," he said, "and has a very specialized terrain, no overhead cover, and, for a force of any size, a series of defiles through rimrock." In opposing stationing a new division at Knox, he argued, "With one armored division already here, the terrain would be overcrowded." The additional 50,000 acres authorized in the Land Act had not yet been purchased, although negotiations were in progress. Chaffee's recommendations for the stations for the two new divisions, instead, were the Beauregard area in Louisiana, a military reservation of 1,500,000 acres, and Pine Camp, New York. "We have had little or no experience in cold weather and need it badly," he said in explanation of his latter choice. For a subsequent station for an armored division, he recommended the desert section of southern California.

It was at this time that Chaffee laid down the initial objective for the Armored Force—to be ready for combat by October 1st.

CHAPTER NINE

Now Is No Time to Die . . .

I

If news of the war abroad had been grim in June, 1940, there was even less cause for cheer in October. While America watched uneasily on the western side of the Atlantic, the tentacles of the Axis monster were reaching greedily in new directions. The long struggle in the deserts of North Africa had begun with the invasion of Egypt by Graziani. The Italians had invaded Greece from Albania. England was groggy from blows struck by the Luftwaffe in the Battle of Britain.

Domestic affairs in the United States, by comparison, in that russet-colored month of autumn seemed piddling and irrelevant. The pre-election fight between the "barefoot boy" from Indiana and the colossus from the Hudson was in its last stages of mud-slinging. The name of the first conscript was drawn from a fish bowl by a group of solemn-looking officials. In Kentucky and Georgia, the 1st and 2d Armored Divisions took to the field for their first maneuvers.

To observers of this demonstration of the armored might of the foremost automotive country in the world, the scene was not overly impressive. Though the force had almost doubled in size since the preceding July, yet thousands more were needed to bring the divisions to their full strength. Moreover, the recruits were obviously green and inefficient, and lacked equipment. More disheartening than even this to the harrassed officers of the Armored Force, however, was the absence of their

183

Chief from this first assemblage of his armored troops. If he had only been away on one of his countless conferences with the War Department, they would not have worried so much. But they knew he lay desperately ill in the hospital, "with no more than a good fighter's chance to dirty his face again."[1] The illness of the previous spring, from which he had not allowed himself properly to recover, plus the furious activity of the last preceding months, were exacting their toll from his body, the leanness of which had often prompted reporters to dub him "The Army's Thinnest General." Acting Commander of the Armored Force in Chaffee's stead was first General Bruce Magruder, then General C. L. Scott, who came up from Benning to take over the job.

For three years General Scott had led troops in the 7th Cavalry Brigade (Mechanized), and for more years than that had been associated with the first armored chief. He was one of the few officers in the United States Army who understood the principles of armored doctrine and, as one of Chaffee's hand-picked high commanders, was acquainted with his plans for the future of the Armored Force.

"The most complex fighting organization in the world," Chaffee had declared on the eve of his illness, "is the armored division. It is built on the principle of every man having his battle station and being supremely good at it." When, however, mishaps at maneuvers revealed that the armored troops, from generals down to privates, were far removed from such a state of perfection, the new acting commander resolved upon a program of intensive training for the ensuing months.

In an organization as complex and specialized as an armored division, its very life hinged on the teamwork and coordination of its component members. No tank drive alone could succeed without the help of its artillery and infantry. When the bellies of its tanks were empty, it demanded fuel from the supply service. It was as helpless as a blind man on a city street corner without the eyes of its reconnaissance, and without the bridges of its engineers the smallest river could halt it in its tracks. Smoke from the mortars of its chemical warfare troops hid it from the enemy. To attain such perfect communion of all the arms required the proficiency of each man at his job, from the general down to the tank driver and machine gunner, and their complete coordination. The armored division was actually an enormous combat team, which was the sum of numerous, smaller, integral combat teams, though Chaffee frequently objected to the use of these two infantry words in connection with the armored division.

The task confronting General Scott, therefore, was the transformation of a mass of straggling recruits and soldiers, many of whom had never seen a tank before, into a brisk, cohesive, armored unit. This was no over-night procedure, but rather the result of months and months of ceaseless, unrelenting practice. German panzer troops had astonished the world with their superlative discipline and training. American soldiers could not afford to be less well prepared. Accordingly, upon completion of the field exercises in October, the acting armored chief, with General Chaffee's direct approval, specified that for the balance of the calendar year "special emphasis would be placed on training of the individual, the vehicular crew, the platoon, the company, and the battalion"[2] readying the two divisions for maneuvers with other troops the following spring and fall and of training the cadres for the 3d and 4th Armored Divisions to be activated in the spring of 1941.

Though the necessity for teamwork keynoted the training rules for the armored divisions and no place was allowed for grand-stand plays and prima donnas, yet evidences of good American initiative and self-reliance were never discouraged among its troops. In this, the preachings of Chaffee on the occasion of the first meeting of the officers of the Armored Force were being observed. He was talking of the men in the tank crews, the gun and infantry squads, when he said, "The association of that small group of men will demand, on the part of the enlisted men, more initiative, more self-reliance, and more guts than in any other branch of the Army . . .

"Now as to leaders for these groups. We have to have them and you have to have them. Discipline is an absolute necessity. We must have the keenest and most alert men, who are not always waiting for orders, and who are not looking out of the window when orders are being given. They have to be hard guys and able to take it physically because it is an exhausting job.

"The only way to make these recruits into fine soldiers is to know your own job—by knowing it better than any man in your organization—being a past master at it. Be a better tank driver or motorcyclist than any man in your organization—or more fit with the rifle and bayonet—the best commander. Be fit for your job. Remember you can't fool the American soldier. Study and then set an example from top to bottom of keenness, smartness, and attention to duty."

Thus those early months following the organization of the Armored Force, in Chaffee's absence from the helm, were a period of intense training. Aside from the time-honored principles of leadership, physical fitness, and other basic requirements, there were stressed: "development of cross country mobility, combined arms teamwork with particular attention to coordinated action with the Air Corps, antiaircraft defense, and fire and maneuver by small units." It was a time of hard work and plodding practice, which left the men tired and sore at the day's end.

"If a thing like this illness had to come to me," said Chaffee, "I don't think it could have come at a more opportune time, when all of our preliminary organization is going well and training is under way, and when the main cause for any slowing up is awaiting of further materiel." At that time, of course, he could not foresee that not until March, 1941, would he return to his post.

One of the problems bearing on the mind of the sick general that had nothing to do with routine training, however, was the organization of additional GHQ tank battalions, which, by virtue of the War Department directive of July 10, 1940, were included as a part of the Armored Force. The stated role of the battalions said Chaffee in 1940, was "to afford additional attacking power either to armored divisions or to infantry or cavalry divisions," and they were to be trained "to be immediately adaptable to inclusion in larger groupings." Since even the most ardent cavalryman agreed that their tactical doctrine and organization should be definitely infantry in character, joint responsibility for effectuating this was placed upon both the Chief of the Armored Force and the Chief of Infantry.

Though later destined to play a large and important part in the theatres of war, in July, 1940, the total number of reserve tank battalions under the command of the Armored Force was exactly one, the 70th GHQ Reserve Tank Battalion (Medium) stationed at Fort George G. Meade in Maryland, and even this lone battalion was then suffering from the last stages of personnel malnutrition. Though originally organized with a cadre of 18 officers and 582 enlisted men, by the end of July, 1940, 319 were absent from training on detached service, special duty, summer exercises, or were sick or otherwise militarily incapacitated.

Such was the sad condition of this potentially powerful unit when news came to Chaffee early in August that War Plans of the War Department General Staff called for many similar battalions as special task forces, though no provision was made for their organization. The armored chief was immediately aware of the inherent threat to his armored divisions for he knew that, in the absence sufficient battalions, the armored divisions would have to supply these troops; and it was in considerable agitation that he dispatched a letter of protest to Chief of Staff Marshall. "So already they are contemplating breaking up our divisions to fritter them away for small purposes," he wrote indignantly. "G-3 has set up no additional GHQ Reserve Tank Battalions so far. At least four more GHQ Battalions should be set up at once. We will have materiel."

On October 5th, the general had dictated from his sickbed a two-page plea to Deputy Chief of Staff, Maj. General William Bryden, reiterating his belief in the need for the "prompt formation of efficient GHQ Reserve Tank Battalions." It was his proposal to utilize eighteen scattered National Guard tank companies to provide personnel for the formation of four tank battalions immediately, with training of cadres for ten more battalions to commence soon thereafter.

Chaffee's insistent representations bore fruit a little over a month later when, on November 25, 1940, the 192d Tank Battalion was inducted at Fort Knox. Three more battalions were organized in quick succession: the 193d at Benning on January 6, 1941, the 194th at Fort Lewis on January 22d, and the 191st at Fort Meade on February 3d. To coordinate the five battalions and to supervise their activities, on February 10, 1941, the 1st Tank Group was activated, and senior commanders of the new group were charged with conducting monthly training inspections and tests of the battalions and reporting directly to Armored Force Headquarters at Knox. Inasmuch as the four National Guard tank battalions had been formed by assembling individual tank companies allotted to the various states and it was expected at the time of induction that they would remain only a year in the Federal service, no attempt was made to standardize these units or to make them conform with established tables of organization and equipment. Loosely organized and inefficient as these initial battalions were, yet they constituted a measure of protection for the armored divisions against the greedy demands of Army war plans.

It was but little more than a month later, however, that all of Chaffee's plans for the battalions nearly went up in smoke. On March 20th, the day that "the Grand Old Man [Chaffee was 56] of Mechanization" returned to duty at Fort Knox after an absence of six months, "looking springy and straight and as keen of eye as ever,"[3] he found on his desk a directive, already cleared by the General Staff in Washington and requiring only his concurrence and that of the Secretary of War, which would have removed all GHQ tank battalions from the control and supervision of the Armored Force and placed them under GHQ. It was the intention of the authors of the order to attach the battalions to field armies for combined training and to assign responsibility for the supervision of personnel, training, and inspection to the Chief of Infantry. The only function left to the Chief of the Armored Force was the role of "advisory agent" in the cooperative development of materiel.

Unwilling to agree to the sabotage of his plans, within a week of his return General Chaffee was winging his way to Washington to protest the move personally to the Chief of Staff. He pointed out that the proposed change would result in confliction in developing equipment, competition in procuring supplies and experienced personnel, duplication of schools, and confusion in writing manuals and doctrines. Chaffee's vigorous arguments were heeded to the extent that the directive was modified merely to make the battalions subject to attachment to field armies and to hold the Chief of Infantry and the Chief of the Armored Force jointly responsible, as before, for development of their tactical doctrine.

Nor was this the only point of attack upon the Armored Force, for termites were busily at work elsewhere in its foundations. In the basic memorandum of the previous July, Chaffee had secured the "exemption of the Armored Force from everything in the Corps Area except routine supply" and the definite provision that maintenance funds would be allotted directly to the Commanding General of the Armored Force. Upon his return to duty, he found that determined attempts were being made in Washington to withdraw such special powers from the armored chief and to restore them to regular maintenance channels. Spearheading the movement were moguls of the Ordnance Department, who resented such encroachments upon their prerogatives.

In a terse letter to Major General Richard C. Moore, Deputy Chief of Staff, however, Chaffee bluntly quenched the arguments in favor of the change. Said he, "Only the Commanding General of the Armored Force is familiar with instructions as to equipment of task forces and with the priorities given to the equipment of divisions. Only he is familiar with the maneuver

demands that are placed on divisions by GHQ. Only he is familiar with the implementation, with critical items, of new armored
divisions and GHQ battalions. Only he is familiar with the
amount of loaned materiel, as long as it is short on the whole,
to the School and Replacement Center, by divisions, and so is
familiar with the wear and tear on the several types and groups
of materiel, particularly tanks, and only he is in a position to
know the logical and necessary redistribution of maintenance
funds to meet the situation at this time.

"Probably when we are all equipped equally that could be
made a routine matter," he concluded, "but it is not now." And
there, temporarily, the matter rested.

Another tempest swirled around the Armored Force
Replacement Center, which, in the spring of 1941, was going at
top speed with over 5,000 enlisted men being fitted for service
in the armored units. Included among the center troops were
men being trained for the armored infantry regiments, the signal, ordnance, medical, and every other component that, combined, were the ingredients of an armored division, and it was
this phase of the center that was under attack. Representatives
of the various arms of the service in Washington contended
that the Armored Force Replacement Center was duplicating
the work of their own existing training centers where superior
instruction in highly specialized equipment was available, that
all troops except "strictly armored elements" (tank and
armored reconnaissance) should be withdrawn from Knox and
assigned to the replacement centers of their own branch.
Armored Force leaders fought back, and the battle was on.

Since teamwork was the keynote of the Armored Forces
from top to bottom, and coordination of all troops the essence
of its success, it was necessary, declared officers of the Armored
Force, that all the combined arms receive training together.
This was conducive to an esprit de corps which, in itself, as
every military man knew, was as potent as any weapon. A real-
location of weapons and equipment peculiar to the Armored
Force would violate principles of economy of equipment, Gen-

eral Heard, head of the Center, stated. Moreover, Armored Force Replacement Center instructors understood armored doctrines and procedures with which teachers at other replacement centers were unfamiliar, and training was based on field needs rather than academic maxims. Dire delays and an added administrative burden were predicted should the new system go into effect. General Scott, a lifelong exponent of combined arms training, jumped into the controversy with characteristic fervor. Staff officers of the Armored Force visited each branch replacement center and, with one lone dissenter, reported that training at Knox was superior. General Chaffee, again ill with a recurrent attack of his sickness, rose from his bed to make a personal plea to General Marshall.

"The only argument I can find in the G-3 paper, which recommends discarding a successfully operating system of training replacements for the Armored Force for one which, in my opinion, will not stand up under either peace or war conditions," he said "is a matter of capacity at Fort Knox." This argument Chaffee considered specious. Already the center was training 5,000 men, and was setting up facilities to train 5,000 more. If it outgrew that capacity, "we will make room," promised the armored chief, "either by moving the 1st Division to a cantonment area in the newly acquired land to the west of Fort Knox or to some other station."

The Armored Force leaders, however, lost their fight. On August 26, 1941, it was directed that henceforth only tank and armored reconnaissance troops would be trained at Knox.

In a letter to his doctor shortly after his return to duty, Chaffee summed up the enormous work and limitless energy involved in guiding the destinies of the Armored Force. "I find many problems confronting me out here which will take time and effort and a lot of traveling to get settled," he wrote. "I have countless inspections that will have to be made all over the country. I feel that we are facing very serious days, and we can afford to lose no time getting ready, and really ready, for any contingency . . ." Chaffee was thus preparing for the war that

he sensed was not far off, and in his program there was little
promise of respite for one who so lately had been intimate with
death. Though there had been "real progress" in his absence,
yet no one realized more keenly than he the time and advan-
tages lost, for which he would have to account with redoubled
energies in subsequent months.

A little more than three weeks later—on April 15th—the 3d
and 4th Armored Divisions were activated at Camp Polk, La.,
and Pine Camp, New York, respectively, and "I had the pleasure
of seeing each train carrying the cadres pull out from Knox,"
wrote Chaffee to Colonel W. M. Grimes. In command of the 3d
Division was General Alvan C. Gillem and of the 4th, General
Henry W. Baird. Though officially dubbed divisions, actually
they possessed a strength of some 3,500 each. But understrength as the existing divisions were, the organization of two
more was contemplated in the early fall. Likewise, the cadres
for ten additional GHQ tank battalions were under instruction
at Knox, to be ready to go to their stations in June.

A bare statement of such facts, however, does not give a
complete picture of the difficulties involved in putting together
the troops of the force. Besides being green and awkward,
recruits arriving at the post were oft-times of such low mental
substance that no amount of schooling could drum into their
skulls an understanding of the intricacies of a tank engine or a
gun periscope or a radio. While an effort was made to have
high mental standards set for recruits for the Armored Force,
it was never as fortunate in this respect as the Army Air Forces,
which was successful in getting a large percentage of Group I
conscripts with ratings of over 130 in the Army General Classi-
fication Test.

Likewise, the same high type of man was desired for officer
material for the tank force, but in the nine-fold expansion
which occurred in the year following its inception, not every
one could be hand-picked. Some idea of the officer personnel
problems can be gathered from a letter that Chaffee wrote to
General Marshall on April 4th, 1941, just three weeks after his

return to Knox. "Out of 3,665 officers assigned to the Armored Force to date, 3,024 are Reserve Officers who have had absolutely no previous experience to speak of. Of the 651 Regular Army Officers, 116 have some previous tank or mechanized cavalry experience. 435 have now had six months or more with the Armored Force. 100 have no previous experience."

Both the Chief of Staff of the U.S. Army and the Chief of the Armored Force agreed that the blitz force was no place for "Plaza Toros," but rather for men of "imagination and aggressive mentality."[4]

"Ever since the earliest experiences with the old Infantry Tank Board, when it was under General Rockenbach and I used to see them standing around arguing about the size of a bolt hole to the point where they never got any tanks and never thought about tactics, I have dreaded the same thing happening in any force that I had anything to do with," Chaffee told his chief. "And from the earliest days I have made it a principle to go on to tactical exercises of any kind that were available, no matter what the materiel at hand has been. I can illustrate this by the Riley maneuvers of 1934, when my combat cars were represented by old Franklin 1.5-ton trucks with a large yellow band painted on them, and again last fall when I set the objective to those armored divisions that they must be ready for field service by the 1st of October, no matter what their equipment was.

"To date, we have rejected no officers because of lack of experience with tanks and mechanized cavalry. Rather, we have fought to keep from accepting mediocre officers lacking in vision and energy, even though they had previous experience. As an example, the following officers have been recently assigned as regimental or separate unit commanders or chiefs of staff: Col. R. E. McQuillin, Lt. Col. Wogan [later a major general in command of the 13th Armored Division], Col. W. H. Morris [later a major general and commander of the 10th Armored Division in Europe], Lt. Col. R. R. Allen [later a major general and commander of the 12th Armored Division in Europe], R. W. Strong, Nalle, Hasbrouck [later a major general in command of the 7th Armored Division in Europe], W. H. Walker [later a lt. general in command of the 20th Corps of Patton's Third Army]. "These officers," continued Chaffee, "are all tops in their branches and have had wide experience both in staff and command other than armored units, but they have been with us only a few weeks to a few months, just long enough to get fairly well informed on organization and equipment through a refresher course of duty with existing units."

Yet despite a desire expressed by the Chief of Staff that the Armored Force be pumped full of "new blood," on May 12th General Chaffee was forced to plead with the War Department for "some brigadiers," for which there existed "four vacancies in the divisions."

The life of the armored chief was further complicated by the thousand and one other duties attendant upon the head of an important new force. Those close to the general were aware of the many demands on his energy and time, and sought to protect him as much as they could. Ernest Harmon, the future general of armored fame in Tunisia and Europe, said to him, ". . . If you only made three or four basic decisions a month your judgment and value is such that such work would be invaluable to the Force. However, instead, you are harassed with a thousand petty subjects . . . You need some one to guard you against all the wolves, the handshakers, the boys who want you to know they are doing something, etc. . . . Big problems should only come to you fully presented in writing, with all the facts so you can quietly study. . . ." Colonel Harmon was right, but as affairs of the Armored Force then stood, such an arrangement was impossible. The fledgling organization needed the strong, steady hand of a vigilant chief.

On April 8th, the Chief of Staff, General Marshall, arrived at Fort Knox for a day and overnight visit. On April 17th, General Chaffee flew to Fort Benning for an inspection of the 2d Armored Division, then under the command of George Patton. Upon his return he journeyed to Detroit to witness the ceremony of presenting the first M-3 Medium 31-ton tank by the Chrysler Corporation to General Wesson, the ordnance chief.

It was this new medium tank which brought Chaffee face to face with an argument that was raging within the ranks of the armored divisions themselves. As the war in Africa progressed and antitank methods improved, the arms and armor of the tanks became increasingly heavy. Seeing this development abroad, there were those among the armored men who declared that the organization of the armored division should be changed. Instead of having two light tank regiments and one medium tank regiment, they advocated two medium tank regiments and one light tank regiment, and the consequent stepping-up of medium tank production. The eye with which Chaffee surveyed the newly unveiled Medium M-3, however, was not entirely unjaundiced. Who yet knew what it could do in action? From where he stood, it appeared to have "barely satisfactory performance characteristics." Moreover, there was talk of increasing its weight, a move which Chaffee feared would decrease the speed and maneuverability of the tank to the point where it would interfere with the movement of the rest of the armored division. To sacrifice mobility of action to heavy guns and heavy armor was anathema to this mechanized general, who believed that a combination of all three—mobility, firepower, and shock action—was the key to the success of the division. It was not strange, therefore, when Chaffee refused to recommend the shift from light to medium tank regiments, until the M-3, or its successor, had been proven by experience.

Meantime, the stream of visitors at Knox did not lessen. On May 14th and 15th, Secretary of War Stimson was the distinguished guest of the Chaffees. His "thank-you" letter written to Mrs. Chaffee indicated that he had been well entertained. "We arrived safely yesterday in Washington with memories of a very pleasant visit to Fort Knox in our minds," he wrote. "Your hospitality was most gracious and helped to render my inspection trip a very refreshing bit of vacation. We all greatly enjoyed your delicious dinner and the pleasant evening we spent afterward under your roof. And last but not least, I shall not forget the beautiful rock garden. Sometime when General Chaffee has perfected his water supply and does not have to be so thrifty in his treatment of your needs, I shall hope to come again and listen to the gurgle of your fountain!" Mr. Stimson was referring to another water shortage then confronting a greatly expanded Knox. Although Chaffee was then taking measures "to improve the situation," not until "new wells come in during the summer" would there be water enough even "to wash vehicles," let alone waste it on a fountain for the delectation of visitors.

On May 17th a party headed by Mr. Marshall Field, "for whom the Office of Public Relations has demanded attention" arrived at Knox, and the following day came Congressman Buell Snyder and his Committee.

On May 25th, the armored chief flew to Pine Camp to inspect the new 4th Armored Division.

Then at last came the day when the last ounce of the general's once phenomenal energy was spent, and he returned to his bed, never to rise again. A month and a year from the day he had become the Chief of the Armored Force, newspapers carried the stark announcement of his relief from the post at the head of the force he had created.

II

The passing of the "Father of the Armored Force" has not gone entirely unremarked by posterity, however. Named in his honor were the newest, fastest, light army tank and Camp Chaffee, Arkansas, one-time station of the 6th and the 14th Armored Divisions. Three days after his death on August 22d, 1941, there was presented before the assembled House of Representatives in Washington, by the Hon. J. Buell Snyder, a "statement" which had been prepared by Chaffee the previous May. It was noteworthy in that it contained some of his most "significant" recommendations regarding the future of the Armored Force.

"The Armored Force of combined arms are at present the most powerful means of offensive action," he declared. "Given a suitable terrain for operations, the most effective defense against such armored forces would seem to lie in more numerous and more powerful similarly organized armored forces." He, therefore, advocated the immediate expansion of the U.S. Armored Force to four armored corps of eight divisions, and its establishment as a separate arm of the service.

"An Armored Force must be manned and led by thoroughly and specially trained personnel," he said. To stabilize its soldiery and to insure its proper training, he advocated that recruits destined for the Armored Force be inducted to serve for three years instead of one, and that officers remain with the Armored Force instead of being transferred to other branches. "An officer," he said, "cannot be expected to give undivided attention to bettering himself professionally for duty with the Armored Force when he does not know what day he will receive orders returning him to duty with foot infantry or horse cavalry units."

To equip the armored divisions, he urged that the manufacturing program of the country be accelerated. "As materiel and supply have dominated recent battlefields," he said, "so have they dominated the development of the Armored Force. Its initial organization was governed by the type and quantity available; its future organization and rapidity of expansion will be dictated by timely execution of adequate manufacturing programs. It is essential that we manufacture the most modern type of fighting equipment for today and, concurrently, develop more efficient types for tomorrow. We are all too familiar with the long and precious time required to develop, tool for, and manufacture new types of critical items of equipment. We are also familiar with the uselessness of an army which is second best in materiel."[5]

But the recommendations of the late General Chaffee to which the Congressmen were respectfully giving ear did not stop there. Pointing to the successes of armored troops in Europe, he called for the formation of U.S. "Armored Armies."

These he described as armored divisions organized into corps, with attached motorized divisions. "The great German victories in France and in the Balkans were won by offensive operations of armored armies supported by combat aviation. Former defensive methods cannot be successfully used against these armored operations. Defense against such operations can be made only by armored units of equal or superior power."

Thus read the forthright "statement" of the first armored chief months before Pearl Harbor!

CHAPTER TEN

Prologue to Combat

I

On August 1st, 1941, Major General Jacob L. Devers, field artillery officer and the youngest Major General in the army's land forces, was named the second head of the Armored Force.

"My assignment to command the Armored Force came to me as a complete surprise over the telephone one morning from the Big Chief," wrote Devers to General Van Voorhis, whose Chief of Staff he had been for a year in the Panama Canal Department. "As I sat back in my chair to catch my breath after hanging up the telephone, the first thought that occurred to me was—General Van Voorhis is going to get a big laugh out of this."

When the two of them had sat sweltering in their quarters in the steaming heat of Panama, discussing the blitzkrieg war in Europe and the American mechanized cavalry brigade at Knox, such an eventuality must never once have crossed their minds, particularly since Devers had reportedly never been convinced of the use of an Armored Force. Yet the appointment of the artilleryman to lead the Armored Force, despite his lack of faith and any previous connection with its destinies was no accident, nor should it have been surprising.

In the German blitzkrieg of Europe, dazzling headlines had featured the exploits of tanks, airplanes, and infantry. Even mechanized engineers had attained a small share of glory. Overshadowed almost completely by these more spectacular performers had been the third "big stick" of the attack: artillery. By the summer of 1941, however, the importance of artillery and gunnery in mechanized warfare had emerged in all its stark clarity. One of the factors contributing to the English victory over the Italians in Lybia had been its superior armored armament. In the German attack on the British in the spring of 1941, this advantage had been reversed, and in every encounter the British found themselves outgunned. Against German tanks armed with 50mm and 75mm cannons, they could throw only their machines armed with 2-pounder (39mm) guns, which, by comparison, were as toy terriers to a Dobermann-Pinscher. The 88mm guns that the Germans had used as an antiaircraft gun in the war in Spain, they now produced as an antitank weapon, for which the British had no counterpart. Throughout the war the 88s continued to be the dreaded nemesis of Allied tanks. Similarly, the English light gun carriers were no match for the German 75mm self-propelled guns, "though so long ago as 1925, we had a well-designed, self-propelled 18-pounder (75mm) gun," bitterly declared General J. F. C. Fuller, who, for just as many years, had been warning the British Army against just such a predicament as they now found themselves in. The inevitable result of the British inferiority in firepower had been a retreat before the more powerfully armed Afrika Korps and the surrender in a few short months of nearly all of the territory they had won from the Italians.

No less significant to military observers was the defensive aspect of artillery in mechanized warfare, as revealed by reports from the battle fronts of Russia in that portentous summer of 1941. When war between Germany and Russia was declared in early summer of that year, and the well-oiled Nazi military machine began to drive into Russia at the rate of 30 to 40 miles a day, the rest of the world prepared itself for another blitzkrieg à la Poland and France served up with typical Hun garnishings. Wagers were laid by responsible men that the Germans would be knocking at the gates of Moscow in a month. Realists declared that three months would be a better bet for, after all, Russia was a mighty big country. Moreover the unfor-

Prologue to Combat 201

gotten record of her bumbling war on Finland in 1939–40 seemed to indicate that the Russian Army then was no more competent than it had been in 1917.

Not many weeks later, however, it began to appear that "sly" Russian defense tactics were proving slightly embarrassing to the arrogant German warriors—nothing serious, to be sure, but annoying, like flea bites to a mastiff. When the Germans had broken through Russian front lines, instead of retiring in confusion or surrendering as the French had done following the collapse of the Maginot Line, the Russians had retreated to other predetermined areas of defense, spotted like fortified islands far back into the Russian steppes. Thus, though the Germans pressed ever forward, they always seemed to come upon more Russians ready to fight them, and their lines of communication and supply stretched longer and thinner. It was then that the bypassed areas of resistance—towns and villages—swung into action. Instead of submitting peacefully to the invader as had terror-stricken Polish, Dutch, Belgian, and French victims of their previous "hell-on-wheels" attacks, the rude Russians produced a variety of weapons out of secret caches and proceeded to make life exceedingly uncomfortable, not to say uncertain for the rear-line German soldiers. Though the losses resulting to the Germans from such unorthodox (from the point of view of previous World War II campaigns) and unexpected defense tactics were not enough to affect them seriously at the moment, yet they eyed with some misgivings the surprising numbers of destroyed Panzerkampfwagens that lay strewn across the steppes—victims of strategically emplaced Russian artillery and antitank guns.

The careful curtain of Soviet censorship concealed actual details of the weapons employed by the Russ; yet this much was apparent: that guns were again playing a deciding role in mechanized warfare, this time in defense.

In view of such developments abroad, and the known faults in the structure of the artillery organization of the armored division, the choice by Chief of Staff Marshall of a man with an artillery background to lead the Armored Force was quite understandable.

The original organization of the armored division contained one regiment of 75mm howitzers of four batteries of six howitzers each, which was used to support the armored brigade (tanks), and a separate battalion of 75mm howitzers of three batteries of four howitzers each, which was provided for the use of the division commander with the infantry regiment as a combat team or in a general reinforcement role wherever needed. Although division headquarters originally contained an artillery section of two officers and four enlisted men to assist the division commander in technical employment and control of divisional artillery, there was no centralized command for the artillery of the armored division. The regiment and the battalion had no common commander, nor could the regimental commander exercise the necessary leadership when the situation demanded.[1] That the first armored chief recognized a change in this structure might be necessary was revealed two months after its organization, when he said in September, 1940: "It may be that it will prove better to regiment these two . . . but it is one of the many things that can only be determined by trial." With the introduction of the 75mm gun on the new medium tank then in the process of construction, it appeared even more probable to Chaffee that the armored artillery regiment would "be taken away from the armored brigade and become a divisional unit for general support." The Chief of Artillery entertained no doubts or hesitancy whatsoever on the matter, however, and as early as November, 1940, was urging that three artillery battalions be formed into a single regiment, as was the practice in the triangular divisions, and that a unified, single command be established. With this recommendation, General Scott, then Acting Chief of the Armored Force in Chaffee's absence because of illness, concurred. But in the hectic first year of the tank force's existence, plagued as it was by the problems of the initial expansion and training climaxed by the fateful illness of its Chief, the organization of the artillery component of the division remained untouched, and there matters stood when General Devers took the helm of the Armored Force.

The faulty structure of the armored artillery, moreover, was not the only weakness of the initial set-up. In preparing tentative tables of organization for the armored division in June of 1940, General Chaffee had specified a change from the 75mm howitzers then possessed by the artillery of the 7th Cavalry Brigade (Mecz.) to 105mm howitzers. When plans for the armored division had emerged from the inner sanctum of the War Department General Staff in Washington, however, he found that they provided for the equipment of armored artillery with the 75mm guns, in spite of his recommendation. The telephone wires between Knox and Washington hummed with protests, as Chaffee made known his objections to this provision, and it was not long before the General Staff acceded to his demands for the 105mm howitzer for the armored artillery batteries.

While the strength of the artillery component of the armored division was thus much improved by the switch to 105mm howitzers, yet certain Armored Force leaders felt they had only partially solved the problem of the right equipment for mechanized artillery. Prime mover for the howitzer was an 8-man, armored half-track carrier. But reports from the battle fronts indicated that what was needed was a self-propelled artillery gun that could move abreast of, or practically at the heels of, the tank. The Armored Force Board early foresaw the possibilities of using a 105mm howitzer on the medium tank chassis, with the thickness of armor reduced to give greater cross-country mobility, but nothing was done about it until artillery officer Colonel Edward H. Brooks (later a major general and commanding officer of the 11th Armored Division, then Chief of the VI Corps of the Seventh Army in Germany) took the initiative and outlined to the Armored Force Board a program for equipping armored artillery with this type of weapon. Colonel Brooks asked the board for the assistance of Captain Louis Heath, and together they drew up the characteristics of the proposed vehicle. Colonel Frank R. Williams, Armored Force liaison officer and later President of the Armored Board, assisted by pushing the plan at the Aberdeen Proving Ground, Maryland, where the Ordnance Department develops and tests most of its equipment.

The arrival of General Devers at Fort Knox resulted in the speedy untangling of many artillery knots and gave fresh impetus to the brave, new, 105mm howitzer-medium tank chassis experiment. It was not many days after Devers moved into his new headquarters overlooking that impressive Kentucky post that he announced his decision that there would be three battalions of armored artillery similarly organized and equipped. He likewise expressed his enthusiastic support of Colonel Brooks' pet project, which thenceforth was rushed to swift completion.

At an Ordnance Technical Committee meeting in November, 1941, the go-ahead signal was given on the construction of two pilot models of the self-propelled howitzer for early test by the Armored Force Board. Three months later the pilot models were ready and the tests began. Day and night the Armored Force Board relentlessly put the newcomer through its paces over roads and cross-country. On the third day the gun was fired, and the tests were finished. On that same day, the Armored Force Board, Ordnance officials, and General Brooks, in conference assembled, approved the basic idea. It was a decision fraught with more significance perhaps than any of them dared dream. Four days later, the pilot model, marked with chalk to indicate certain modifications, was shipped away for production, and even before the drawings had been completed, the American Locomotive Company was at work upon the new vehicle. By the summer of 1942, the first howitzers were in the hands of troops.

When British General Montgomery, in October, 1942, launched his offensive in North Africa against the Afrika Korps at El Alamein, he possessed two surprise weapons the new American General Sherman medium tank and the new self-propelled 105mm howitzer, designated the M-7 and nicknamed the "Priest" by the British because of its pulpit-like silhouette. Thirteen weeks after he began his attack, Montgomery entered Tripoli after an advance of 1,300 miles. It has been declared by both English and American officers alike that General Brooks' "baby", which first saw the light of day at Fort Knox, "played a tremendous part in the defeat of Rommel."[2]

It was directly through the efforts of General Devers that another innovation—"eyes in the air"—was introduced into armored artillery. The tank was like the cowboy of Wild West days, whose life, especially in the movies, was as long as his shooting hand was quick. The success of a tank drive hinged directly upon the ability of its artillery to destroy the antitank guns before the antitank "killed" the tank. The position of artillery observers in the armored division hence was no bed of roses. They rode right up in front where they could see the most and where the action was thickest. When the tanks encountered antitank resistance, they radioed the position of the obstacle back to the big guns of artillery. Split-second adjustment of the artillery guns to the indicated point spelled the difference between victory and defeat.

If aggressive artillery observation on the ground was so vital to success, reasoned Devers, why wouldn't artillery observers in the air, where they could see more and see farther, give the artillery an even greater advantage. While each armored division possessed a squadron of observation airplanes, which acted as the eyes of the commander, yet too often the number of planes actually furnished were less than adequate for his purposes and none could be spared for artillery observation duty. Accordingly, Devers undertook to secure additional planes for the division to serve as a part of the artillery. His efforts were crowned with success when, on June 19th, 1942, the Armored Force was authorized to include eight liaison planes as an organic part of the armored artillery of the division.

II

The organizational structure of the armored division received its first real shakedown in March, 1942, when the Army Ground Forces was established, and the Armored Force became a part of it along with all the other land forces of the Army except service and supply. In the changes which were made in the armored division, an attempt was made to correct the faults that had appeared in the year and a half of its existence, and to adjust it to meet armored developments in war.

The Army maneuvers of 1941, in which the 1st and 2d Armored Divisions had participated, had revealed an unbecoming unwieldiness in the armored brigade organization that was out of place in a supple, fast-paced, steel division. In practice, the division commander issued his orders to the brigade commander, who, in turn, set up the combat teams—thus involving an unnecessary link in the chain of command. The 1942 change, therefore, abolished the brigade form of organization and substituted the regimental form instead. The division was set up into two combat commands, each headed by a brigadier general. No troops were placed under the permanent command of either brigadier, but rather the division commander gave each of the two a task force suitable for the particular mission set forth. The new setup thus possessed greater flexibility than before, and delegated duties to the leaders of the combat commands which released the division commander for his real job of planning the overall strategy and of commanding the reserve.

More significant than this change, however, in the striking echelon of the armored division was the reversal of the original ratio of two light tanks to one medium tank, whereby twice as many medium as light tanks were provided for the revised division. This was the eventuality that General Chaffee had foreseen the year before, but which he had refused to approve until the medium tank had demonstrated its effectiveness. By March of 1942, however, it could no longer be denied that the medium tank was destined to be the major performer in the North African theatre of war, and that with the medium M-4 tank, the American armored divisions could "eat the cake of heavy protection, and have mobility too," as Hechler put it. The new tables of organization also reduced the number of tank regiments from three to two each composed of three battalions: two medium and one light.

A regiment of infantry armed with Garand rifles and riding in armored half tracks had been included in the original organization of the armored division. Its duties were things that infantry alone could do in war. "Infantry is ideal for outposts, for mopping up, and for holding ground until the last drop of the hat," General Chaffee had declared in September, 1940, summarizing the uses for armored infantry. "It is especially suited for helping to organize the ground for future defense and for taking over those situations when movement stops in the mobile fight, and there will frequently be such situations when tanks will want to break off the fight and withdraw under the protection of the infantry to refit, to rest, to reorganize, to gas, while the infantry keeps the enemy out of your hair.

". . . the infantry will be called on many times to develop a doubtful situation. When the reconnaissance has brought you in the outline, but still the details are lacking—when you don't know where this or that or the other antitank weapon is and targets are not yet disclosed for your artillery, machine guns, and bombardment aviation, you must use the infantry to apply the necessary pressure to bring out the details.

"This infantry is going to be very useful in stream crossings—first, the infantry will establish the bridgehead; then comes the H-10 or the pontoon bridge, and then the armored vehicles. That is the way we cross unfordable streams."

As the war unfolded abroad and antitank resistance
increased, British and German tank generals employed more
and more of such infantry in the mechanized battles. Sometimes it walked ahead of the tanks to probe the enemy defenses
and to clear the path for armor. Sometimes it fought beside
them. Sometimes it followed behind the tanks, though so
closely as to be practically on the exhaust pipes. Teamed with
armored artillery and armored engineers, it comprised the bul-
wark of antitank defense.

The effect of such growing importance in the armored
combat team was the addition of an extra battalion of infantry
to the infantry component of the armored division in the 1942
reorganization. Later, as infantry became more and more
prominent in the mechanized fight, the need for a reservoir of
readily attachable armored infantry battalions became apparent. Accordingly, an armored "group" form of organization was
designated for tactical control of separate infantry battalions.
The infantry in these battalions were identical with the armored
infantry battalions in the armored division in employment,
operation, and organization, and constituted a potentially powerful reserve force for armored leaders. During March, 1943,
three such groups were activated.[3]

Meantime, a peep into the backyard of the infantry branch
of the service revealed that elderly matron in the throes of a
rejuvenating Madame du Barry course of stream-lining. The fat
pack on the foot soldier's back had been reduced from eighty
to forty-five pounds. In his hands was a new rifle that could fire
twice as fast as the time-honored old Springfield. The number
of men in the infantry regiment was reduced by one-third, but
new artillery and antitank weapons increased its firepower.
Most wondrous of all, however, was the contemplated motorization of several infantry divisions.

The new motorized divisions were designed to be "a cross
between the present armored and infantry divisions"[4]—composed of bantam cars, three regiments of infantrymen riding to
the battlefield on wheels, machine guns, mortars, antitank can-

nons likewise transported, 106 light and medium tanks, 37mm antiaircraft guns, and "quantities of new tank killers—75mm howitzers on a self-propelled mount. The role announced for the motorized divisions by the Chief of Infantry was even more interesting.

"The primary role of the divisions," he declared, "is the support of armored forces. There are three missions that may be given to motorized divisions acting in support. Such motorized divisions may protect the rear of an Armored Force envelopment. They may be used to protect the inner flank of an Armored Force envelopment. Or they may be used to form a base of support for maneuvering mechanized forces.

"We should also consider the mission of motorized divisions with regard to the main forces. Here their mission will include the task of holding critical terrain areas until stronger forces arrive. Again, used together with the Armored Force, motorized divisions extend the scope of operation of the larger units to which they both belong and insure to these parent units the freedom of maneuver they must have . . .

"We should habituate ourselves to thinking of the whole category of fast troops—armored forces and motorized division alike—as a single unit of combat."[5]

Such trends in U.S. infantry and such statements by its chief were a far cry from the bumbling backwardness of the infantry divisions in the Plattsburg maneuvers of 1939, when infantrymen had not understood the tactics of the small tank brigade from Knox, let alone the means by which to resist it. They assumed even greater meaning in view of the pronouncements of Colonel S. L. A. Marshall and General J. F. C. Fuller, both of whom blamed the failure of the German tank offensive in Russia partly on the lack of sufficient motorized infantry. Actually, the force of combined motorized and armored troops which the Chief of Infantry permitted himself to describe was, in effect, an armored army, the likes of which, under Patton and Bradley, streamed across France in the breakthrough at St. Lo, and was in line with repeated urgings of armored leaders

since late 1941 that one division of motorized infantry be
included in each armored corps.

Other portions of the armored division anatomy that
underwent alterations in the 1942 reorganization were the
armored reconnaissance battalion, in which three armored
reconnaissance companies and a company of light tanks were
substituted for two companies of scout cars, a company of light
tanks and a company of infantry; the supply and maintenance
outfits, which were unified by the establishment of division
trains controlling maintenance and medical battalions; and the
GHQ Reserve Tank Battalions, which General Devers termed
"the lost children" of the Armored Force.

Following the activation of the four new tank battalions in
response to General Chaffee's request early in 1941, making a
total of five such battalions then existent, the need for a tank
group headquarters "to coordinate activities, develop tactics
and technique, and to act as command agencies in the theater
of operations"[6] soon became apparent. The use of the tank
group in mass was also contemplated for specific tactical missions. Accordingly, on February 10, 1941, as previously related,
the 1st Tank Group to supervise the five battalions was established. When more new battalions were formed, the 2d and 3d
provisional tank groups were organized on May 26th, 1941.
The tank battalions were scattered so widely over the country,
however, that, even with the new group setup, proper supervision proved difficult and they were more or less left out in the
cold in the matter of equipment and training. Moreover, the
fact that the Chief of the Armored Force and the Chief of
Infantry were both charged with responsibility for the development of their tactical doctrines did nothing to clarify an
already murky state of affairs. "As I remember the situation
(which was always confusing)," recalled the battalion commander of the 70th Tank Battalion, "we were under Headquarters Third Corps Area for administration (I made a play for
exempted status) and directly under the Armored Force for
training. Later we were assigned to the 1st Tank Group, and

from that time on we never had a clear picture of just who was controlling our destiny. . . . I do remember that at one time we were getting directions from so many headquarters—five as I recollect—that I drew a Rube Goldberg diagram. Also we were changed from medium to light and back again so often that we couldn't keep up with the changes. I think the last time this happened we were on an alert status with the Amphibious Force Atlantic Fleet and consolidated with an infantry antitank battalion on maneuvers in North Carolina at the time. That sounds facetious but is a fact. . . ."

It was just such a situation as this which led General Devers to declare early in 1942 that "we must take prompt action to bring them (the tank battalions) into the fold and to be in closer touch with their needs and problems." Eventually the battalions and groups were reorganized to include three battalions per group with the three battalions located at one station, while the provisional tank groups were re-formed and made permanent in February, 1942. At the same time, the internal organization of the battalions was changed to make it conform as nearly as possible with battalions in reorganized armored regiments in the new armored division, for the purpose of making the two completely "interchangeable."

It was these "lost children" of the Armored Force that ultimately wrote their names in blood beside those of the foot infantry divisions in the hills and plains of Italy and during the breakthrough in the fields of France, where they "kept up the slugging match against fanatical resistance whenever found that kept gaps open, that prevented the enemy piercing the sometimes critically narrow corridors."[7] The employment of the tank group in mass however, failed to materialize at any time during the war, and "was therefore a useless setup, tactically," said General C. L. Scott.

Throughout all the early pronouncements of the first armored chief, there appeared the statement that aviation must closely support all armored actions. It was a precept, however, that plagued his successors, and proved more easily said than done. No one denied that air support was vital to armored success; the question was: how to go about teaming up the two arms. Their predicament was all the more galling in that time and again the Germans had effectively demonstrated that they knew the answer.

Soon after the reorganization of the armored division in March, 1942, a new system for coordinating the tank-plane team went into effect. It was a procedure so involved in red tape that it wound up by defeating the very purpose for which it had been intended. Field Manual 31-35 outlined the steps that were followed in getting the planes up to the tanks. First, the Air Request Party transmitted the request for air support to G-3 Air at division headquarters, whereupon a consultation took place between G-3 Air and an air force representative. The request then went to the armored corps headquarters, where another conference ensued. If the request was approved, the call went to the airdrome and the planes took off. By the time they arrived at the scene of action, however, more than likely the situation for which they had originally been requested was then "ancient history."

Such roundabout routine also hamstrung the British fighting Rommel in North Africa, according to reports by General C. L. Scott, who observed the fighting in the Middle East from March to July, 1942. Conversely, the general reported the German front-line troops as being able to secure action from their air support within 15 to 20 minutes, sometimes less. Upon his return to America, he proposed that the bottlenecks in our system be removed by establishing simple oral communication from forward ground units direct to the air squadrons. Not until the American troops were in France, however, was such a system worked out. Under the setup finally developed by the 12th Army Group, air force officers rode in forward tanks equipped with a special radio able to talk to the supporting planes, with the result that, when needed, planes were in action in a matter of minutes.

The provision in the original Armored Force organization which attached an observation squadron to each armored division likewise was a headache in actual practice. Moreover, a sufficient number of planes never were actually attached. After some experimenting, in 1943 the air force set up "reconnaissance groups" to do the work of the observation squadrons.

Subsequent to the establishment of the Army Ground Forces, direct contacts between the Armored Force and the War Department General Staff practically ceased. New regulations decreed that matters pertaining to the Armored Force should pass through Army Ground Forces channels, the same as for the other outfits that comprised the new Army organization. The liaison office in Washington, created specially for the Armored Force, was abandoned, and the officers therein became members of the Requirement Section of the Army Ground Forces staff. According to the historian of the Armored Force, there is indication that these former Armored Force liaison officers received specific oral instructions from General Clark that they were to act in a new role as Ground Force staff officers rather than as representatives of the interests and viewpoint of the Armored Force. The kid gloves were doffed in the handling of the Army's tanks. Henceforth they were just another member of the Army's combat team—and, in the opinion of some, a badly neglected member at that.

III

On the next to the last day of November, 1941, Army umpires, with an audible sigh of relief, officially declared the end of three months of battle maneuvers in the South. They had been the largest and most ambitious war games hitherto undertaken by the Army; and they had exposed with dreadful clarity the sad condition of American troops. The conscripts were raw and resentful. They were waiting only for the day when their term of military service would expire. The National Guardsmen were enthusiastic and ill-trained. With innocent exuberance they transgressed the strictest military rules of combat. Regular Army troops were trim and disciplined. But their ranks were spread too thin to hide the glaring deficiencies of their less soldierly comrades. Observers shook their heads grimly and hoped that war would not come soon.

When the war came, however, a week and a day later, before maneuver troops barely had unpacked their bedrolls, it was obvious that mollycoddling days in the Army were over and that training would begin in earnest. Criticisms noting the faults seen during maneuvers were dispatched to all headquarters, and an intensive training program for ensuing months outlined. After what they had witnessed in the "war" in the Carolinas just past, Army chieftains knew that the only way to build a sound organization out of the conglomerate material at hand was to start from scratch and work up. Accordingly, the new schedule called for small-unit training as phase number one, followed progressively by company, battalion, and finally regimental drill. No branch of the service was deemed of such excellence as to be exempted from the program. All were included—infantry, artillery, cavalry, and the armored force.

Only the 1st and 2d Armored Divisions had engaged in the big maneuvers—the 3d, 4th, and newly activated 5th Armored still being engrossed in the problems of getting organized. Though "the aggressive spirit shown by Armored Force units as a whole" had been commended by maneuver officials, and though "pistol-packin' Patton," commanding general of the 2d Armored Division, had provided priceless copy for newspaper reporters witnessing the war games, yet the armor, too, had been guilty of the same defects that had characterized the performance of non-armored units of the Army. "In general," declared Armored Force Headquarters, in forwarding the criticisms to its commanders, "the omissions are attributable to the inexperience or lack of training of company officers . . .", a condition it proposed to correct in the rigorous training period which was to follow.

The high point of the Armored Force training program proved to be the Desert Training Center. In January, 1942, General Patton was made head of the I Armored Corps. Soon thereafter, he was assigned the task of finding a spot somewhere in the southwestern part of the United States resembling the desert and mountainous regions of North Africa, where armored divisions could prepare to meet Rommel's crack Afrika Korps. For days Patton and his party flew over California, Arizona, and Nevada, until he finally found a triangle of land that looked just right: miles and miles of blistering heat, volcanic cones, barren mountains, and dry, dusty lakes. It was as desolate and bleak as any place in the world, and inhabited only by coyotes, big horn sheep, and rattlesnakes. General Lesley McNair and General Mark Clark approved his choice, and 30,000 square miles, stretching from Desert Center, California, to Yuma, Arizona, to Searchlight, Nevada, most of it already public lands, were acquired as the desert proving ground for American tankers, and General Patton became its first commander.

The area was so vast that whole campaigns, using small armies, could be planned and executed in full scale, and two armies could travel four hundred miles without ever once encountering each other. It was to this huge, barren waste that the 2d Armored Division journeyed in the spring of 1942 to rehearse for the impending battle. Here, under the blazing desert sun, which sometimes raised temperatures to 150 degrees inside a tank, the "armoraiders" wheeled and clanked. Men fainted and machines broke down as Patton drove them mercilessly. Tests were conducted with salt tablets, special diets, and dehydration. Engines which overheated were discarded for desert warfare, while special insulation was developed to prevent scoring of bearings and other moving parts in sandstorms. The troops, from the general on down, slept in tents when in camp, which was not often; and on the ground beside their tanks or under their trucks, when on maneuvers. They learned to go without sleep for thirty-six hours at a stretch, and to determine direction by the sun and the stars. It was during this stern prologue to combat that the 2d Armored earned its nickname, the "Hell on Wheels" Division.

Conspicuously absent from the desert center was the other partner of the original Armored Force, whose prelude to battle, meantime, had taken a different and somewhat more glamorous course. Easter, 1942, saw the 1st Armored Division entraining for a port of embarkation, and, in due time, landing in the British Isles. It was then under the command of Major General Orlando Ward. A visit paid to the American tankers by King George and Queen Elizabeth soon after was a far cry from the sun and sand of the desert, which were the lot of their sister division. And gratifying, indeed, was the article about them in Collier's by the ubiquitous Quentin Reynolds, who predicted that "American armor was destined to make a name for itself," after he, too, had visited them. Even the new name of the 1st Armored Division had a more romantic and effete flavor than the rough sobriquet of its twin. It was now called "Old Ironsides."

As the two elder sisters of the Armored Force prinked and perspired preparing for their debut in the theatre of war, the numbers of the once-small armored family began steadily to wax. On December 7th, 1941, there had been five armored divisions in varying stages of undress. In the months following, money and men poured into military posts throughout the country, and one after another more steel divisions were born.

On February 15th, 1942, the 6th Armored Division was activated at Fort Knox, then moved to Camp Chaffee, Arkansas. Its first commander was Brigadier General Wm. H. Morris. Later, it was transferred to Camp Cooke, California, and commanded by Maj. General Robert W. Grow.

Two weeks later, on March 1st, the 7th Armored Division was organized at Camp Polk, Louisiana. Major General Lindsay McD. Silvester was its chief. Later it went to Fort Benning, Georgia.

On April 1st, 1942, the 8th Armored Division was formed at Fort Knox as a training unit. It was headed by General Wm. M. Grimes, who had assisted in the organization of the 4th Armored Division at Pine Camp the year before. From the start, the 8th functioned as a cadre training division exclusively. It became a regular combat armored division in February, 1943, when the newly organized 20th Armored Division took over the training job, and the 8th moved down to Camp Polk.

On July 15th, 1942, the 9th and 10th Armored Divisions were activated simultaneously, the former stationed at Fort Riley, Kansas, the latter at Fort Benning, Georgia, later at Camp Gordon. Major General Geoffrey Keyes was named commanding general of the 9th and Maj. General Paul W. Newgarden commanding general of the 10th.

On August 15th, 1942, the 11th Armored Division was created at Camp Polk, Louisiana, with Brigadier General Edward H. Brooks of M-7 fame in command. Five days later the III Armored Corps was activated at this station, making Polk the largest Armored Force post in number of units stationed there. Willis O. Crittenberger was named as its chief.

On September 5th, the IV Armored Corps was organized at Indio, California, under Major General Walton H. Walker.

Ten days later, on September 15th, the 12th Armored Division saw the light of day at Camp Campbell, Kentucky. Its "Old Man" was Major General Carlos Brewer.

On October 15th, 1942, the 13th Armored Division was formed at Camp Beale, California. Commanding general was John B. Wogan.

Three more divisions—the 14th, the 16th, and the 20th—remained to be activated before the Armored Force would be complete, and such was the official armored picture on November 8th, 1942—the day the 1st and 2d Armored Divisions were baptized by fire on the shores of North Africa.

CHAPTER ELEVEN

Operations Torch and Husky

I

The surprise Allied invasion fleet, which carried the first Yanks to a Western Front in World War II, converged on the North African coast in three prongs. The Western Task Force under General George Patton sailed three thousand miles across the Atlantic Ocean and landed on the shores of French Morocco. A part of this gray, silent convoy had transported the tanks and men of the 2d Armored Division, still tanned and tough from their hard months of desert training. It carried units, also, of that harassed sire of all tank battalions—the 70th—which was extricated from administrative red tape with barely enough time to make its Port of Embarkation. Farther toward the east, on the same day, the 1st Infantry Division and a part of the 1st Armored Division poured ashore in the Oran sector of Algeria. Until they set sail from the British Isles, where they had trained for six months, the men of Old Ironsides had believed they were preparing for a European invasion. They did not know that in secret conclave high Allied chiefs still declared their armies unready for this undertaking. Still farther eastward, the British First Army, veterans of Dunkerque, debarked from their vessels at Algiers with armor, infantry, and artillery. The curtain had risen on the Allied campaign to drive the Axis out of Africa.

Although American General Mark Clark had lost his pants off the African shores only a few weeks before in an effort to secure an unopposed landing for the Allied troops, the French welcomed the foreigners arriving at their ports with blazing

guns instead of with open arms. While, in the east, Algiers capitulated to the British Army with only a gesture of resistance,
French Moroccans treated Patton's men to a lively sea battle
and rough handling by the batteries on shore. In the three days
of skirmishing that followed before the French Resident General, Auguste Nogues, arrived at Patton's headquarters to surrender, all but one of the French ships that had engaged the
invading fleet had been sunk or beached and American tanks
had performed their first missions under hostile fire. It was the
tanks that had fought and defeated the 32 French tanks which
had come to the assistance of the beleaguered French troops. It
was the tanks that had captured the airfield and held it until
the infantry arrived. It was the tanks that had spearheaded the
advance on Casablanca, French Morocco's only modern city. "I
was with the group that landed . . . sixteen miles north of
Casablanca," wrote Hal Boyle, AP correspondent, "and I saw
them surround that great port and prepare for a razing attack,
when the Vichy defenders capitulated before the guns of this
mighty steel ring." On November 11th, General Patton, therefore, had occasion for a three-way celebration: Armistice Day of
World War I, his fifty-seventh birthday—and the successful conclusion of his first World War II engagement.

At Oran, similar scenes were being enacted by the tanks of
the 1st Armored. It was Company C of the 13th Armored Regiment that spearheaded the advance on La Senia and met the
enemy eight miles inland from the beachhead. It was a sub
tank force of Combat Command B that captured the important
airfield at La Senia. It was this same force that assisted in the
assault and capture of Oran, and it was through the headquarters of this tank force that the surrender of the harbor defenses
and the French fleet was effected.

The Americans had proven what they could do against half-
hearted, inadequate opposition. It still remained to be seen
how they would fare against a seasoned and superbly equipped
front-line enemy.

Though the invasion had not been unopposed, yet resistance had been weak and sporadic, and the Allied troops had landed with organizations and equipment almost intact. It was this fact that led the Allied command to resolve upon a bold gamble. Tunis and Bizerte, key cities of Tunisia, lay only 400 miles to the east of Algiers, and 700 miles from Oran. Important rail and highway junctions, rich, thriving, and surrounded by natural strongholds of defense, their possession would be invaluable to the Allies as a base for air operations against the "soft underbelly" of Europe and against the rear of Rommel's troops, then retreating helter-skelter westward across Lybia toward Tunisia before Montgomery's Eighth Army. Instead of cautiously stopping to consolidate invasion gains and to await vitally needed supplies, it was therefore decided to send the most mobile American and British troops against these two points at once in a mad race to seize them before the Germans did. The odds were against the success of their plan, they knew. They were short on transport and blitz supplies, and it would be weeks before the harbors could be cleared of sunken French ships and materiel landed in adequate amounts. Moreover, they possessed no forward air bases from which to operate against the enemy. Not the least of the hazards threatening the success of the undertaking was the fact that Axis troops in force were stationed across the Strait of Sicily, only 150 miles from Tunis and Bizerte. An airborne operation across this small stretch of water—a feat in which the Germans had so often demonstrated their adeptness—would effectually forestall the ambitious hopes of the Allies.

Despite all the risks inherent in the situation, however, General Anderson at once set forth for Tunisia. His initial step was to dispatch British and American parachutists ahead to seize advance airports and key points. A spearhead of mobile infantry and armored troops followed across the northern reaches of Algeria and on into Tunisia. Included in this force was a part of Combat Command B of the 1st Armored Division, which had dashed 300 miles from Oran to join the eastward push. Another Allied spearhead moved southeastward toward Gabes, a strategic town on the coast at the southern entrance of Tunisia from Lybia. A company of Combat Command B was apportioned to this drive. The rest of the 1st Armored Division arrived in North Africa in the middle of November. Such piecemeal use of the armored division was characteristic of its employment in Tunisia until the last few weeks of the campaign—a practice which proved costly to the Allies and against which armored leaders had warned again and again. Meanwhile, to protect the Allied rear from Axis attack through Spanish Morocco, Patton's Western Task Force was to remain in French Morocco, and that is where it stayed throughout the Tunisian campaign.

As the Allied columns rolled into Tunisia, they ran up against Nazi patrols and then met German advance units with new, heavy tanks. It began to look as if the Axis had succeeded in beating Anderson in his race. But the Allied troops defeated the German resistance and pushed forward. By the end of November, they had crawled through narrow passes along the Atlas Mountains, across ancient Roman bridges, through gray-green olive orchards as far forward as Djedeida, 15 miles from Tunis, and beyond Mateur, only 18 miles from their other objective, Bizerte. They were standing on one of the great historic regions of the earth—land dotted with battlefields and ruins of the Roman and Carthaginian empires. Behind them were steep, rugged hills cut through by streams and valleys. Before them lay the flat coastal plain stretching down to the blue, sparkling waters of the Mediterranean. Though Anderson's supply lines were attenuated to a mere trickle and his air support was at best sporadic, success seemed imminent. One more swift, hard punch would take him to his goal.

Then, at the beginning of December, in the hills around Mateur and Djedeida, the Germans risked their first big encounter with Allied armored advance units. While Axis planes bombed and strafed, German and Allied tanks met in furious clashes. The combat-ignorant tankmen of the American armored division fell into many German traps and lost quantities of new and badly needed equipment. The Allies were forced from their advance positions. It was the first Allied setback in the North African campaign, and the more bitter because success had loomed so handily. Moreover, troops in southeastern Tunisia had also fallen short of their objective.

In the skies over Tunisia, the Luftwaffe reigned supreme, while report had it that a thousand men a day were being flown or ferried across the straits to bolster the Axis defenses of Tunis, Bizerte, and Gabes to the south. Against this growing tide of Axis strength, Anderson could only show dwindling supplies and lightweight equipment. When the rains came in mid-December, turning roads into quagmire and further bogging down transport, an Allied breakthrough was out of the question, and the British First Army settled down on a line running north and south through Medjez-el-Bab, some 20 miles to the west of the farthest positions they had occupied in the hopeful early days of the drive. The chastened but somewhat wiser American armor was removed from the muddy arena of war and passed to the British First Army reserve.

The bold gamble for Tunis and Bizerte had failed, but not before the Allies had occupied all of Tunisia save a thin coastal strip some 50 miles wide extending the length of the eastern seaboard of the country. This narrow corridor of land, bounded on the north and east by the sea, on the west by jagged hills and winding valleys, and on the south by a marshy lake, hills, and a 15-mile-wide gateway held open by the Germans for Rommel's retreating Afrika Korps, was the stage upon which the future battles of the Tunisian campaign were fought.

II

If the news of the war emerging from Tunisia in the ensuing winter months was bitter vetch for Allied mouths to chew, not so the reports of events that were occurring elsewhere in that far-off continent. In January, 1943, at Casablanca, Roosevelt,

Stalin and Churchill met in historic conference, and men of
the 2d Armored Division felt pleased when they caught a
glimpse of their Commander-in-Chief. Miles to the east, meanwhile, Montgomery's Eighth Army was making cheerful headlines by continuing its chase of Rommel's desert troops across
the north of Libya. Here were no rains to mire the armor, no
hills to defend the retreat, but hard-packed sand and good
coastal roads, down which the tanks and trucks and armored
cars sped. When finally the Axis troops scrambled through the
door leading into Tunisia and pulled it firmly shut in Monty's
face, the war entered a new phase.

Whereas only four short months before Axis troops had
been threatening Egypt, the Suez Canal, and a possible junc-
tion, if Stalingrad fell, with German troops in the Middle East,
now they were holed up in a tight little corner of Tunisia, thousands of miles to the west of Suez, on a piece of land around
which an Allied noose was pressing ever tighter day by day. On
the south stood the Eighth Army, facing the 15-mile-wide gate.
At the north, entrenched along the Medjez-el-Bab line was the
British First Army, still commanded by General Anderson.
Guarding the 150-mile-long central sector was an odd assortment of French and American troops under American General
Fredendall. His French soldiers were poorly equipped and his
American men unseasoned, and there were only enough to
spread them out thinly up and down the front. Little action,
however, was anticipated in this sector; but it was here, on Feb-
ruary 14th, that United States troops experienced Gethsemane.

Two main passes sliced through the bald, scrawny hills in
the central sector to the coastal plains behind Rommel's back.
One lay to the north through the Ousseltia Valley; the other to
the south was the Faid Pass. If the Germans did strike at the
central sector, of the two passes the Ousseltia Valley region was
deemed the most likely point of attack, for a successful lunge
there would cut straight to the rear of the British First Army
and isolate it from the rest of the Allied forces. Reconnaissance
appeared to confirm German activity at this point. Conse-

quently, the bulk of the American-French strength was concentrated in this sector of the front, including Combat Command B of the 1st Armored Division, while Faid Pass was left to be held by a handful of American paratroopers, units of Combat Command A of the 1st Armored Division and some French infantry, which was established to guard the pass itself.

When the Germans suddenly appeared in the Ousseltia Valley and overran French positions, the Allied premise seemed to be confirmed. To the rescue went Combat Command B supported by attachments from the 1st Infantry Division, also scattered piecemeal over the whole long front and, with the 1st Armored Division, constituting the American troops fighting in that sector. The positions were restored, but the armored troops continued to cruise up and down the front in anticipation of a German counterattack at the same point, as was the customary German procedure.

The thrust to the north, however, proved to be only a feint to throw the Americans and French off guard. When, on Sunday, February 14th, crack units of veteran panzer divisions began to pour through Faid Pass onto the barren plain beyond, the real direction of the German attack became all too evident. Light as defenses were at this point, the situation was made even worse for the Allies by the fact that American troops, composed of infantry and armored detachments, had just relieved unequipped French troops in the area. Their heavy equipment had barely arrived, they were still tinkering with communications, guns were newly emplaced, and they were not even acquainted with the ground they were to defend, when the Germans came roaring at them in two blitzkrieg columns protected by a ceiling of planes overhead.

The inevitable debacle was described in terse sentences by American newsmen: "What hit the Americans was the same machine employing the same tactics that shattered the French armies in the spring of 1940. First dive bombers smashed down from the bright Tunisian skies in long, screaming dives. The Americans took to their foxholes. The tanks sped up in V formation with great 52-ton Mark VI's spearheading them . . . and the gunners were overrun before they had had time to fire more than a round. Allied aircraft was noticeable by their absence. The American armored strength was apparently scattered battalion by battalion along the front. The Nazi units thus sliced through the thin American lines in all directions . . ."[1]

"On Tuesday, the American counterattack, spearheaded by what was left of American armor" failed, and a general retreat was ordered. Withdrawing to the line of the mountains to the north and west, the U.S. troops gave up an area of 4,000 square miles, including the important towns of Gafsa, Feriana, Sid bou Zid, and Sbeitla. "Officially losses were admitted to be substantial. Berlin claimed 'annihilation of the 1st Armored Division'."

Actually, just in time, Combat Command B with American infantry and artillery had arrived from the Ousseltia front to join forces with the shattered remnants of the 1st Armored Division at Sbeitla. There they covered the withdrawal of their tired, stricken comrades from Sbeitla, established outposts guarding the twisting, granite-walled defile that was Kasserine Pass and held them until relieved by elements of the 1st Infantry Division, and then retired to the west to the Tebessa Mountains to reorganize, refuel and to cover the extreme right of the American forces.

Not since Pearl Harbor had U.S. soldiers faced such black hours. When they had landed in North Africa, self-confidence and cheerful cockiness had been an American trade mark, and boasts had not been infrequent that an American soldier, with one hand tied behind his back, could lick any five Nazi supermen. Events in the early days of the war had somewhat checked but in no wise dissipated their exuberance. Now the very flower of American armored and infantry regiments was tasting grim, bitter defeat, and they found it baffling and degrading.

Rommel's panzer troops had halted before Kasserine Pass, but across the mountains and through the valleys only a few score miles to the west lay a huge American base overflowing with valuable supplies, and not far to the north was the rear of the British First Army. Another successful lunge by Axis soldiers would disintegrate the whole central sector and divide British and American forces.

The situation was critical, and the Allied high command poured reinforcements to the south to help stem the Axis onslaught. From the north came a British armored brigade. From Oran came word that the 9th and 34th Infantry Divisions were moving to the battle. An S.O.S. went out to the air forces to forget about bombing Italy for a while and fly down Kasserine way. General Sir Harold Alexander, newly arrived deputy allied commander, appeared on the scene exuding confidence, and on February 20th, "an allied spokesman said the tide had turned."[2]

It was on that same day that the German attack was resumed. First a deadly artillery barrage was laid down on American positions guarding Kasserine Pass. Then Axis infantry strongly attacked. Before nightfall, U.S. soldiers were again retreating, and the Pass belonged to Rommel. Then, on Sunday morning, February 21st, just one week after their surprise attack at Faid, Nazi armor roared out of Kasserine Pass. With eyes squinting into the morning sun, American and British troops watched the panzer force fan out in two powerful columns over, the plain on which they stood. It looked like a repetition of the battle of Faid.

What happened then is described by an eye witness of the battle:

> One column struck northwestward toward Tebessa, big American base, 35 miles distant across the Algerian border; the other lunged toward Thala, tiny Arab village 20 miles to the north.
>
> The Americans got their supreme trial on the road to Tebessa in the southern half of Hamra Plain [General P. M. Robinett, who commanded Combat Command B of the 1st Armored Division during this engagement calls it 'Foussana Plain'.], to which most of

the battered forward armor had already withdrawn from the other side of Kasserine Pass. Here Fredendall's forces stood amid defenses in depth consisting of infantry and tanks, plus all types of fixed and mobile artillery from 37mm to 155mm guns, much of it emplaced in the surrounding hills.

The Hamra [Foussana] Plain is egg-shaped, with a wide base at the northeast and a pointed top at the southwest. Four secondary roads lead out of it. The whole thing is bounded by towering broken cliffs swept by scattered rain clouds . . .

Our forces held the lower half of the Plain and all the mountain positions, which German mobile forces bypassed in order to engage and disintegrate our armor on the plain itself and force a withdrawal of the entire line. Part of our armor had arrived in the nick of time that morning to support what tank destroyer and infantry units we had disposed on the plain at that moment. They were holding the line at the dry river bed gouging the middle of the plain.

Just ahead and below us on the smoke clouded plain we could pick out American Sherman and Grant tanks maneuvering with light tanks and tank destroyers toward Axis reinforcements pouring on to the battlefield. Our infantry and antitank guns had taken positions in deep wadies behind the mobile forces, while heavy artillery, which had already moved into the bottom of the plain, lobbed shells into the enemy movements.

Meanwhile a few 88mm guns that the Germans had brought through the Kasserine gap began to bombard the entire plain, not laying down any specific barrage but alternately concentrating their fire on our tanks and into our infantry positions or trying to reach out for a counter battery duel. We could hear the heavy bursts of our artillery, the occasional barks of our rapid fire antitank guns, the roar of our tank engines . . . and, amazingly, the engines of the unarmored supply trucks and jeeps which rushed gloriously into the fray behind the troops, either to service them or to feed them hot food from rolling kitchens . . .

Some of the new and heavier guns which we began to hear were either the German 81mm mortars or 210mm field pieces. Tanks asked for aerial support and soon behind the smoke haze we could hear the crescendo of the German antiaircraft fire, then dull whoomps of American bombs.

Several of our tanks reported in code that they were taking action to try to complete the trap around 4 German and 2 Italian tanks, all of them Mark IV's (mediums with 75mm guns), German Mark VI's (56-ton heavies)—2 of which were on the plain and 8 of which had gone toward Thala—didn't seem anxious to come into close contact with our armor, probably because their flank defenses were still too weak and because our tank boys, after successfully engaging several, found Mark VI's wouldn't move unless screened by light tanks and armored cars.

We listened to the tank commanders on the radio while watching the valley as dusk settled, adding gloom to the noise of the battlefield. Then suddenly like a mushroom a ball of fire rose from the distant left hand side of the plain, burned fiercely and lengthily, and then another and another until six brilliant flames with heavy oily smoke over them marked the end of the Axis tanks the American forces had trapped. The sky was dominated by Anglo-American planes.

The tide of the battle had turned on the Hamra plain. The metallic radio voices from the tanks registered excitement. It was the emotion of victory, the emotion of knowing that they controlled the next phase of the battle . . .[3]

On the plain in the north, the British, too, had won their fight, and by Tuesday morning Axis forces were retreating through Kasserine Pass. Allied planes bombed and strafed the retiring columns from overhead. On the ground, what remained of American armor followed through the pass. But so efficient was the Nazi use of mines in delaying pursuit that Rommel's retreat was as successful as his attack, and the withdrawal was accomplished with the Axis forces almost intact.

The defeat of the Americans at Faid and Kasserine was the subject of frank scrutiny and earnest conversation by Allied chieftains. "Faulty intelligence and consequent faulty disposition of troops" were blamed for the initial defeat. Yet just as much to blame was the fact that Fredendall simply did not have enough troops wherewith to establish the kind of defenses in depth he needed at the vulnerable points in the long central sector. He and his staff were posed with the question of determining at which of the two points the Germans would strike and then concentrating the major strength of the American-French forces accordingly. Had the unlucky American general possessed two or three more well-equipped divisions of armor and infantry, the outcome of the Axis thrust might well have been far different. When the two met on Foussana Plain and Rommel was finally turned back, Fredendall had just such reinforcements of massed armor, infantry, and artillery that would have spelled the difference between defeat and victory in the beginning. Not to be forgotten, however, is an equally responsible factor in the blunting of the Nazi spearhead at Foussana. Rommel was just as starved for troops as Fredendall. Though he had detached strong units of panzers from his desert army facing Montgomery, and though additional veteran troops had arrived from Europe, yet he did not possess sufficient reserves to "exploit the breakthrough and extend the gains" made by the tanks at Faid. As a result, the farther the panzer columns went, the less formidable became their sting. Rommel's attack was like a strong-topped vegetable thrusting forth from a firm, but tiny root on a weak and watery stem. Had this not been so, it is quite likely that even the hasty though soundly constructed Allied defenses on Foussana might have been pierced.

It was generally conceded that the inexperience of the American soldiers likewise contributed to the defeat. Many of the troops had never been under combat fire. When enemy planes and guns attacked in force, instead of sticking to the defense of their posts they made a wholesale dive for the nearest foxholes. Lower echelon commanders too often lacked training and ability to coordinate their men. Attacks, as a result, were apt to be straggling and sloppy, with none of the dash and precision of the battle-wily Nazi veterans. Axis successes served to enhance the front-line legend that Nazi troops had the best weapons, and soon U.S. troops lost confidence in their own equipment. Enthusiastic reports of newsmen, describing German wonder guns and tanks, did nothing to disabuse them of this idea.

No Yankee soldiers suffered greater wounds at the hands of the Nazi maulers, however, than did the American tankmen of the "Old Ironsides" Armored Division. The wrecked hulks of brand-new General Shermans and General Grants were grim markers on the roads from Faid to Kasserine, down which the erstwhile "pride and joy" of the Armored Force had been forced to flee. Thousands of casualties had thinned its ranks. Worst of all, however, had been the jolting blow to Yankee self-confidence.

It can be safely said, nevertheless, that American armor had been worsted in battle, not through any lack of personal bravery on the part of the soldiers, but because practically every major tenet laid down for its employment had been disregarded. Instead of being massed in strength, it had been so widely scattered along the front that it would have taken a week to send a post card from one company of tanks to another. Instead of being backed up by its team-mates, infantry and artillery, too often the tanks were sent in to fight it out alone. Instead of vitally needed air support, there had been practically no Allied planes in the sky until the last days of the battle. The consequent battle array of American tanks had been veritable "sitting ducks" for Rommel's panzers.

Nor did the American tankers courage in battle compensate for their inexperience in Nazi ways. Tricks that once, but no longer, had singed Montgomery's warwise desert rats were again used at Faid against the Americans with deadly effectiveness. Tank survivors of the battle ruefully described the Nazi traps they had watched their comrades fall into. "Generally they try to suck you into an antitank trap," said one officer. "Their light tanks will bait you in by playing around just outside effective range. When you start after them, they turn tail and draw you within range of their 88mm guns. First they open up on you with their guns in depth. Then when you try to flank them, you find yourself under fire of carefully concealed guns at a shorter range . . ."[4] Another U.S. soldier, a sergeant of the 1st Armored Regiment, told how he had seen at Sbeitla a group of Germans attack, dressed in American uniforms and riding in captured American half-tracks. "They get you in," he said, "and then they give it to you."

On the home front 3,000 miles away, news of the American tank reverses sharply jarred the reverential awe with which the general public regarded that vehicle, and no one was surprised when President Roosevelt revealed that tanks had been moved down on the priority list. The *Cavalry Journal* expressed the opinion of many military men in an article which declared: "The dominance enjoyed by armored forces in 1939 and 1940 is over . . . It is another example of the old story of firepower versus armor. Firepower always wins in the end." And Jack Belden, ace *Time* war correspondent wrote "Tanks! How futile they appear face to face . . . with ambush-emplaced guns." The most reasonable voice of the crowd, perhaps, was that of Major General Alvan C. Gillem, Jr., pioneer Armored Force man. Shaking his head at the stories that tanks had had their best day, he said, "Used in the proper combination, tanks are demoralizing and effective. And in an armored division, tanks are used in the proper combination. Fighting an enemy is like hunting birds. You've got to 'bird dog'. Flush out your enemy and then do your shooting. Send your experts out to find and tap the mines, locate the antitank guns and destroy them with your artillery, and then send your tanks against the infantry. And while you are doing that your men are learning more about their own job of setting effective mines. Naturally, if a tank is sent into mined areas and against concealed antitank guns, it will be blown up. Many tools are available to the armored commander, and they will do their job provided they are properly used."[5]

III

One of the repercussions of the American setback in southern Tunisia was a change in the top commander of the American forces on the central front. Through all the long winter months back in Casablanca, General George S. Patton, Jr., had been fretting to be in the battle in Tunisia, the while chained to his desk a thousand miles from the fray. When the 1st Armored Division suffered large casualties and lost much equipment in the initial phases of the campaign, he had siphoned many of his officers and men and their tanks from the 2d Armored Division as replacements, and had wistfully bade them godspeed as they marched eastward. Time and again at his headquarters he had boasted what he would do to those "Nazi so-and-so's" on the battlefield. And not many days after Kasserine, Eisenhower gave him the chance to make good his words.

To this man, then, one of the original hand-picked leaders of the Armored Force, was given the job of preparing the damaged central sector for its part in the impending Allied offensive and of retrieving the American losses.

The day that Patton faced his new command, he must have realized the size of the job he was tackling. The men before him were unshaven and hollow-eyed. Their uniforms were dirty and torn. When they laughed, which was seldom, it sounded empty and self-conscious. Their whole dejected appearance was the very synthesis of defeat.

Thanks to their new leader, within less than a month this tattered, forlorn crew had been transformed into a brisk, cohesive outfit ready to follow him to the ends of the earth—a not unlikely place for Patton to wind up. He planned his campaign carefully, massed his tanks on a narrow front, and started after the enemy. First he retook the Sbeitla valley to the east of Kasserine Pass. Then, on the night of March 17–18, the American 1st Infantry Division, commanded by former cavalryman General Terry Allen, struck the first blow of the Allied offensive that ended in Tunis and Bizerte.

Traveling 45 miles to the south in trucks, the 1st Infantry Division attacked Nazi-held Gafsa at dawn. The surprised enemy retreated 18 miles eastward to El Guettar without a fight. Three days later Allen's men had seized El Guettar and were pushing into the steep, treacherous hills beyond. Here they were no more than 12 miles from a narrow pass down the valley to the east, where the hills opened a grudging gateway to the coastal plain behind Rommel's back. Their triumphant advance was halted abruptly, however, when, after withstanding counterattacks by the 10th Panzers for four days without relief, they were forced to fall back to El Guettar.

Meanwhile, the 1st Armored Division had thrust northeastward from Gafsa and captured Maknassy. But here, too, they were stopped by the sharp hills, which lay between the town and the lowlands stretching to the sea. For many months this last series of hills had been in Nazi hands and were all too well organized for defense to be taken without long bitter fighting.

The American spearhead was blunted, the attack paused, and Patton prepared a new plan. Instead of continuing to attack at both Maknassy and El Guettar, he decided to concentrate on forcing the way to the pass east of El Guettar and then loosing his armor through the gap. Accordingly, the 1st Infantry Division was assigned to clear the hills on the north of the val-

ley, the 9th Division the hills on the south, and again the 1st
Armored Division was split up and half of it shifted to El Guettar. If Patton's forces could break through, Rommel would be
trapped in the south between him and General Montgomery.

German resistance held firm, and the plan never succeeded. Though the veteran 1st Infantry achieved its objectives
on schedule, the green, inexperienced 9th, in its first offensive
combat, failed to clear out enemy pockets from the hills that it
captured. When the armor tried to move forward, it was
stopped by fire from the unsubdued guns that the 9th had left
behind. And there it was when Rommel's troops, retreating
before Monty's army, passed by on the coastal road only a few
miles away to a juncture with General Von Arnim's forces facing the British 1st Army in northeastern Tunisia.

The Axis line now stretched in an arc some 120 miles long
and 50 miles wide, backed up against the Mediterranean Sea.
It contained an area 4,320 miles square, less than the size of
Connecticut. The plateau upon which Tunis and Bizerte lay
was girdled by the inevitable rugged Tunisian hills cut through
by river valleys and canalized roads. It was terrain that promised the Yankee troops the same kind of difficult and varied
fighting that they had encountered elsewhere in Tunisia—
artillery duels, infantry assaults, hand-to-hand combat, tank-
infantry teams, and armored thrusts. The only difference was
that now school was over, and the Americans who fought in the
final phase of the campaign were confident graduates of battle.

The second stage of the offensive began on April 23d, the
same day the Allied air force flew a record 1,500 sorties to
attack enemy positions. The biggest surprise of the day, however, was the appearance of the American II Corps, comprised
of the 1st, 9th, and 34th Infantry Divisions and the 1st Armored
Division, on the northernmost sector of the front on the left
flank of the British First Army, where it had been moved in a
lightning shift from southern Tunisia. Equally unexpected was
the fact that the II Corps had a new commander. General Omar
Bradley replaced General Patton, who dropped out of sight in

the first of his several highly publicized, Axis-worrying disappearances of the war. The 1st Armored Division was also headed by a new general. In the fighting around Maknassy in March, General Orlando Ward had been wounded. To take his place, Major General Ernest N. Harmon, pioneer Armored Force leader who had come to the 7th Cavalry Brigade (Mechanized), in 1939, was summoned from Casablanca, where he had been serving as commanding general of the 2d Armored Division.

Objective of the Americans was, first, Mateur, then Ferryville and Bizerte. These glistening, white Tunisian cities lay beyond green hills bristling with enemy guns. To clear a path for the tanks down the valleys between the hills was the task that confronted the infantry. For two weeks they assaulted and smashed through the enemy defenses. Where the terrain was too rugged, jeeps were discarded for mule trains. It was savage and gruelling combat, and "they found," said John Lardner, "that life was just one djebel (hill) after another, and each ridge higher than the last." Then on May 6th, Allied armor all along the line from the north to the south broke through the hills and struck out to the sea. By four o'clock the next afternoon, in a blitz blow executed with lightning speed, the seven-month campaign was over.

The last days of the campaign saw the 1st Armored Division for the first time employed intact and in mass to perform traditional missions. It spearheaded the advance on Mateur and made reconnaissance in force on the hill mass east of Mateur, which led to the main assault of May 6th. It was the 1st Armored Division which started the final offensive that drove on to Ferryville and led to the fall of Bizerte, then cut through in two swiftly moving, hard-hitting prongs to the northeast and east to the coast. It was the "1st Armored Division," said Ernie Pyle, "that made the kill and got the mass of prisoners [38,000 according to an official bulletin released by the Secretary of War]." Its success was ample testimony to the soundness of the teachings of its founders.

IV

Plans for the step to follow the Tunisian campaign had been initiated by the Allies long months before the final battles of Bizerte and Tunis. It was on January 23d, 1943, to be exact, that top Allied generals, meeting in secret conclave at Casablanca with the Heads of State, transmitted the message to General Eisenhower which pointed the direction of the next attack upon the Axis.

"The Combined Chiefs of Staff have resolved," read the communication, "that an attack against Sicily will be launched in 1943 with the target date as the period of the favorable July moon."

Though considerations of Luna introduced a somewhat romantic overtone in the preparations for Operation HUSKY, as the invasion of Sicily was dubbed, there was only deadly intent in the convoy of dark ships that silently converged on the shores of Sicily on the night of July 10th. The moon had just "favorably" disappeared beyond the western horizon. Unfavorable heavy winds that had plagued the crossing from North Africa were dying down. Hours before, glider and parachute troops had flown overhead and dropped inland behind enemy defenses. And in the hearts of the shadowy figures aboard the rocking boats, there was little but grimness and fear of the bloody reception that might be lying ahead.

Troops of the invasion force were a mixture of combat veterans and raw soldiers. Units of the British Eighth Army, commanded by General Montgomery, landed on the eastern coast at Cape Passero. They constituted the right prong of the landings along a 100-mile stretch of coast, and were aimed at Messina to the north, along the route where the main battles were expected to occur. Their landings went almost unopposed, and soon they were entering ancient Syracuse, where, 2,154 years before Archimedes had perished by the sword of an invading Roman. Then, on the plain before Catania, they were stopped in their tracks, with that port and railway center and rugged Mt. Etna standing formidably between them and their goal.

Canadians of the Eighth Army landed on the Britons left. They drove inland against light resistance, and complained that there was not much fighting to do.

Three American infantry divisions and one armored comprised General Patton's Seventh Army, which tackled some 35 miles of Sicilian coast to the Canadians left. They landed in three sectors. At Scoglitti, the 45th Infantry Division, new in combat, splashed ashore and raced inland to capture Vittoria, twelve miles away, and to make a juncture with the Canadians. The splendid 1st, only American infantry veterans of Tunisia in the invasion force, and still commanded by General Terry Allen, landed near Gela. Here also landed the grizzled, veteran 70th Tank Battalion on the morning of July 10th, to fight and die alongside the 1st, for it was at this point that the Germans concentrated their fiercest resistance. German leaders had anticipated an Allied invasion attempt at just this spot. Crack armored troops had therefore been assembled in force in the neighborhood. On D-Day plus 1, they unleashed their attack, catching the 1st Infantry Division with some 40 artillery pieces and 15 antitank guns in position to fire, and a handful of tanks. Only the excellence of American artillery and naval gun fire from the boats offshore saved the action, which Chief of Staff Marshall, in his report, termed "the most critical moment of the invasion." At Licata, meanwhile, to the west, the combat force commanded by General Lucian K. Truscott had an easier time. There landed the 3d Infantry and the 2d Armored Divisions.

The task that confronted these Allied invading troops was the conquest of a piece of land in the Mediterranean about the size of our state of Massachusetts. Its terrain was as varied as had been that of Tunisia, except that its mountains were even more rugged and steep. From the relatively flat coastal region upon which they stood in the south, the land pushed up to the north from a knobby, wheat-carpeted plateau to jagged cliffs and peaks rimming the island's north shore. It was toward these forbidding, natural, mountain fortresses that the Americans and British faced, for in their shadow lay the two prizes of Sicily, Phoenician-founded Palermo and Messina, the latter but three miles across the water from the toe of Italy. With their capture would come the fall of that island stepping-stone to the continent.

In the first two days of the invasion, 80,000 men, 7,000 vehicles, and 300 tanks were landed. During this time and for the next five days, units of tanks of the 2d Armored Division operated separately under several commands, assisting the infantry in capturing towns and consolidating their gains. Then, on July 18th, with the beachheads secure, the Allied air force dominating the skies, and one-quarter of the island in Allied hands, the 2d Armored was assembled as a division and held in readiness for a lightning thrust. Leader of the armor was Major General Hugh J. Gaffey, artillery expert who had served with the pioneer 7th Cavalry Brigade (Mechanized) under General Chaffee, and but lately had acted as Chief of Staff for General Patton during the months he commanded the American troops in Tunisia.

Two days later, the capture of Enna severed the road and railway nerves through central Sicily, and the American armor was released, shooting to the west and north toward Palermo. The result was what General Patton exultantly described as "one of the fastest-moving operations of its kind in the history of warfare." It was faster than the German blitzkriegs of 1939–40. "I was with a leading reconnaissance unit of this headlong armored spring," wrote Hal Boyle, AP war correspondent.[6] "We jumped off from a point east of Castelvetrano and swung in a giant arc across a mountain ridge to Palermo, entering it twenty-two hours after the attack began. En route, this column smashed three separate strong points with hardly a pause. It was led by a general who fought all through the Tunisian campaign in another outfit. His seizure of Palermo, one of the neatest bits of armored surgery in the Mediterranean campaign, cut Sicily in two and ended all German resistance in the western half of the island." The American officer who accepted the surrender of Palermo for the Seventh Army was Major General Geoffrey Keyes, Patton's Chief of Staff and another erstwhile leader of the 7th Cavalry Brigade (Mechanized). July 22d must have been a red-letter day for these pioneer men of armor in the Sicilian fight, for again an armored division had demonstrated what it could do when it was employed according to the rules of sound procedure by men who understood them.

With the fall of Palermo, four-fifths of the island was in Allied hands and German resistance was pushed into a small triangle some 60 miles wide at the base and 70 miles deep on each side on the northeastern tip of Sicily, in which lay the focal point of Messina. In it was centered the worst terrain of that island's rugged regions, wherein the Germans were solidly entrenched in the most strategic places. The djebel fighting that the infantry had learned in Tunisia was the order of the day henceforth in Sicily, with the only difference that here the hills were higher and steeper. It was this kind of combat that completed Operation HUSKY on August 16th, just 39 days after the Sicilian invasion.

CHAPTER TWELVE

"Tanks or to Hell with It"

I

The conclusion of the Tunisian and Sicilian campaigns, which had witnessed the progress of American tankmen from the desolation of defeat at Faid and Kasserine to the intoxication of victory at Ferryville and Palermo, far from inducing unanimity of opinion on the question of the tank and the armored division, found military men as divided in thought as they were in the old, pre–Armored Force days. Pointing to the brilliant successes of armor under Generals Harmon and Gaffey, proponents of tanks urged stepping up the production of tanks instead of dropping them on war priority lists, and dispatching more armor to both the Atlantic and Pacific battlefronts. They protested that tanks were being relegated to a back seat at a time when they should be leading the fight. Others argued just as vigorously that the heyday of the tank was over—that its value on the battlefield had been neutralized by tank-busters and new methods of defense. In the combat arenas of the future, they foresaw no major role for an armored division and urged that they be broken up. By far the majority of sober observers, however, believed that the work of the armored division had just begun—that with some organizational changes to meet altered battle conditions, they would perform just as spectacularly as ever. Newspapers publicly speculated on the future role of the armored division, and when General Jacob L. Devers was removed from the command of the Armored Force late in the spring of 1943 and sent to the European theatre as commander of the U.S. forces there at a time when nothing was going on, Army gossip had it that he had been "kicked upstairs" as a result of colliding with Lt. General Lesley J. McNair, Chief of the Army Ground Forces, on the matter.

Out of the crucible of war, however, one incontrovertible fact had emerged: that instead of being welded closer together by their combat experiences, tankmen and doughboys regarded each other with greater mutual suspicion than ever before. At a time when teamwork was an essential to success, each had persisted in a course of rugged individualism on the battlefield, for which they had paid dearly with lost lives and wrecked equipment. "In Africa, Sicily . . . ," declared Major General John W. O'Daniel,[1] "came recurring complaints from the infantry that the tanks had 'failed to show up,' had 'pulled out when the going got tough.' At the same time, tankers were making similar complaints about the Doughboy—'They wait for us to win the fight and then they walk up.' 'They don't take out the antitank guns because the AT guns don't shoot at infantry.'" Actually, it was a situation for which neither was responsible. They were both simply the victims of an accelerated program of mobilization that had been forced to cut training corners in raising an army from a few hundred thousand to millions in only a few months' time.

As early as the 1941 maneuvers, the need for combined infantry-tank training had been recommended as a part of regular Army education by General C. L. Scott. Pearl Harbor, however, disrupted all carefully planned schedules and brought men into the army so fast that it was barely possible to give infantry divisions the basic essentials, let alone an added course in fighting with tanks. Again in 1942 Colonel Edwin K. Wright, Assistant Chief of Staff, G-3 Armored Force, reiterated to top military leaders the necessity for "combined infantry division-tank battalion training emphasizing the tank support of infantry divisions in the attack."[2] Though Army Ground Force chieftains agreed wholeheartedly with the colonel's sage recommendation, little to effectuate the plan could be done immediately inasmuch as the still-adolescent Armored Force was in the throes of its first reorganization. Moreover, there was no equipment to spare for such a program. Consequently, divisions destined for the North Africa campaign went overseas without being exposed to this valuable pre-combat preparation. Indeed, many a doughboy on the Tunisian front had never been closer to a tank than on the sidewalk of his home town watching one go by in an Armistice Day parade. Nor was such ignorance of tanks confined to the ranks of the divisions. Commanders of foot troops were usually just as uninformed and inexperienced on the subject, unless they had been lucky enough to have served with infantry tanks in pre-war days. It was common, in Tunisia, for infantry commanders not to include commanders of tank units attached to their outfits in staff conferences and plans. The reported battlefield misunderstandings between the two arms were therefore inevitable.

Matters were not improved any when grimy-faced, dog-tired doughboys, slugging their hearts out against the Tunisian djebels, saw masses of tanks sitting behind the lines, waiting for them to make a hole for the armor to get through. No one had ever explained to them the principle of armored exploitation of an infantry breakthrough. All they saw were the tanks in hiding while they did the fighting. They had watched them bog down in mud and run out of gas in the first fighting in Tunisia, when they had been counting on the mobile firepower of their tanks to lead the way for them. They remembered what had happened during the Allied Tunisian offensive in March, when the 1st Armored Division had tried to push through the hills to the coast beyond Maknassy, and failed. There hadn't been enough infantry around to punch the holes through the German lines for them was the official explanation. Then had come the final stage of the battle of northeastern Tunisia, and the culmination of their resentment. After they had done all the hard work of blasting through the passes and cleaning out the hills, the 1st Armored had swept through the gap, captured Ferryville, thousands of prisoners, and practically all the glory.

It was small wonder, therefore, that doughboys hated tanks—both German and American.

From the moment tankmen had joined "Old Ironsides," on the other hand, the "speed," "mobility," and "fire power" of an armored division had been drilled into their heads. Training for a slow slugfest, with tanks and assaulting infantry inching forward together, had never been included in their curricula. That had been the job designated for the GHQ Reserve Tank Battalions of the Armored Force. With few such battalions available for the campaign in North Africa, however, just what General Chaffee had warned General Marshall against as far back as August, 1940, occurred: The 1st Armored Division was split up and frittered away into small units assigned to assaulting infantry in the hills of Tunisia. The result had been doubly disastrous. Not only were the tankmen unprepared for the new duties with which they were confronted, but when masses of armor were needed, they were not there. Faid and Kasserine bred a greater mutual dislike than ever before.

If the war had bred mistrust and suspicion between tanks and infantry, however, just as surely had the artillery become the big brother of the Army. In the execution of its combat tasks, it had been aggressive, expert, and cooperative. Time after time, prompt action by its observers and gunners had retrieved both tanks and infantry from grave predicaments; and nothing made its colleagues in battle more comfortable than to know the artillery was close by. It was in the battles of Faid and Kasserine that the 68th Armored Field Artillery Battalion, veteran outfit of early mechanized brigade days, won its battle spurs by saving the battered remnants of the 1st Armored Division. A report of the War Department citation awarded to the battalion a year later, in describing the action, read:

> On the 15th (February), the combat command, which the battalion was supporting, was attacked in the rear and flank by German tanks, at least 16 of which directly attacked the battalion. That unit, however, remained in

position, and by delivering direct fire on the tanks, the attack was broken and several Mark VI (heavy 56-ton) destroyed.

On the night of February 16, enemy tanks again threatened the position of the combat command. Direct fire from the battalion was effective, repulsing the enemy with the loss of three Mark VI tanks and permitting the combat command to reorganize for further defense.

The next day the battalion was given the mission of covering the withdrawal of the remainder of the Division through Kasserine Pass. Through its direct fire it slowed the enemy advance and made possible the successful retirement of hundreds of men and salvage of equipment, which otherwise would have fallen to the enemy.[3]

As the campaign progressed in Tunisia, the reputation of artillery continued to wax. In the decisive stages, military observers estimated that German infantry units were suffering an average of 50 percent casualties from murderous U.S. artillery fire. Indeed, so proficient was the handling of their guns by the crews that German prisoners were heard to ask about the new automatic artillery gun. At the battle of El Guettar in March, four U.S. artillery battalions panicked a force of 32 German tanks advancing upon American positions, causing the crews to abandon their vehicles. Nor soon to be forgotten was the performance of American artillery on the beachhead at Gela, Sicily, when fire from its guns and from the naval batteries of the convoy boats offshore turned back attacking crack German panzers and saved the day for the Allied invasion. To truck-drawn artillery was given the credit for having knocked out most of the tanks in World War II up to that time. Equally respected were the self-propelled 105mm and Long Toms (155mm).

The confidence and admiration with which U.S. soldiers regarded their own artillery, however, in no wise lessened the wholesome respect which the djebels and wadies of Tunisia had taught them to feel for the same branch of the German Army, especially their 88mm. It was this weapon which too often had proven to be the down-fall of American armor. "Find German 88 Guns or Die" was the warning of men of the 1st Armored Division to tyro tankers in training back in the States. "Four 88 guns, if dug in," declared a colonel of that same outfit, after several months of fighting on the North African front, "are a match for any tank company. They are the most wonderful things to camouflage I have ever seen. They are very low to the ground. You can watch the fire coming in, little dust balls on the ground give them away and show how low they are. They just skip along the ground. If a tank can find them, you can get them out. Over 1200 yards, there is no use worrying about them. Their shells bounce off the medium tank at that range. Under 1200 yards, watch out. The enemy's gunnery stinks at long range. I feel that our men are better—but I would say the gun is worth four tanks."[4] And wrecked carcasses of Sherman and Grant tanks, rusting on the plains and in the passes of Tunisia, attested to the bitter truth of the colonel's statement.

It was, in fact, this effectiveness of artillery, both friendly and enemy, against tanks that lent substance to the argument in certain quarters that the tank's sun was setting. They predicted that, to protect themselves from enemy guns, tank armor would grow thicker and speed proportionately less, a process that would continue until the tank had virtually immobilized itself and it was no more than an expensive, relatively stationary, steel fortress for the few men inside its belly. Such an eventuality was not new in history. It had happened to the knight in armor, who had so weighted himself and his horse down with metal trappings that he had ultimately destroyed his usefulness. When the 56-ton German Tiger tank appeared on the Tunisian scene, their prophesies seemed to be correct.

The initial success of the new Axis monster gave rise to a series of exaggerated stories of its prowess and invincibility. Allied soldiers regarded the Tiger with awe, and "Not one

American tank has been reported as having hit one," cabled a war correspondent to the home front, using the same article to state that soon the U.S. Army would match the Tiger at the front with even bigger tanks. Armored leaders, however, had different ideas on the subject. It was true the Army had developed a heavy tank—but it was their belief that such a tank, because of the difficulties inherent in its weight, did not belong in an armored division. They took the stand that what the medium and light tanks lacked in weight and protection was more than offset by their mobility, backing up their contention with innumerable examples from military history of a small, agile army defeating a larger, less mobile foe. Though well aware that the Tiger tank was an impressive vehicle, they nevertheless were inclined to think that, once the novelty of the behemoth wore off, G. I.'s would not find it so formidable as they thought.

It was not, however, a view unanimously shared by fighting men abroad. In mess halls, in canteens, in officers' clubs, wherever, in fact, groups of combat troops foregathered, there raged an eternal debate on the relative merits of American vs. German tanks. The seeds of the argument were sown in the early stages of the campaign in Tunisia, when green American troops emerged from their first encounters with German tanks and guns on the wrong end of the fight, and G. I.'s and correspondents joined in touting German panzer wagons and in derogating American tanks. Actually, there existed some grounds for complaint. Several of the American armored units were still riding in General Grants, predecessors of the General Sherman M-4 mediums, whose riveted construction and limited traverse of the 75-mm gun had proven inefficient and unsatisfactory in combat. By the time the men of "Old Ironsides" drove triumphantly into Ferryville, however, the soothing effect of victory had healed the wounds of defeat, and most American tankers were willing to swear by their equipment, providing they had enough of it. But there were still those who swore that, tank for tank, the Germans still held the edge and that in any

duel they would come out the victors, to which the classic reply
was, "Stay away from enemy tanks, man. Let your artillery knock
them out." The debate, however, persisted through Sicily, into
Italy, up through France, and finally into Germany, and when
the whistles signaled V-E Day, it was still going on.

II

Changes in the U.S. Army, promulgated in War Department
Circular 256 in the early fall of 1943, were a natural result of
combat experiences abroad, and army chiefs indicated the reorganization was made with five considerations in view:

  a. To secure the maximum use of the available man-
     power.
  b. To permit overseas transport of a maximum of fighting
     power.
  c. To provide greater flexibility in organization in keeping
     with the principle of economy of force and massing of
     military strength at the decisive point.
  d. To reduce headquarters and other overhead in order
     that command functions may keep pace with modern
     communication and transport facilities.
  e. To provide commanders with the greatest possible
     amount of offensive power through reduction in pas-
     sive defense elements.

Keynote of the new Army set-up was flexibility, and revised
tables of organization provided the second major revamping of
the Armored Force in the three years of its existence.

Most striking innovation in the armored division was the
abolition of the regimental organization and the reduction, by
half, of the tank battalions. As a result of this change, the "three
musketeers" of the armored division were made equal in
strength: three battalions of tanks, three battalions of armored
infantry, and three battalions of armored artillery. It was the
answer to the improved antitank weapons and technique which
had developed since the blitz days of Poland and France, and

military leaders explained that, far from indicating the eclipse of the tanks on the battlefield, it merely meant increased support for them. Actually, the U.S. Army was not the first to shape up its armored organization in this fashion. As early as 1941, the German Army in Russia was reported to be using smaller numbers of tanks in its armored divisions in proportion to infantry, to combat the effective Soviet "area" type of antitank defense, which proved so frustrating to the victory-proud panzers, while in 1942 the British armored divisions in North Africa had been reorganized into smaller divisions comparable to Rommel's, which also were lighter in tanks and heavier in infantry than U.S. armored divisions.

Though regimental troops disappeared from the armored division, the combat command feature was retained. This provided for two headquarters "capable of controlling a variable number of tank and infantry battalions," and a reserve command headed by a colonel who was charged with the supervision of infantry training and the control of division reserve. Later, in European operations, it was customary to use the division in three combat commands, additional headquarters troops having been added to the division to function as a third combat command headquarters.

Also affected was the division's organic supply battalion, which was eliminated from the new division. Each battalion was made self-sustaining instead.

Another change was the reorganization of the reconnaissance battalion to include four reconnaissance troops, an assault gun troop, a light tank company, and headquarters and service troop; and its rechristening with the name of Cavalry Reconnaissance Squadron (Mecz.). This Armored Force component was manned chiefly by erstwhile horse cavalry devotees, and so at last the longstanding feud between the horsemen and the tanks was satisfactorily settled.

Crux of the changed army pattern, however, was contained in the terse War Department statement that "the new organization of the armored division is in accordance with the principle that armored and infantry divisions will operate together in a corps." While there was nothing new in this idea, the first armored chief having declared in 1940 that "the greatest benefits will accrue from the close cooperation between armored divisions and combat aviation . . . (with) other *large* bodies of *normal* troops,' yet it constituted a rededication to the program of wedding the tanks and infantry into a closely knit, smooth-working combination, a situation which had not hitherto obtained in American battle array abroad, save in the closing days of the Tunisian campaign and in the pattern of General Patton's Seventh Army which had conquered western Sicily.

To implement the union, it was decreed by War Department Circular 256 that "the motorized division as a separate type of organization" be eliminated and that training "of all infantry divisions in movement by use of the troop transport battalion" be substituted instead. Thus every foot soldier division, by the attachment of six companies of trucks, could easily be turned into a motorized division to support a fast-moving armored drive, should the battle picture so develop. Likewise, tanks were to be trained to act in a dual role by making the new armored division tank battalions and the general headquarter reserve battalions interchangeable and prepared to support infantry divisions or to act as replacement units for armored divisions. An important phase of the new regime was to be emphasis on the already-too-long delayed training of the tank-infantry team, involving close cooperation between tanks and assaulting foot troops.

Cognizant that team-work between the partners rather than grand-stand plays by individual members provided the key to victory for the new, stream-lined army against a totalitarian foe, bosses of the Ground Forces served notice of their intention to reduce the Armored Force from its princely position as semi-independent head of sixteen powerful armored divisions to the status of a common subject of the military ground machine by abolishing, on July 2, 1943, its proud title and calling it, instead, the "Armored Command." Similarly, on October 1, 1943, the II,

III and IV Armored Corps, all with two or more armored divisions under their command, were redesignated the XVIII, XIX and XX Corps respectively. While the immediate effect on the troops of changing the name of the Armored Corps was small other than shifting shoulder patches in the Corps headquarters, it gave added emphasis to the impending tank-infantry training program and a hint of even more drastic changes in the future.

On September 3, 1943, Italy had been invaded, and already plans for the not-far-distant invasion of Normandy, calling for many potent packages of armor, were in the making. No time, therefore, was wasted in executing the War Department orders, and by November 1st all but three of the U.S. armored divisions had been stripped down to its new, stream-lined, battle dress. (These three were the 1st, 2d, and 3d. Later, the 1st was changed to conform with Circular 256, but the 2d and 3d remained according to the 1942 reorganization. These were known as "heavy" armored divisions, the other 14 as "light.") Tanker strength siphoned from the old divisions was used to form new battalions, many of which were destined to be organized into armored groups and assigned to corps containing infantry divisions, while infantry divisions were assigned to erstwhile armored corps. Coincidentally, work went on apace in preparing a field manual designed to show how to use infantry and tanks together.

The teams that brought the Axis to its knees a year and a half later were being forged.

III

Reaction to changes in the Armored Force was mixed in military circles, and a statement of the conflicting views is an expression of the years-old argument that had prevailed on the question of tanks. Though, according to some, the new developments were the outcome of a healthy evolution to meet altered conditions, a sizable group of tankmen and others felt that "someone is sniping at us" and that there was a campaign

on to deemphasize the role of armor in general and the
Armored Force in particular. It was their contention that tanks
were again being subordinated to infantry in the U.S. Army and
that we were deliberately throwing away our superiority as an
industrial nation by almost entirely stopping the production of
tanks and other armored equipment. Their views were voiced in
the semi-official publication of the tankers, *The Armored News*, in
an editorial titled "(A) Tanks or (B) To Hell With It":

> Arguments about the relative importance of air, armor,
> artillery, or infantry in winning the war usually get about
> as far as arguments in religion. Perhaps, if we put this
> down in A.B.C. fashion, somebody, including ourselves,
> will see what we are driving at.
>
> A. We read about the tough time the Marines had on
> Tarawa—and, in the same breath, how the New York
> National Guard took Makin. The Marines went ashore
> ahead of tanks at Tarawa, convinced that air had soft-
> ened up the Japs. They had about 3,700 casualties.
>
> At Makin, the tanks went in ahead of the infantry,
> gave the infantry a beachhead, and the casualties ran
> around 300.
>
> B. War correspondents reported that, of the platoon
> of tanks which apparently went ashore at Tarawa, three
> were knocked out fairly quickly, but the other two just
> blistered the Nips. Dick Johnston of U.P. noted that the
> two tanks . . . accounted for at least 600 Japs, a couple
> of steel pillboxes, an ammunition dump or two and
> 'indirectly cost them (the Japs) Tarawa a little sooner
> than otherwise would have been the case.'
>
> C. The War Department's Tunisian critique said that
> the only trouble with tanks was that they weren't used
> in large enough numbers.
>
> That's the way it goes.
>
> The theory of armor revolves around the job of
> bringing fire power to the enemy with a minimum of

loss to our own personnel. That doesn't mean that any-body expects tanks to win the war; it does mean that the nation has a perfect right to expect that armor will be employed under any circumstances where its use can do the job and save lives. Why let the infantry be cut to rib-bons if a few tanks could knock out the pillboxes and automatic weapons that are doing the damage? . . .

. . . it becomes apparent that our future lies in whether we decide to kill men or machines. We can make tanks and guns and armored personnel carriers by the thousands, but with all our ingenuity, we've never been able to figure out how to produce men on the assembly line basis.

It's a question with armor of either using it and using it properly—or just saying to hell with it and keep on winning the war the hard way. . . .

As proof of their belief that that was just what the U.S. Army was continuing to do, they pointed to the battle of the Anzio beachhead, where they declared that American infantry was fighting a slow war a few feet at a time instead of over-whelming the foe with armored force. "Our Army," they said, "is committed to and talks offense, but it has been trained by officers who know only the trench position warfare of World War I. Hence the results at Anzio." While their statement was true that progress of the war was slow in Italy, where only the 1st Armored Division was fighting, what they did not know, until it was revealed in General Marshall's report, was that no large armored forces could be spared from preparations for the Normandy invasion to help with the Italian fight, which was always regarded as a diversionary action, albeit king size, of the main operation in western Europe.

The further fact that the organization of no more armored divisions was being contemplated at a time when German panzer and motorized divisions in Italy outnumbered the Allies five to two and when the Russians were reported never to be

willing to risk battle on a major sector without the equivalent
of twenty armored divisions (more than in the whole U.S.
Army) was used as another indication that certain top echelons
of command were wilfully bent on relegating armor to a back
seat, no matter what the cost of such a move might be in terms
of doughboys' lives, or that there existed a woeful ignorance of
the requirements of mobile warfare in high military places. No
less cause for alarm was that the diminishing of armored influence was occurring before enough tank battalions had been
organized to match infantry divisions, even on a one-battalion-
for-one-division basis. A target for further criticism in the organizational change was the removal of the supply battalion from
the armored division—a move which many perturbed tankers
pessimistically opined would stop their tanks before the Germans did. The only protection against future encroachments
and guarantee that the armored case would be heard, they felt,
was the addition of a special armored section to the War
Department staff and more representation and power in Army
Ground Force councils.

Any hopes that might have been entertained for a restora-
tion of the Armored Command to its original semiautonomous
status, however, were summarily ended on February 19, 1944,
when Lt. General Lesley J. McNair announced the change of
the Armored Command to the "Armored Center in further-
ance of the policy of placing armored units and establishments
in normal command channels." Under the new set-up, the
Armored Center at Fort Knox, comprised of Headquarters,
Armored, Center, the Armored School, and the Armored
Replacement Training Center, was assigned to the Replacement and School Command of the Army Ground Forces at
Birmingham, Alabama, while the Armored Board was ordered
to operate directly under Army Ground Forces Headquarters.
Duties of the new Armored Center, according to McNair, were
the continued inspection of training and equipment of the
Armored School, Armored Replacement Training Center, and

armored units which were assigned or attached to other elements of the Army Ground Forces.

With all armored units by then assigned to the command of corps or armies, it was obvious that the Armored Center had dwindled to a mere shadow of the powerful Armored Force it had once been. Commenting on the changes, however, Major General Charles L. Scott, commanding general of the Armored Center, said: "The big mobilization period is over for all army commands. All (the changes) are logical, sensible, and economical in the use of overhead personnel and have been applied equally to other special commands which, like the Armored Command, have completed their major mobilization missions. From now on our big job will be the training of replacements to keep the ranks filled overseas.

"(Physically), it is merely a change in terminology. Everything will go on here (at Fort Knox) about the same as before. We will lose only about 400 of our approximately 46,000 military population.

". . . Contrary to some ill-informed press articles, there is nothing in these changes that is prejudicial to armor or intended to detract from its important functions in battle."

Though the words of General Scott were designed to reassure troubled tankmen everywhere, yet his concluding statement was read with considerable dubiety by many, who were inclined to feel that armor had been delivered into the hands of a domestic enemy. When the new Armored Field Manual 17-36, featuring the employment of tanks with infantry, was published, they thought they saw their worst fears confirmed.

They need not have worried, however, for both U.S. armored divisions and tank battalions were poised on the threshold of overwhelming glory.

CHAPTER THIRTEEN

Continental Cavalcade

I

The saga of tank fighting during the first two months of the Allied invasion of France, June and July, 1944, was the story of individual tanks—of a "swimming tank" that looked like a small infantry assault boat in the water, and of General Shermans and of light tanks that fought, sometimes singly, sometimes in pairs or quartets, with crouching, creeping G.I.'s. The action was played out in "the highest winds and roughest seas in twenty years"[1] on the beaches of Normandy, and in cruel, pelting rains and on sunny, summer days through its fertile orchards and green fields, each neatly bounded on four sides by a diabolic hedgerow.

The DD tank (Duplex Drive), as the amphibious tank was called, constituted one of the secret invasion weapons of the Allies. Developed early in the war by a British inventor, it was a 40-ton vehicle with a waterproofed hull, fitted with a canvas screen which could be raised or lowered. When the screen was raised, it extended above the turret; and since only a foot or two of the canvas wall was visible above the water when the tank was afloat, hence its boatlike aspect. When it reached shallow water, the screen was lowered, and the "boat" metamorphosed into a full-fledged fighting tank. Twin propellors at the rear, which were driven by the tracks of the tank and which could be swivelled left and right for steering, propelled the DD through the water, while the compass, periscope, and escape apparatus, with which the webfooted tank was accoutred, were in the best of naval tradition. Thorough pre-invasion tests had demonstrated that the tank could be launched from landing craft several miles offshore in fairly rough seas, and could go four or five miles an hour in still water. And impressed by its possibilities as an invasion vehicle, the Allied High Command had ordered the manufacture of many thousands to assist the infantry on D-Day in clearing the Normandy beaches.

Though the DD tank was a baby of World War II, yet the idea was by no means new. As early as 1920 the British had built one experimental model of an amphibious tank, while in June, 1921, that far-sighted American inventor, J. Walter Christie, completed his first version of a swimming tank. In June, 1922, he completed a second model, and in November, 1923, his third and final machine. A perusal of its specifications reveals that the vehicle weighed 7 tons, could go 7.5 miles an hour in water, 18 miles an hour on tracks, and 30 miles an hour on wheels. It was armed with a 75mm gun, had two propellors for operation in the water, and was steered by varying the speed of the propellors or tracks. An astonishing demonstration of the tank was given for General S. D. Rochenbach, U.S. World War I tank leader, one cold December day in 1922, when it success-fully swam across the Hudson River.

> The demonstration started at Hoboken, N. J., crossed the 23rd Street Ferry, thence to Broadway, then up Broadway to 74th Street, thence out Riverside Drive to 205th Street. With the assistance of a motorcycle police squad, the streets were kept cleared and the machine ran on its rubber-tired wheels at the rate of 30 miles per hour," wrote General Rockenbach. "At the Dyckman Street Ferry, the machine was moved on the ferryboat and was transported across the Hudson and ran from the ferry on the very narrow cinder road bordering the river. Its tracks were put on with heavy grousers, and thus the machine turned from the road up the steep bank of the river between the Palisades. Its climbing

ability was something remarkable, and it continued to ascend for 100 feet, where the earth ended against the precipice. It then descended the bank much easier than the spectators, who were slipping and sliding, reached the road, turned abruptly to the left, went along the river for some 30 feet, and then descended a 6-foot stone wall into the Hudson River. It crossed the Hudson under its own power, but instead of the driver directing the machine to its designated landing place on the east shore, he headed south of the same and on getting across the river, faced a sheer stone precipice. At the time of crossing the river, the tide was going out very rapidly, and the very worst possible for the machine to encounter. The driver turned his machine up the river and buffeted a tremendous tide and current successfully for over a mile. He then headed for the shore, reached a 20-foot rock revetment of the New York Central Railway Lines, ascended that, flopped down on the railway tracks, turned south on rails and ties, and continued along the railway line until he reached the crossing at 205th Street. . . . it was the most remarkable performance that I have ever seen or heard of . . .

While perhaps Mr. Christie's tank might not have fared so happily had a locomotive appeared to contest its passage down the railroad tracks, yet Rockenbach's report of the successful one-tank invasion of New York City convincingly attested the amazing powers of the intrepid machine. Though more proof was scarcely needed, it further demonstrated its abilities by swimming the Potomac. The tank, however, was not purchased by the Government but was later destroyed, and one learns with interest that the plans were sold to Japan. Nothing more was done to provide the Army with amphibious tanks until 400 DD tanks were built in the United States at Eisenhower's command (to supplement the British-manufactured DD's) for the invasion of France.

The churning seas which the Allies encountered in the English Channel on D-Day, however, not only sent thousands of miserably sick G. I.'s to the railings of their convoy boats, but had the effect as well of reducing the effectiveness of the amphibious tank. The assault forces landed on five beaches— the British and Canadians at the left on the so-called Sword, Juno, and Gold beaches, the Americans on the right at the Omaha and Utah beaches. Invasion plans called for the DD tanks to swim to shore with the first troops, but the angry waves said otherwise. Though determined Americans and Britons launched the tanks offshore in the teeth of the storm at the Sword, Utah, and Omaha beaches, the sea took its revenge. At the Sword and Utah beaches, tanks managed to land, but late. At the Omaha beach, where German resistance was the strongest and their assistance was most desperately needed, all but two sank in the water. At the Gold and Juno beaches, no attempt was made to swim the tanks in. Instead, the landing craft beached and unloaded the DD's directly on the shore.

Despite such bruises and buffetings at the hands of Neptune, the swimming tanks that managed to reach land performed heroically. Rampaging among German pillboxes and knocking out enemy guns, they "are estimated to have saved the lives of 10,000 Allied soldiers."[2] A full measure of praise for their service was accorded to them by the Supreme Commander, General Eisenhower, in his report to the Combined Chiefs of Staff, when he declared, "It is doubtful if the assault forces could have firmly established themselves without the assistance of these weapons."

The amphibious tanks, however, were not the only armor landed on that stormy day in June. Five infantry divisions, plus two follow-up infantry divisions, with all their attached armor, artillery, and other reinforcements were to comprise the initial invading force. In round figures, Eisenhower proposed to land, during the first two days of the assault, 176,475 personnel and 20,111 vehicles, including 1,500 tanks, 5,000 other tracked vehicles, 3,000 guns, and 10,500 other machines from jeeps to bulldozers. Actually, by nightfall of D-Day, despite the handicap of the weather, there had been landed in the American beachhead sectors three infantry divisions (the 82d and 101st Airborne had also been flown inland) with their attachments as designated, while behind them were being disembarked a steady stream of additional divisions. ". . . the comparatively light casualties which we sustained on all the beaches except Omaha were in a large measure due to the success of the novel mechanical contrivances (the DD tank, the "flail" tank, which cleared paths through mine fields at the beach exits, and the British AVRE) which we employed, and to the staggering moral and material effect of the mass of armor landed in the leading waves of the assault," wrote General Eisenhower. It was teams made up of the infantry and tanks so landed on D-Day and thereafter that helped to gain a foothold on the beaches of France; then for six long weeks fought together through the hedgerows of Normandy to "establish the lodgement area"— living space for an overgrowing invasion body.

The bocage (thicket) country of the Cotentin Peninsula lying to the south of the invasion beaches furnished the setting for the "lodgement" operations. It was a region dominated by hedgerows—"a ditch and wide hillock, sometimes twelve feet high, planted with bushes and trees to keep the topsoil from washing into sunken roads, with which the area abounds."[3] The effect may have been picturesque, indeed, to a casual tourist, but not so to American soldiers, for each pretty, little field surrounded by its hedgrows each about four hundred yards apart, constituted a miniature battlefield within a natural defensive wall that had to be taken by assault. The Allied answer to the Nazi antitank and machine guns in the hedgerows was a combination tank-infantry team play.

When American troops went into action on the Normandy front, the U.S. Army Ground Forces tank-infantry team training program was barely eight months old. Indeed, only three months had elapsed since the publication of the new tank manual "covering the doctrine and tactics of the employment of separate tank battalions with infantry elements of the infantry division" in attack. By the time it had arrived at all headquarters, most of the infantry divisions and their tank battalions that were to fight in France were already in England, on the high seas, or en route to ports of embarkation. Obviously there had been little or no time to put the program into practice; hence the result was that, as the G.I.'s and tanks fought side by side among the hedgerows, they developed their own S.O.P.'s, while all sorts of ingenious ideas were devised to insure a smooth-working, harmonious marriage.

To overcome the suspicion and dislike between the two, and to foster their mutual acquaintance, it became the rule for commanders to try to keep the same group of tanks attached to the same group of infantry. They messed together, slept together, and fought together. Sometimes G.I.'s hitched rides on their tanks or buttoned up inside them. Within a few days after the landing in Normandy, it became general practice to fasten to the outside of a tank a telephone hooked into the tank's intercommunication system, and in some cases radios were furnished to tanks so they could tune in on the infantry channels. A plan was devised for emergency supplies for the infantry to be carried on the outsides of the tanks.

Joint tactics employed by one corps, which did hedge fighting from D-Day, were described thus:

> An effective infantry and tank team play . . . had one platoon of tanks, divided into two waves, to support the infantry. The first wave of tanks took positions in the most advanced hedgerows held by our troops. As the infantry advanced down the flanking hedgerows, toward the hedgerow held by the enemy, the two tanks shouldered their way through the hedge and sprayed the enemy position with machine guns. Under cover of this fire, the infantry advanced toward the German-held hedgerows, using the flanking hedgerows. When they reached the flanks of the enemy hedgerow, the infantry

worked toward the center of it, cleaning out the Germans as they joined forces. The second wave of tanks stayed one hedgerow behind the first, in position to support the attack and to give protection against the sudden appearance of krauts on the flanks. They also protected the first wave of tanks by working on any German bazookas or AT grenade launchers who were trying to knock out the tanks. Once the hedgerow was clear, the first wave of tanks worked up to it and the second wave took the position formerly occupied by the first. The process was then repeated and the advance went on.[4]

For this kind of fighting both medium and light tanks were used.

To prevent the advance from halting when the tanks had to withdraw for refueling and resupply, tanks were often used in double teams—one at the front and one in reserve at the rear. The leading tanks would fight until their gas and ammunition were exhausted. When they retired to the rear, they would be immediately replaced by their doubles, and the action would continue with no interruption.

The intimate alliance of tanks and infantry begot effective results in the form of territorial gains and a hitherto unknown sense of responsibility for the welfare of each other. As the G. I. became familiar with the highly individual personality of his iron teammate, he learned to place a true value on its capabilities and to understand how it could help to save his life if he protected it properly from antitank guns. Likewise, the tankers came to appreciate the infantry's bazookas and bullets. Not only in the hedgerows of Normandy but across the whole of France and Germany as well, these two found a job to do, breaking holes in enemy lines, keeping open critically narrow corridors, and capturing bypassed towns.

If General Chaffee had been alive to witness the slugging matches of these tank-infantry teams, it would have occasioned

him no surprise, for time after time he had expressed to his colleagues, and finally had stated officially in his 1939 War College
speech, his belief in tanks "to have a continuing and important
role in the close support of assaulting infantry—a role which is
separate and distinct in thought, conception, method, and
equipment from the role of mechanized forces. Mechanized
cavalry or panzer corps," he said, "do not take the place of
properly supported battle infantry, which is needed in quantity
in any army." When, in the summer of 1940, all tanks, both cavalry and infantry, were thrown into the Armored Force, it was
with this realization that Chaffee designated the organization of
separate tank battalions for close infantry support and
expressed his opinion that a special heavy tank should be developed for test in this service. In the first frantic expansion of the
Armored Force, however, when personnel and supplies were
concentrated in the organization of armored divisions at the
expense of the tank battalions, heavy tanks were shelved in
favor of mediums and lights.

It is interesting to speculate at this point on what might
have been the fate of tank battalions and heavy tanks had the
Chief of Infantry been successful in his attempt to wrest control
of the battalions from the Armored Force in the spring of 1941.
Would the tank-infantry team training have begun earlier than
it did, or was the infantry branch, like the Armored Force, too
busy teaching recruits the bare rudiments of marching and
shooting to have squeezed out the time in its limited schedule
for such additional activity? And would the assault-minded
infantry have pushed the production of a heavy tank, with
which to equip these battalions, or would they have spurned
such a monster as did speed-minded armored leader Patton
and General J. L. Devers, who declared that, if armored units
had heavy tanks, they would be weighed down by special bridging equipment and their speed cut immeasurably. Early in 1944,
the development of the T26EI heavy tank—weighing 43 tons
and armed with a 90 mm gun was announced. Reports from
the European theatre of war in 1944 and 1945 indicated certain

powerful infantry commanders as favoring its employment arid it is likely that had the defeat of Germany taken longer these heavy tanks would have found their way to the front in substantial numbers. As it was two months before the war's end, a total of only 250 of the heavy tanks had been produced in America.

Hindsight reveals that what these GHQ tank battalions had needed in their early days was a sponsor, high in the councils of war and exclusively concerned with their special needs and problems. It likewise seems probable that, had tank battalions supporting infantry gone into action equipped with heavy tanks, there would have been no debate on the relative merits of German versus U.S. tanks.

II

It was on July 25th, just forty-nine days after D-Day, that General Bradley mounted the offensive at St. Lo, which, in one day, changed the complexion of battle from bunts to blitz. The plan was for the English and Canadians to engage the strong forces of German infantry and panzers on the left at Caen, while the Americans struck a hard blow against the enemy on the right. With good luck and good weather attending, the rosiest hope of the Allied commanders was for a breakthrough to Avranches on the threshold of the Brittany Peninsula, some forty miles to the south. Here a special airborne operation was prepared to be launched at the enemy's rear, to assist the ground troops to pierce any strong resistance they might encounter.

The attack commenced at midday on the heels of a stunning air bombardment, when three divisions of infantry of the VII Corps moved forward in force through the hedgerows. Though the going at first was slow and difficult, by midnight they had crossed the key Periers–St. Lo Road and pushed a sizable wedge through enemy lines, thereby opening the way for the armor clanking impatiently in the rear. For months the tankers had been training for just such an eventuality, and they didn't intend to muff it. Moreover, they knew that the Allied

chiefs had staked their strategy on an armored breakout to
Brittany.

Allowing the Nazis no time, therefore, to regroup their
retreating troops, bright and early the next morning the
armored thrust began, when tanks of the 2d and 3d Armored
Divisions surged forward through the gap. With them they carried their own ammunition and fuel, infantry riding in trucks
and atop tanks, and bulldozers with which to cut through
hedgerows and build roads. In command of the 2d was Major
General Ernest N. Harmon and of the 3d, Major General Leroy
Watson. Overhead the sky was filled with planes. That day
instead of pursuing its own princely way, for once the Allied air
power was at the beck and call of the ground forces, indefatigably bombing, strafing, and reconnoitering enemy formations
and strongholds in the path of the advancing tanks. It was a
combination that proved as unbeatable then as it had in 1940,
when it was the Germans who were moving across France. Town
after town fell to the Americans, while the Nazis retreated
southward in confusion. Pockets of resistance bypassed by the
tanks were mopped up by the infantry, following closely on
their heels. Sweet as their success was to them, however, tankers
were even more pleased by the armored tactics of the Germans,
who, in Normandy, frantically hurled their tanks into the fight
piecemeal, as the green Americans had done in North Africa at
Faid Pass and Kasserine, with the same unfortunate results.

Meanwhile, a few miles to the west, the 4th Armored Division and the 6th Armored Division, spearheads of the American VIII Corps, were repeating the successes of their tank
colleagues in the VII Corps. On July 27, the towns of Periers
and Lessay were taken. On July 28th, the 4th Armored, commanded by Major General John Wood, captured Coutances
and 4,500 prisoners, then raced onward with the 6th Armored,
commanded by Maj. General Robert W. Grow, to the Sienne
River, which was crossed the next day. Then, on July 31st, just
six days after the Allied offensive began, the 6th Armored took

Granville, the 4th Armored rode into Avranches, and they saw nothing in front of them to bar their way into Brittany. It was here, in the midst of the flame and smoke of battle, that the American Third Army was officially born, though most of its units already had been in action for days.

The appearance of a new U.S. Army on the breakthrough front was no surprise to anyone, except perhaps to the carefully protected American public. Weeks before, the Germans had announced the establishment of General George Patton's headquarters in an orchard in Normandy, and soon after the offensive began at St. Lo they had stated over the radio that two armies, one commanded by Patton, were fighting in that area. Eisenhower's official designation of the VIII, XII, XV, and XX Corps therefore, to constitute the U.S. Third Army under Patton only served to confirm what the enemy had been broadcasting for days. Under the new setup, Lt. General C. H. Hodges replaced Bradley as commanding general of the First Army, which was now comprised of the V, VII, and XIX Corps, while General Bradley assumed command of both armies.

Not even the occasion of its birthday, however, halted the onward sweep of the new Third Army, for on that very day—August 1st, to be exact—the 4th Armored Division, "speed demons of the Third Army," as they aptly came to be called by newspaper correspondents, captured the dams of the Selune river and crossed into Brittany, thereby rendering superfluous the projected airborne operation intended to assist them. Once inside that peninsula, the armored spearheads fanned out like a Fourth of July skyrocket, one shaft-the 6th Armored-shooting westward toward the Atlantic seaport of Brest, 140 miles away, and twin shafts of the 4th Armored darting southward toward Nantes straight across the neck of Brittany and eastward behind the backs of the embattled Nazis in Normandy, toward the heart of France. By August 10th, infantry divisions, following in the wake of the armor, had completely overrun the Brittany Peninsula and were heading in the direction of Paris. It was obvious that Third Army speedsters had outstripped expectations of the Allied High Command.

While Third Army exploits were bagging the lion's share of the headlines in newspapers throughout the world, the activities of the British and the U.S. First Army on its left flank, though less spectacular, made Patton's pronged push possible. From Chabourg to Chaumont, English and Canadian soldiers pinned down German troops in force in bitter defensive combat, and at Mortain, barely more than a stone's throw across the hills from Patton's narrow corridor of supply, troops of the First Army, including three infantry divisions, the 3d Armored Division, and a part of the 2d Armored, steinmed a savage Nazi counterattack designed to break through to Avranches behind Patton's back. When it became apparent that the German attempt had failed, it was then that the Allied chiefs determined to utilize spearheads of Patton's easterly advancing forces to try to encircle the enemy armies in Normandy. Overnight, objectives changed, and a whole corps shifted its direction to turn north.

On the night of August 12th, the 5th Armored Division of the XV Corps of the Third Army arrived at Argentan, which became the lower "lip" of a pincers almost completely enclosing a whole German Army and thousands of tanks. Five days later the Canadians took Falaise, which became the upper "lip." Taking its name from these two towns, there ensued the "Battle of the Falaise—Argentan Pocket," which ended the fighting in Normandy only two and a half months after the invasion. Meantime, the remaining corps of the seemingly ubiquitous Third Army, each spearheaded by an armored division, continued their headlong drive toward Paris and the Seine.

In his authoritative expositions on armored warfare, General J. F. C. Fuller has many times referred to what happened on the plains of Arbela in 331 B.C. as a classic blueprint for blitzkrieg in 1940 A.D. In this battle, Alexander's heavy infantry and heavy cavalry on the left held the Persian "battle body" of

Darius "in a clinch," while Alexander and his light cavalry "struck at a weak point on the right, broke through, and then wheeled his horsemen to the left . . . whereupon the whole of Darius' army (reputed to be a million against Alexander's 45,000) was swept by panic." In the breakthrough at St. Lo, one sees Fuller's conception of true armored tactics proven correct by an almost exact duplication of the events at Arbela. While the English and Canadians held down the main body of Nazi troops on the Allied left wing by heavy concentrations of infantry and infantry-tank teams (heavy cavalry), American troops broke through on the more lightly defended right, where speedy armored divisions proceeded to demoralize the enemy in the rear areas.

Fuller has likewise propounded the battle of Cannae between Hannibal and the Romans in 216 B.C. as a second "grand maneuver in present day armored fighting."[5] In this historic set-to, Hannibal routed the Roman right wing cavalry with his own cavalry, then enticed the Romans into a pocket, whereupon he attacked them on both flanks with infantry and with cavalry, returning from pursuit, in the rear. This classic action Fuller has termed "envelopment," and, in perusing the execution of the Falaise—Argentan entrapment, the analogy between this modern maneuver and the ancient battle of Cannae is also apparent.

Thus, while methods were changed by the tools of modern war, the ideas of generals on how to win battles were the same as they had been 2,000 years before. There were the same masses of infantry on which to hinge the action; the same mobile forces with which to penetrate to the rear and spread in all directions; and the same factor of surprise which all three winning generals employed to trick his opponent and turn the battle in his favor. There were the same strategical plan, the same masterful maneuver, the same demoralization of the enemy. Only the spears and horses of Alexander were different from the shells and tanks of Eisenhower. The chief thought that arises from such a comparison is an astonishing one: that the battles of World War II were more akin to those of Arbela and Cannae than of World War I, from which had disappeared mobility, surprise, and generalship.

III

The liberation of Paris on August 25th by the French 2d Armored Division of the Third Army heralded a new phase of the campaign, though no pause in the pace of the advancing Allied armies. With the Germans in pell-mell northward retreat, the victorious, confident British and American troops jumped across the Seine, into territory full of nostalgic memories for many a hoary-haired World War I campaigner.

Moving forward on a line stretching from the Channel coast inland some fifty miles to Vernon were Monty's men of the Canadian First Army and the British Second Army. Straight toward the Lower Rhine region they went—the Canadians taking, on the way, Rouen, Dieppe, which fell to forces that had fought in the ill-fated raid of August, 1942, and Ostend and Dunkirk; the British racing through Amiens, Albert, Bapaume, Doullens, across the Belgian border into Lille and Antwerp, in an armored dash of some 195 miles "as the crow flies" (Eisenhower) in less than four days. By September 12th they were fighting within the regions of Holland.

Marching abreast with the British, on their right, toward the German border was the American First Army. The drive was made on a three-corps front, spearheaded by the 2d, 3d, and 5th Armored Divisions. "We're the guys who took Soissons and Chateau Thierry," tankers of the 3d Armored Division on the First Army's right were wont to shout to jeeping newsmen, and indeed this they had accomplished by August 29th, with scarcely time to remember the American soldiers who had found the going somewhat tougher in their encounter with the Germans on those identical spots only twenty-six years before. The next day they hurried on to liberate Laon; thence seventy miles to the northeast into Belgium. To the west, the 2d Armored Division was simultaneously chalking up gains that were equally spectacular. Between the two came the 5th Armored Division, thrusting up from Compiegne. Then, on September 4th, the entire First Army wheeled to the east across Belgium, on into Luxembourg, and seven days later knocked on the door of the Siegfried Line.

The cost of Verdun to General Patton's Third Army, striking to the east from the Seine, on the right wing of the Allied forces, was three American tanks. St. Mihiel, scene of the first all-American offensive in 1918 in which Patton had led the 304th Tank Brigade into action, fell soon thereafter. At Sens, the 4th Armored Division surprised the German garrison taking sun baths. The arrival of the American tanks was their first inkling that U.S. troops were anywhere about. But in the middle of September Patton's tanks ran out of gas only a hop, skip, and a jump from the German border in the neighborhood of Metz. It was a condition that obtained from the British sector in Holland to the Swiss frontier.

The biggest problem posed by the success of the Allied armored drive through France was no tactical or strategical one, but rather the question of supply. "Approximately a million gallons of gasoline were needed at the front every day to enable the armored columns to maintain the headlong rate of their advance," and time and again, in their reports of the war in Europe, General Marshall and General Eisenhower refer to the "herculean task" of getting this much fuel up to the tanks. In the first days of the breakout, fleets of two and a half-ton trucks, loaded with supplies picked up at the beachhead dumps, trailed close behind the wheeling, speeding spearheads of armor and infantry, down the narrow corridor to the south. When the flying columns of the Third Army burst out of Brittany, however, and headed eastward at a rate of fifty miles a day, truck transport was not enough, and Eisenhower, in his determination to keep the tanks rolling, was forced to provide a new kind of delivery—C-47's from the First Allied Army, which had been done out of their job in Brittany and again at Orleans southwest of Paris, by the very tanks for which the planes were called upon to fly gas. By the time the Allied armies were over the Seine, these transport planes were delivering 2,000 tons of supplies a day, sitting down, one every 14 seconds, on narrow emergency landing strips often only fifty miles behind the racing tanks. It was a development that Patton had often predicted in the days before the invasion. As the armor raced farther into France, other measures were devised to enhance the supply system. The Red Ball Express Highway was one of them. This was a one-way road which began at Cherbourg in the tip of the Normandy Peninsula, then swung south and east to the east of Paris, returning thence to the coast by a parallel route. On this highway, some 9,000 military trucks, loaded to the axles, rolled day and night in a never-ending stream at forty miles an hour. And, as fast as captured railroads could be repaired, they, too, were loaded down and sent eastward "nose to tail." Serpentine lines of 6" pipe wound their way across France in the wake of the advancing armies, and by September 20 seven hundred miles of this pipe had been laid connecting beachhead storage tanks with forward points of distribution, which were delivering 4,500 gallons of gasoline a day. Meanwhile, Allied soldiers did what they could to help themselves by utilizing sizable supplies of fuel captured from the retreating Germans.

Yet, despite all such prodigious efforts and contriving, it was impossible to deliver enough supplies for the armored rat race to continue into Germany. While First Army troops did succeed in piercing the dragon-tooth-studded West Wall near Trier and Aachen in mid-September, this was done by slow-moving infantry teams supported by tanks, engineers, bulldozers and tank destroyers, with only feeble thrusts by the hitherto irresistible armored divisions. Torrential rains, which began to fall in October, turning roads and fields into quagmires, further completed the blunting of the spearheads. By December, action all along the front had bogged down into a slow war of artillery bombardments and infantry assaults.

IV

A white, Christmasy landscape furnished the backdrop for the Nazi's last, big show. The scene was a humpy, wooded, 75-mile-long sector between First Army-held Aachen and Trier, a line thinly garrisoned by the U.S. 9th Armored Division, the 4th, 28th, and 106th Infantry Divisions—the latter mostly farm boys fresh from the rolling fields of Camp Atterbury, Indiana, only the month before. The time was December 16, 1944.

There was a gala, festive spirit pervading the frontline troops that day. It was a Saturday; piles of Christmas packages were arriving from home; and G. I.'s were busy with nothing more important than devising ways and means to provide whiskers for Santa Claus in the camp show. There was even a rumor that Bing Crosby was going to be on hand to sing "White Christmas" for them. Luckier G. I.'s were back in Paris on furlough, strolling on the boulevards and buying Lucien Lelong perfume for their girls in the U.S.A. Even General Bradley had departed from the front for a conference on replacements at General Eisenhower's headquarters.

All unwarlike thoughts were abruptly ended that day, however, and for grim days thereafter, by the sight of enemy tanks suddenly nosing onto the horizon. Though few realized it then, they were the vanguard of eight crack panzer divisions aimed right through the center of the weak Aachen—Trier line. On their heels came two panzer-grenadier and fourteen infantry divisions. It was German blitz in the same style and setting as in 1940. Its purpose was to split the Allies and throw their campaign into disorder.

The green 106th bore the brunt of the enemy attack, and quickly gave way before the powerful panzers. One Nazi tank brigade, operating in captured American equipment, served to increase the Americans' horror and confusion. By the following day, Allied positions along a forty-mile front had been overrun. Eisenhower and Bradley, meantime apprised of the breakthrough, ordered the 7th Armored Division to reinforce the north shoulder of the penetration and the 10th Armored, the south flank. The action of these two armored divisions in the ensuing critical days won more laurels for American armor and special praise from both Marshall and Eisenhower in their war reports. "The splendid stand of the 7th Armored Division at St. Vith," which denied the Germans that important area during the early days of the attack, was "in the finest American tradition," wrote the Chief of Staff of the U.S. Army. No less unstinted was Eisenhower's praise for the 10th Armored and 101st Airborne, who "held the vital road center at Bastogne, although completely surrounded for five days and under constant attack by forces many times superior in strength."

Though even more divisions were rushed to the front—the 11th Armored, which had just arrived in England, was hurriedly trans-shipped to France, along with the 17th Airborne and additional infantry divisions—and a corps for counterattack was collected under General Collins, as the week progressed, the German advance through the First Army's center continued. More strength was needed to halt the Germans, and the order went out for Montgomery's men on the north of the salient and the Third Army on the south to join the attack. Almost overnight Patton wheeled his men, who had been in the midst of an attack of their own on the Saar to the east, to a north and slightly westerly direction with scarcely a pause, to begin hammering on the German left flank. "It was a brilliant military accomplishment including corps and army staff work of the highest order," Marshall said.

Nevertheless, by the day before Christmas, the enemy had driven into American lines almost sixty miles toward the Meuse near Celles, and it looked very much as if he were going to get across that river. Headquarters everywhere were permeated with the greatest gloom, and there were rumors of sharp dissension between British and American top chiefs. Substance seemed to be lent to such whispers when it became known that Field Marshal Montgomery had been given almost all of General Bradley's command except the Third Army and the XIX Tactical Air Command. And, as usual when affairs turned against them, criticism of Allied tactics and equipment flew thick and fast. At this crucial moment, it was a decision by Major General J. Lawton Collins, according to reports by both Hanson Baldwin of the Times and by Iris Carpenter, British war correspondent, that turned the "breakout into a break-back."

The circumstances attending the incident would have done credit to any Hollywood scenario. It was a cold, clear Christmas Eve, and the villain, in the shape of the crack Nazi 2d Panzer Division, was fast approaching the hero's doorstep. At headquarters a conversation between two men was taking place— one was General Hodges; the other, General Collins.

"The boss (Monty) says I can withdraw across the Meuse and give up the east bank to those so-and-so's, but I don't want to," said Collins to Hodges.

"It's up to you to call the next play," said Hodges. "Do what you want to do."

"So I please myself," Collins said. "Give me General Harmon, and his 2d Armored Division."

He got General Harmon, who drove up with his tanks after a breathless, 100-mile dash around the rear.

"I want you to jump off tomorrow morning," Collins told General Harmon, "and 'take the Panzer' out of that Second Panzer Division. All set?"

"Hell, yes," replied General Harmons.[6] So far he hadn't lost a battle with his tanks—not since the day he had replaced wounded General Orlando Ward as pinch-hit commander of the 1st Armored Division in North Africa—and he didn't see why the battle next day should be any exception.

It wasn't. By Christmas night the Nazi drive to the west had been stopped.

Thenceforth, the battle news continued to improve. Allied planes, which had been grounded by fog during the first six days of the offensive, now filled the sky. The shoulders on each side of the 45-mile-wide salient were still holding firm, preventing Von Runstedt from widening his breakthrough. On December 26, the 4th Armored Division, under its new commander, Major General Hugh J. Gaffey, broke through to the defenders of Bastogne. Eight days later Eisenhower began his counterattack to push the Nazis back from the bulge.

In the blow aimed to eliminate the enemy salient, the Germans were hit on three sides. The Third Army attacked from the south from Bastogne. The British Army hit the nose of the bulge from the west. The First Army advanced from the north—and so did the North Wind, leaving in its wake 9 above zero temperatures, deep, drifted snow, and icy roads. What had been difficult terrain before was now much worse, thanks to the perverse weather. In the First Army sector, four divisions were engaged: the 83d Infantry teamed with the 3d Armored, the 84th Infantry teamed with the 2d Armored; and the effect of the blizzard on the first days of attack by the two latter divisions was described by Sgt. Theodore Draper one of the G. I.'s serving with the infantry division:

> Our zone was cut in half by a small stream, the Aisne. As a result, at least in the first six days, there were two distinct sectors and the 2d Armored Division started the attack with two combat commands abreast—combat command A and combat command B. In turn, each combat command was made up of three task forces. The set-up was complicated, evidence that the terrain was complicated . . . Although originally planned as an armored offensive with the infantry in support, the battle of the Ardennes bulge quickly became an infantry attack, primarily, with armor used only as the ground permitted. To that extent, this may be a contribution to the story which is not only typical of the rest, but which also traces the main line of the thrust.
>
> Icy weather caused the tanks to skid and act like drunks. Every time a tank skidded, a column was held up . . .

The main objective of the day was Devantave, and
between them and this point were a cluster of woods
and a hill. The tanks could not go through the woods,
and our infantry had to push ahead. We got through
the woods safely, and 88s were waiting. We had to pull
back. Light tanks were used to evacuate the wounded.
Nothing else was possible in the snow . . .

By the time we took Devantave, it was clear that the
original plan which gave the infantry a supporting role
was not working out. The terrain and the weather were
against it and they won. The victory of the elements
gave the infantry the main job.[7]

Throughout the ensuing weeks, the grimy, tired-eyed
doughboys slogged ahead over snow-covered minefields,
through white-mantled forests, and up the steep, icy sides of
stubbornly defended hills. Water froze in their canteens, and
the men built fires on the steel bottoms of their trucks to thaw
themselves out and to heat their rations. Wounded often froze
to death before they could be picked up. Medics carried their
morphine under their armpits to prevent congealing.[8] But by
the end of the long, cruel month, the Allied lines were back
where they had been before the German attack.

V

Lying in front of the Rhine, there is a narrow strip of land—in
some places fifty miles or so wide—that is the western border
of Germany. Fortified by the Siegfried Line and natural barriers of thick, dark forests, wide rivers, and rough mountains, it
contains such handsome prizes as the Saar Basin, the Roer
dams, centuries-old cities—and the western approaches to all
bridges across the Rhine leading into the heart of the Reich.
The next phase of the Allied offensive called for the capture of
this region and the destruction of the enemy forces within it,
preparatory to seizing bridgeheads across the Rhine which

would require special amphibious operations, for no one, even in their fondest dreams, expected to find any of the bridges across that river left intact.

Ranged along the German border for the drive, from the north to the south, were seven Allied armies. Near the Lower Rhine, farthest to the north, stood the Canadian First Army, with the British Second Army on its right flank. Down the line, in front of the Roer river, was the U.S. Ninth Army, commanded by General Simpson. Immediately to his south was the U.S. First, charged with seizing the Roer dams to prevent the enemy from flooding the troops farther down the river. Below the First, confronted by such formidable obstacles as the heavily forested Hunsruck mountains, four rivers to be crossed, and extensive minefields, was the U.S. Third Army. In the southernmost sectors were Patch's U.S. Seventh Army, which had come all the way up from southern France via the Mediterranean to fight for the Saar Basin, and the French First Army, to which three American infantry and one armored (the 12th) division had been given "to carry the brunt of battle by an attack between two French corps."

Attacks began early in February; but atrocious weather, difficult terrain, and bitter enemy resistance slowed the advance to a mere crawl. In the north, soggy ground and floods prevented the use of the four armored divisions and five armored brigades, which General Montgomery had assembled for a swift, violent blow. Instead, his infantrymen worked themselves forward a yard at a time, sometimes waist-deep in water. Down the line, flood conditions in the Roer delayed the river crossing of the Ninth and First Armies for two weeks. Meantime, all through February, the Third Army hacked and bulldozed through the rough ground, building its own corduroy roads as they went along, the while hurling strong invective at a kind of fighting for which Patton and his men had little taste. To the south, an understrength Seventh Army made practically no progress at all, while the French Army on its right, having reached the Rhine, was engaged in "aggressive defense." Then, in the first week of March, there occurred a series of armored explosions in the First and Third Army sectors that abruptly changed the whole complexion of the offense.

Following the crossing of the Roer, operational plans of the high command called for the capture of Cologne by the First Army and, at the "appropriate moment," a strong attack to the southeast to the Rhine, there to converge with a Third Army force heading up from the south. On March 5, according to schedule, the 3d Armored and the 104th Infantry were entering Cologne, whereupon the III Corps, spearheaded by the 9th Armored Division, was dispatched to the southeast to join with the Third Army. Proceeding smartly apace in the execution of their mission, it was noon of March 7, that a small advance outfit of Combat Command B of the 9th Armored Division drew up on high ground overlooking the little town of Remagen, perched on the west bank of the Rhine. They were on their way to a point farther up the river and had paused only to do a little reconnoitering. What they saw below them, however, transfixed them to the spot, for "here," in the words of General Eisenhower, "occurred one of those rare and fleeting opportunities which occasionally present themselves in war, and which, if grasped, have incalculable effects in determining future success."

The river, at this point, was about a thousand feet wide, and across it, standing proud and undamaged, was a great bridge— the only one left intact by the Germans up and down the entire Rhine. It was the double-track Ludendorff railroad bridge leading across the river to the village of Erpel, and locomotives still chugging over it indicated how completely unaware of the fact the Germans were that the Americans were close by.

The fortunes of war had placed Lt. Colonel Leonard Engemann of Minneapolis in command of this fated little group of 9th Armored G. I.'s who stood gazing excitedly down upon the beautiful sight. No one had to tell him, or them, what the seizure of the span would mean to the Allies. It was a moment of decision for the colonel. Should he wait for orders from his commanding officer, Brig. General William Hoge, and for rein-forcements, which were miles away, or should he try to take the bridge at once? Colonel Engemann did not hesitate. Minutes later, the task force was rolling down the hills into Remagen. The Germans were still asleep, and the Americans took the lit-tle town with no trouble. By midafternoon they were on the approaches of the bridge. Across it they could see the 600-foot-high, sheer, basalt cliffs on the other side, forming a natural barricade for the enemy, but they did not falter. When they were halfway across the bridge, the Germans suddenly woke up and tried to dynamite it. Something went wrong, and the bridge did not go down. By late afternoon, the Americans were across, and word of the brilliant coup was flashed back to Eisenhower. Though the Allied Supreme Commander had contemplated no thrust across the Rhine at this point, the cap-ture of the bridge altered his plans; and by the next day thou-sands of men, guns, and tanks were jamming the roads to Remagen. Two weeks later, the tentative toehold of the plucky tankers of the 9th Armored had been expanded into a bridge-head 25 miles long and 10 miles deep, with three corps lodged therein ready to strike.

Meantime, tankers of the Third Army, anxious not to be outdone by their armored brothers to the north, broke out of the rough country that had practically immobilized them all during February, and embarked upon some spectacular doings of their own. It was on March 5 that spearheads of the 4th Armored charged through a gap in the hills made by the infantry and headed for the Rhine. In fifty-six hours they had slashed their way to Koblentz, capturing a German general en route. A few miles above them, the 11th Armored Division roared toward the Rhine on a parallel route, thence to a junc-tion with First Army troops, likewise bagging a Nazi general on the way. Motorized infantry followed close on their heels, protecting the armored flanks against possible counterattack, mopping up bypassed areas of resistance, and taking care of the thousands of German prisoners.

Those eventful early March days also saw the British and Ninth Armies in the north move to the river Rhine, thus leaving only the U.S. Seventh Army short of this goal. The matter was soon remedied, however, when the offensive to seize this last area west of the Rhine remaining in enemy hands began on March 15. While the Seventh Army attacked along the front between Hagenau and Sauerbrucken, Third Army units suddenly hooked downward toward the enemy's rear—the object being to catch the Nazis in a giant trap. The appearance of Third Army troops in the Seventh Army sector caught the Germans, who had expected them to go to Remagen, by complete surprise. On March 16, a spearhead of the 4th Armored Division, still celebrating its smash to the Rhine near Koblentz only the week before, broke through for a gain of 32 miles, deep in German-held territory. Thenceforth, resistance crumbled, and the occupation of the last remaining territory west of the Rhine degenerated into a race between armored divisions of both American armies to see who could capture the most.

By March 25 all the land west of the Rhine was held by the Allies. This simple statement denoting the conclusion of the drive to close the Rhine did not mean any pause, however, in the forward sweep of the victorious armies. Rather, the battle had continued across the Rhine without interruption, even while the Germans were still resisting in the Saar, when, on the night of March 22d, General Patton had effected his surprise crossing of that river. Using his own "navy"—"big plywood assault boats which he had lugged up the Moselle Valley and over the mountains at night, hiding them by day from aerial observation," he had sent his U.S. 5th Infantry Division over the Rhine to the east bank, where they had landed before the Germans realized what was going on. And when the 4th Armored Division erupted out of the bridgehead three days later in another spectacular drive of 27 miles straight into the heart of Germany, the Nazis were powerless to stop them.

In the last month of the war, all sixteen of the American armored divisions were in the European theatre of war—fifteen of them on the German-Austrian front (the 1st Armored Division was on the Italian front). Normal practice was to include an armored division—sometimes two—in each corps, to act as the spearhead of the advance across Germany. Behind them rode some of the infantry divisions of the corps in German or American trucks or any other conveyance with four wheels and an engine on which they could lay their hands. It was their job to guard the armored flanks, demolish strong points of resistance, and otherwise forward the advance. The attacking forces thus were, in effect, armored armies. Slogging in the rear on foot came other infantry divisions of the corps, to occupy towns, collect and guard the herds of prisoners, and finish off remaining Germans who chose to fight and not surrender.

It was, indeed, a repetition of the tactics employed in the drive through France and fine weather, an excellent road system, and disintegrating enemy resistance combined to make it another field day for American armor. Armored gains of 20 to 30 miles a day were not unusual, and in one sector the tanks moved so fast that bombing lines of tactical aircraft had to be changed every twenty minutes. Huge quantities of booty fell into their hands, while the great numbers of prisoners often proved an embarrassment to the advance. Now it was the Germans who didn't have enough men, didn't have enough equipment, didn't have enough supplies; and who fell into all the traps, and who made all the mistakes.

Spectacle-studded as the war's finale was, however, no performance rated four stars more than the action called "The Envelopment of the Ruhr." This region lay on the east bank of the Rhine between the Remagen bridgehead of the First Army on the south and the Ninth Army on the north. Within it were contained Hitler's coal, iron, and ammunition works, and thousands upon thousands of the flower of Nazi troops stationed there to defend it. It was a tempting prize which the Germans would be unhappy to lose, and one which Eisenhower determined to gain at the earliest possible moment.

Operations to acquire the Ruhr began on March 30—the day the U.S. Fifteenth Army was formed and the Ninth and First Armies were freed to strike into Germany. On that day, tanks of the 2d Armored Division broke out of the Ninth Army area north of the Ruhr in a powerful sweep toward Munster, at the same time that Major General Maurice Rose and his 3d Armored Division roared out of the Remagen bridgehead in a drive that carried them 55 miles in less than 12 hours. When the 3d Armored tanks halted that night for a few hours' bivouac, they had chalked up "the longest armored march in history in one day."[9] On April 1st, the two armored prongs met at Lippstadt, and the encirclement of the Ruhr, described by General Marshall as the largest pocket of envelopment in the history of warfare, was complete. The triumph of the intrepid tankers of the 3d Armored Division, however, was dimmed by sorrow, for their brilliant commander was not with them to share the glory of their achievement. Earlier that same day he had been captured and shot down by the Nazis. His lifeless body was following his conquering armor on a litter carried on the hood of a jeep.

Up and down Allied lines, leaders now prepared for the final, victorious drive. Armor and infantry shared alike in the successes in the closing days of the war, but a special measure of renown was the lot of old "Hell on Wheels" when their outfit was officially credited with being the first American unit to make a bridgehead across the Elbe River, pre-arranged dividing line between the Americans and the Russians. "Yeah, but ask them what happened to it," a Lieutenant Colonel of the 83d Infantry Division, who was riding close behind them in a captured German car, roared to the author. The sad fact of the matter was that two days after the 2d Armored Division drove across the Elbe, they were pushed back again by counterattacking Nazis and, as it turned out, the infantry was actually the first to get across the river and stay there.

On April 26, the first meeting between the Russians and the Americans occurred, when an advance patrol of the U.S. First Army shook hands with Soviet soldiers in the Torgau area of the Elbe. And when the war ended twelve days later, Yankee tankers were viewing sights all the way from Wittenberge to the "Beautiful Blue Danube." They had traveled a long way from their early school days at Knox on the banks of a river equally famous in song, when they and their handful of obsolete equipment had been voted by military classmates as the outfit "least likely to succeed."

Epilogue

War Department
Bureau of Public Relations
Press Branch
April 4, 1946

Cavalry, Armor to Merge, Secretary of War Reveals

The historic cavalry and the comparatively new armored force will be merged into a single "Armored Cavalry" arm in recognition of new developments during World War II, Secretary of War Robert P. Patterson revealed at Fort Riley, Kansas, today.

Personnel for the new "Armored Cavalry," it was stressed, will not be drawn solely from the cavalry but also from other branches and in the same manner as it was drawn for the armored forces.

At a press conference held before ceremonies to dedicate Patton Hall at the cavalry post, the Secretary of War outlined plans for the consolidation, which he said would add to future efficiency of the army.

At Secretary Patterson's request, General Jacob L. Devers, Commanding General of the Army Ground Forces, told the press conference that while it was planned virtually to eliminate the horse from the army, it is contemplated that a small detachment of skilled mounted troops will be maintained to give instruction and train small units for use in rough terrain, and that pack animals will be retained for specialized work.

In response to a question, General Devers said the greatest use to which he had put horses in World War II was as pack trains in the Vosges mountains of eastern France. He said that in Italy pack animals had been used and that quite extensive use of animal transport had been resorted to in Burma.

One of the oldest combat arms of the United States Army, the cavalry was not organized into combat formations of the historic horse-borne type in this war. The only large cavalry unit to see service in this war was the 1st Cavalry Division, which fought in the Philippines and occupied Tokyo after the Japanese surrender. This division, however, fought as "dismounted Cavalry", which is similar in employment to infantry.

Future plans for horse cavalry, while indefinite, take into consideration the fact that over certain types of terrain where motorized elements could not travel, and where mobility greater than that of foot troops is required, animals are the only suitable means of transportation.

Several units in World War II were designated as cavalry, but actually were reconnaissance troops mounted in light tanks, scout cars and half-tracks, similar in their mission to the reconnaissance troops assigned to infantry divisions. These units proved their value on every battlefield.

Notes

All quotations not credited are from the personal files of General Chaffee.

CHAPTER 1.
1. *Tanks* by Col. R. J. Icks.
2. *Les Chars d'Assaut* by Capt. L. Dutil.
3. *Machine Warfare* by J. F. C. Fuller.

CHAPTER 2.
1. Feb. 25, 1928, *Army-Navy Journal.*
2. Biographical sketch by Chas. Mettler.
3. Horace Stebbins.
4. Built in 1929, Successor to T1-E1.
5. Chas. Mettler.

CHAPTER 3.
1. From War Department telegram to Col. Chas. Haffner, Pres., Cook County Chapter, R.O.A.
2. Quote from Hawkins' article in the *Cavalry Journal,* Sept.–Oct. 1931.
3. *Mt. Vernon Democrat,* April 20, 1934.
4. *Kansas City Times,* June 13, 1934.

CHAPTER 4.
1. Chaffee.
2. Jones, Rarey & Icks: *Tanks Since 1916.*
3. Chief of Infantry, *Infantry Journal,* Nov.–Dec., 1939.

4. At the time of Mr. Christie's death in January, 1944, he was
   still engaged in litigation involving failure of the War
   Dept. to pay $30,000 to $40,000 which he claimed was due
   for license fees on modern tanks which have certain
   Christie features, according to the United Press. (*Armored
   News,* Jan. 17, 1944.)
5. *Tanks* by Col. R. J. Icks.

CHAPTER 5.
1. Chaffee speech, 1941.
2. *American City,* Nov. 1936.
3. January–February 1938, *Infantry Journal.*
4. July–August 1939, *Cavalry Journal.*
5. Letter, Chaffee to Van Voorhis, Jan., 1938.

CHAPTER 6.
1. *Louisville Courier Journal,* July 14, 1944.
2. *Time,* August 9, 1943.
3. *Louisville Courier Journal,* August 18, 1939.
4. *New York Sun,* August 30, 1939.

CHAPTER 7.
1. Congressional Record, April 4, 1940.

CHAPTER 8.
1. Statement of Col. Alvan C. Gillen, Jr.
2. Interview by Gillem in Louisville Courier Journal, May 23,
   1943.
3. *History of the Armored Force* by Hechler.
4. Hechler to author.
5. Major Addison McGhee in *He's In the Armored Force Now.*
6. *New York Daily News,* July 21, 1940.
7. *History of the Armored Force* by Hechler.
8. *History of the Armored Force* by Hechler.

CHAPTER 9.

1. *Time*, December 30, 1940.
2. *History of the Armored Force* by Hechler.
3. *Louisville Courier Journal.*
4. Letter from Marshall, March 31, 1941.
5. From the Congressional Record and from excerpts which were not published.

CHAPTER 10.

1. *History of the Armored Force* by Hechler.
2. *Tanks* by Icks.
3. *History of the Armored Force* by Hechler.
4. *The New Army of the U.S.*, August 1, 1941.
5. January, 1941, *Infantry Journal.*
6. *History of the Armored Force* by Hechler.
7. July, 1945, *Infantry Journal.*

CHAPTER 11.

1. *Newsweek*; and Drew Middleton, *N. Y. Times*, March 1, 1943.
2. *Newsweek*, March 1, 1943.
3. Merrill Mueller, *Newsweek*, March 8, 1943.
4. *Tankers in Tunisia* by Brig. Gen. T. C. Camp.
5. *Louisville Courier Journal*, May 23, 1943.
6. *Louisville Courier Journal*, July 31, 1944.

CHAPTER 12.

1. May–June, 1946, *Cavalry Journal.*
2. *History of the Armored Force* by Hechler.
3. *Armored News*, February 7, 1944.
4. *Tankers in Tunisia* by Brig. Gen. T. J. Camp.

CHAPTER 13.

1. Eisenhower's Report.
2. *Cavalry Journal*, May–June, 1946.
3. *Newsweek*, August 7, 1944.

4. *Infantry Journal*, October, 1944.

5. *Infantry Journal*, March, 1944.

6. Taken from a book review of Mrs. Carpenter's book by Charles Poore in the September 7, 1946, *N. Y. Times* with some changes and additions by the author.

7. *Infantry Journal*, May, 1945.

8. *Time*, January 22, 1945.

9. Hal Boyle, May 8, 1946, *AP Dispatch*.

Index

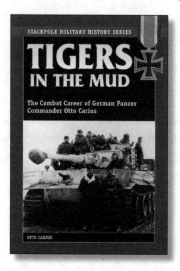

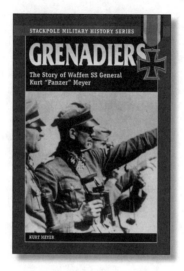

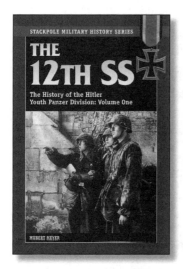 

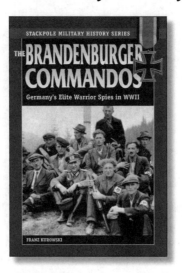

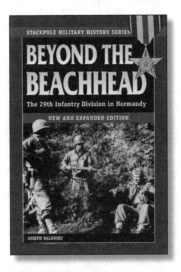

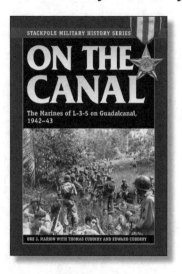